ENGLISH TEACHER'S
Portfolio of
MULTICULTURAL
ACTIVITIES

Ready-to-Use Lessons & Cooperative Activities for Grades 7-12

JOHN EDWIN COWEN, Ed.D.

Illustrations by Marlene Page-Ware

THE CENTER FOR APPLIED RESEARCH IN EDUCATION
West Nyack, New York 10994

Library of Congress Cataloging in Publication Data

Cowen, John E.
      English teacher's portfolio of multicultural activities : ready-to-use
lessons & cooperative activities for grades 7–12 / John Edwin Cowen.
        p.   cm.
      ISBN 0–87628–300–8
      1. Multicultural education—Activity programs—United States—
Handbooks, manuals, etc.   2. Literature—Study and teaching—
Activity programs—United States—Handbooks, manuals, etc.
3. Portfolios in education—United States—Handbooks, manuals, etc.
I. Title.
LC1099.3.C697   1996
370.19'6'0973—dc20   95–25860
                                            CIP

Printed in the United States of America

10 9 8 7 6 5 4 3 2

ISBN 0-87628-300-8

**THE CENTER FOR APPLIED RESEARCH
IN EDUCATION**
West Nyack, NY 10994
A Simon & Schuster Company

On the World Wide Web at http://www.phdirect.com

Prentice Hall International (UK) Limited, *London*
Prentice Hall of Australia Pty. Limited, *Sydney*
Prentice Hall Canada, Inc., *Toronto*
Prentice Hall Hispanoamericana, S.A., *Mexico*
Prentice Hall of India Private Limited, *New Delhi*
Prentice Hall of Japan, Inc., *Tokyo*
Simon & Schuster Asia Pte. Ltd., *Singapore*
Editora Prentice Hall do Brasil, Ltda., *Rio de Janeiro*

DEDICATION

To Dr. Harold Morris, Superintendent
Teaneck, New Jersey, Public Schools

This book was greatly influenced and inspired by the vision of Hal Morris and by his commitment to a global/multicultural education for all of Teaneck's students. This vision is summarized below.

Global/multicultural education develops an awareness of multiple historical perspectives—as well as an understanding of female and male roles—through which students gain knowledge and understanding of the heritage and cultures of diverse nations, societies, and ethnic groups, including their own. By acquiring multiple perspectives, an individual will be able to develop a sense of cultural consciousness, including being aware of the diversity of ideas and practices found in human societies around the world, and the recognition of how one's thoughts and behaviors might be perceived by members of other communities, nations, or ethnic groups.

Through global/multicultural education, the individual will develop the ability to communicate effectively and to appreciate customs and cultural styles different from his or her own. This, in turn, becomes a major means to combat racism, prejudice, and discrimination by placing emphasis on correcting myths and stereotypes associated with different races and ethnic groups.

Teaneck, New Jersey, 1991

ACKNOWLEDGMENTS

Personal appreciation is extended to Connie Kallback for her support and faith in me as an educator and author, and for her persistent encouragement, guidance, and editorial skills. She provided direction and constructive assistance in helping to make this project come to successful fruition.

To Lila Ross for her technological assistance and editorial comments with the proposal for this book. To Linda Kuhran for her tireless and professional, technological ability, and for her tenacious energy in placing my handwritten text on computer.

Finally, to my wife Jay, and daughters Jill and Juliet, I am indebted for your support and patience over the past two years in my efforts to make this book a reality.

ABOUT THE AUTHOR

John Edwin Cowen received a doctorate in curriculum and teaching from Teachers College, Columbia University. Dr. Cowen is currently Assistant Professor of Education and Reading in the Master of Arts in Teaching Program at Fairleigh Dickinson University. He is the former Assistant Superintendent for Curriculum and Instruction for the Teaneck, New Jersey, Public Schools, and has more than twenty years' experience as an English, reading, and special education teacher. Dr. Cowen is author of *Human Reading Strategies that Work* (New Jersey Department of Education) and editor/author of *Teaching Reading Through the Arts,* (International Reading Association). He is also a multicultural, small press publisher of John Edwin Cowen/BRAVO Editions. His poetry and articles have appeared in more than fifty magazines and journals.

Dr. Cowen has served as Editor-in-Chief of the *Reading Instruction Journal* (New Jersey Reading Association) and as a member of the Editorial Advisory Board for the International Reading Association. He is Past President of the New Jersey Reading Association and is a recipient of the Phi Delta Kappa Excellence in Teaching award, and Phi Delta Kappa award for the Teaneck School District's Outstanding Literature-Based Language Arts Program. Dr. Cowen was inducted into the prestigious International Reading Association's President's Club.

ABOUT THE ARTIST

Marlene Page-Ware, an African American artist, illustrator, sculptor, and fabric designer, has taught at Teaneck High School in New Jersey for twenty years. She has exhibited her work in several exhibitions, competitions, and galleries throughout the New York, New Jersey, and Philadelphia area. In 1991, Ms. Page-Ware received the Heritage Gallery Emerging Artist Competition First Place Award. She presently has a print entitled *Children of South Africa* published by the October Gallery of Philadelphia. Marlene Page-Ware is a graduate of Douglass College, Rutgers University, where she received her Bachelor of Arts and Master of Arts degrees in the visual arts.

FOREWORD

MULTICULTURAL LITERATURE: COMPLETING THE HUMAN STORY

To the English teacher the story is familiar enough. John Keats, nineteenth century British poet, after spending an evening reading Chapman's English translation of Greek mythology, is so overwhelmed by this new world of information and knowledge that he is moved to write his famous sonnet:

On First Looking Into Chapman's Homer

Much have I travell'd in the realms of gold,
And many goodly states and kingdoms seen;
Round many western islands have I been
Which bards in fealty to Apollo hold.
Oft of one wide expanse had I been told
That deep-brow'd Homer ruled as his demesne;
Yet did I never breathe its pure serene
Till I heard Chapman speak out loud and bold;
Then felt I like some watcher of the skies
When a new planet swims into his ken;
Or like stout Cortez when with eagle eyes
He stare'd at the Pacific—and all his men
Look'd at each other with a wild surmise—
Silent, upon a peak in Darien.

When I first read this sonnet, I was overcome with ecstasy, much the same as the "watcher of the skies" experiencing a new "planet" swim into view. And I remember the reports of Keats' shouting in delight at the discovery of the new world that excited his imagination. It seemed to me at the time that the essence of being a teacher of English was first to experience directly the excitement of new worlds contained in literature and then to communicate those worlds and that excitement to the students.

Like Keats, we as English teachers have travelled through many exciting "realms of gold." We have read British and American literature and, to some degree, world literature (usually from a Eurocentric point of view). These realms have served us well, and we have been able to use this knowledge to touch students, to move them, and to help them understand what it is to be human; however, it is time for us to breathe the "pure serene" once again, for if we insist on using these familiar realms as the exclusive world to relate to the human condition, we run the risk of losing sight of the new planets swimming before us. Worse, if we cover our eyes to these new planets, we use an exclusive rather than an inclusive approach to life and prevent legitimate expression from being heard.

WHY MULTICULTURAL LITERATURE: A MULTICULTURAL CURRICULUM SEEKS AND ENSURES QUALITY

Anything less than a complete story, picture, or idea is less than a quality experience. Anything less than an approach to feelings, events, history, and stories from various points of view is incomplete. We become something less than excellent if we do not remind our students that there are legitimate, different points of view and that often there are competing theories of truth. If we tell students, for example, that Macbeth's "Tomorrow and tomorrow" soliloquy is the best expression ever of human despair, we, as teachers, settle for partial rather than complete information. Worse, we present information in an elitist context that cuts off the need to examine other similar expressions and belittles and trivializes all other similar human expression. In truth there are countless other powerful expressions of despair. For example, "A Song in Time of Depression," from the Paiute, is but one poem which, taught along with traditional pieces, could reveal to students the universality of an emotion. In general, the Native American culture is excluded from our curriculum and yet rich stories are there to be told. Indeed, Walt Whitman, America's poet of democracy, reminds us in his poem, "Unnamed Lands," of the untapped source of new information the Native American culture contains:

> *Nations ten thousand years before these states,*
> *. . . men and women that like us grew up*
> *And travel'd their course and pass'd on,*
> *. . . What histories, rulers, heroes, perhaps transcending all others.*

MULTICULTURALISM CRIES OUT AGAINST EXCLUSIVITY

Simply stated, a multicultural curriculum encourages teachers to develop ideas, units, concepts, events, or themes from different points of view. For example, a theme such as the father-son relationship should have a wider scope than a traditional single-work study of *Death of a Salesman* by Miller. Some teachers say they have no need to teach African American literature since they have no African American students in their classes. In truth, until we and our students, all our students, are familiar with African American writers—their presence, their contributions, their reality—we cannot truly profess to have a full, complete understanding of American literature or history. Our incompleteness makes us less than excellent, and this same mediocrity results when we ignore other ethnic groups. No intellectual or social value is served when ethnic groups, which constitute a significant portion of this country's population, have their stories and histories routinely ignored or distorted. Ralph Ellison, in *Invisible Man,* used the term "invisible" to refer to the main society's ignoring of ethnic individuals and groups.

Women also have been traditionally subjected to this pernicious practice—being treated as invisible and unimportant. The concept of invisibility at work is seen clearly whether it is in the case of Emily Dickinson, who was viewed as a writer of feminine poetry by male-dominated publishers, or in the case of Celie, in Alice Walker's *The Color Purple,* who, tired of being dehumanized, asserts, "I'm poor, I'm black. I may be ugly and I can't cook . . . But I'm here," the concept of invisibility at work is apparent. Inevitably, in her desire to be recognized as visible and important, Celie expresses her declaration of self-worth and in so doing speaks not only for herself, but for all those treated as though they were invisible and unworthy. More than a century ago, Walt Whitman who understood the concept of invisibility said, "The Americans of all nations at any time upon the earth have probably the fullest poetical nature" (preface to *Leaves of Grass,* 1855). This is no less true today; the European immigrants have been replaced by a new wave of immigrants from Asia, Latin America, the Caribbean, and other non-European countries. Imagine how Whitman's soul would stir at the thought of the new poem, the new miracle these immigrants promise with their hopes, dreams, insights, and stories—their and our realms of gold.

Since multiculturalism does not seek to replace one centrist view with another, but rather to embrace the fullness of the unifying human experiences, a positive side effect is that the comprehensive acceptance and inclusion of multicultural literature into the curriculum increases the potential to promote and serve the common good—not unworthy motives of a democracy.

MULTICULTRALISM IS CONSISTENT WITH CURRENT SOCIAL THOUGHT

The ramifications of the Industrial Revolution, and the psychological theories of Freud and Jung, have served to separate us into observable pieces so that the wholeness of our beings has been disturbed. Beckett, in *Waiting for Godot,* describes this condition in his depiction of four characters rendered inert by their inability to connect with themselves and with each other.

Currently, there are movements crying out for wholeness in medicine, nutrition, social institutions, religion, language, and others. These movements have sensed the intellect's attempt to overspecialize and to categorize and are seeking a natural balance and wholeness. The movement of multiculturalism may be considered somewhat akin to the movement of ecumenism in religion—a movement centered on the concept that individual religious beliefs and practices properly understood and practiced really have more things in common than in particular—those common experiences, stories, and ideas that bind the human family together. Contrary to so many claims by opponents of multiculturalism, a balanced multicultural program does not divide (the word "Balkanize" has even been used) but rather unifies and leads naturally to wholeness.

MULTICULTURALISM TRANSCENDS TIME, PLACE, CULTURE

At a recent gathering of new teachers in our district, I was discussing the universality of literature in relation to a multicultural curriculum. Without identifying the author and title, I read aloud a portion of a short story in which a young man is dying at home where he lives with his mother and father and younger brother. The younger brother, half asleep, begins to imagine wild things, all portending the imminent death of his brother, who is separated from him by a thin bedroom wall. In the middle of his imaginings he is awakened by his father who says, "Son, son, I need your help. Your brother . . ."

At this point I stopped reading. Everyone was riveted to the story. What was most interesting was that not a single person in the audience wanted to know the author or title of the story. What they demanded to know was what happened next. They were engaged in the story and the human experience of a family faced with death (the reading was taken from "Early Dawn," a short story by Seruma, a contemporary African writer). The universality of the feelings and emotion transcended time, place, and culture.

A multicultural curriculum provides the best opportunity to engage the full range of human experiences. In our highly technical age, where we even think of dividing the brain's spheres into left and right functions, we should now—more than ever—look for literature that speaks to the heart. It is in the heart that authors experience their special mystical moments, their epiphanies, and it is in the canon of multicultural literature that we stand the best chance of linking and unifying ourselves to a universal heart.

CONCLUSION

In our travels we have all found valuable realms of gold from which we relate similar fundamental human experiences for our students' learning. Our realms of gold, our backgrounds, our centers, which at one time excited us, have served us well and have allowed us to help countless students in sharing what it is to be human. It is time for us now—as primary transmitters of culture—to broaden our cultural backgrounds to include more experiences, and more opportunities so that we will be able to pass on a fuller, more complete, more accurate and honest account of what it is to be human. We must add to the realms of gold and accept and embrace the new planets swimming into view. We must open wide our eyes, fully embrace the newness and freshness of a whole world of new information and become, as did Keats, ecstatic and alive with the excitement of new knowledge passing before our very eyes.

Flory J. Perini
Humanities Supervisor, Teaneck, New Jersey, Public Schools
Past President, New Jersey Language Arts Teachers Association

ABOUT THIS TEACHER RESOURCE

REAL MULTICULTURAL LITERATURE

What distinguishes this book from others is the *real* award-winning multicultural literature included here, which represents all five major geocultural groups:

1. Native American, 2. African–African American, 3. Latino–Latino American, 4. Asian–Asian American, and 5. Northern European–European American.

Through this literature, students acquire multiple perspectives with regard to values, ideas, customs, and social actions to help them understand and appreciate one another's differences and similarities.

TEN THEMATIC UNITS

Ten complete units, built upon central themes, are presented with an introduction and themes that include (1) Masks Around the World; (2) Awakening the Imagination; (3) Learning from Conflict; (4) Dreams Deferred; (5) What If? Scenarios; (6) Cultural Perspectives Through Poetry; (7) Relationships: Family and Friends; (8) Folk Tales from Different Cultures; (9) Talking to the Animals; and (10) The Play's the Thing. The introductions, addressed to students, may be photocopied to give them information about the theme and selections for that unit.

A variety of genres are included—short stories, articles, essays, poetry, folk tales, fairy tales, allegory, plays, and what if ? scenarios for problem solving.

FOCUS FOR PREREADING

Each student activity section begins with a Focus, or preview to each literature piece; it also provides a biography of each author—including his or her cultural heritage—creating a schema or prior knowledge backdrop for successful understanding.

HIGHER ORDER THINKING (H.O.T.) RESPONSES

The activity questions are designed to elicit Higher Order Thinking (H.O.T.) responses—responses that require students to think analytically and creatively. Many of these activities require small group problem-solving interactions, which encourage discussions, follow-up research, and individual expository writing responses.

CREATIVE PRODUCT

Every activity requires students to engage in an activity that culminates in producing a creative product from a synthesis of previous learning experiences. The creative assortment of activities presented in each unit serves as stimulating, enjoyable encounters for adolescents, and at the same time, serves as *models* and springboards for creative discussion, debate, role playing, dramatic readings, art, and creative writing in several genres.

FLEXIBLE GROUPING AND COOPERATIVE LEARNING

Each unit is designed so that the teacher can fit these activities to his or her style of teaching. Students may work independently, in small cooperative groups, or in whole-class activities. Each unit is designed to help the English teacher, Language Arts teacher, or Academically Gifted teacher provide reading and critical thinking opportunities for students as enrichment or to supplement existing classroom curricula. These units may be photocopied for student use.

THE OBJECTIVES OF THIS BOOK

The objectives of this book are

- to understand other cultures through multicultural perspectives;
- to promote creative thinking strategies;
- to promote creative expression;
- to help students understand abstract reasoning in reading and artistic expression;
- to help students value and learn to use metaphors as a means of expression;
- to select alternative points of view;
- to make connections;
- to draw inductive conclusions;
- to explore and appreciate evocative language;
- to create products, including inquiries, reports, documents, art, and creative writings;
- to work cooperatively in groups;
- to synthesize ideas; and
- to see relationships and contrasts, and to apply or create alternative forms of expression.

PORTFOLIO ASSESSMENT

Finally, this book takes advantage of the portfolio assessment approach. Because the creation of products is the culminating act of each lesson or activity, it is essential that students be required to keep a folder or special notebook—perhaps even a carton—to contain writings, artwork, or other creative projects. It is also necessary that students receive constant feedback from their cooperative group, other classmates, and, of course, the teacher.

John Edwin Cowen, Ed.D

CONTENTS

Unit One

INTRODUCTION TO THEME: MASKS AROUND THE WORLD—3

Unit Two

THEME: AWAKENING THE IMAGINATION—25

Unit Three

THEME: LEARNING FROM CONFLICT—53

Contents

Unit Four

Theme: Dreams Deferred—89

Unit Five

Theme: What If? Scenarios—125

Unit Six

Theme: Cultural Perspectives Through Poetry—143

Unit Seven

THEME: RELATIONSHIPS: FAMILY AND FRIENDS—171

Unit Eight

THEME: FOLK TALES FROM DIFFERENT CULTURES—209

Unit Nine

THEME: TALKING TO THE ANIMALS—241

Unit Ten

THEME: THE PLAY'S THE THING—277

Unit One

THEME:
MASKS AROUND THE WORLD

INTRODUCTION

The creation of masks is an art form that continues from ancient times to today. Masks appear in most cultures from around the world. They are prevalent in each of the five geocultural groups that recur as themes throughout this book. Native American; African and African American; Asian and Asian American; Latino and Latino American; and European and European American are the five major cultures represented in this book. Masks from these cultures are interwoven thematically as symbols and as reminders of different multicultural perspectives, and are presented in a variety of activities through art, literature, and social issues.

MASKS FOR DECEIVING

T.S. Eliot, a famous European American poet and critic, is the author of the well-known poem, "The Love Song of J. Alfred Prufrock." Two lines in this poem comment on the universal characteristics of human nature and personality, depicting how different masks, or faces, are "put on" by people who can change their facial expressions at will:

> . . . there will be time, there will be time
> to prepare a face to meet the faces that you meet . . .

You can, for instance, choose to look sad when you are really happy or you can put on a happy face when you are sad. People often lie or deceive one another, but may give the appearance of being honest or innocent. Have you ever experienced this? Haven't you actually been able to see through such masks? Perhaps you have, on occasion, even created or "prepared" such a face to meet the face or faces that you have wanted to deceive. Masks or faces are worn to conceal our innermost feelings and fears as well. Paul Dunbar, the great African American poet writes of this in "We wear the Mask":

> Why should the world be over-wise
> in counting all our tears and sighs?

MASKS FOR THE STAGE

Actors and actresses are quite good at contorting their faces to create different appearances or personalities. Makeup worn by actors masks reality, and can aid a young person in portraying someone very old, or in acting as a sinister character. The symbols for the theater are masks—one representing tragedy and one comedy. Masks have been worn on stage for centuries, and in every culture. Masks readily transform individuals into different characters or into animals, gods, or mythological figures.

In ancient Greece, women were prohibited from performing on stage, so masks were worn by men in order to play female roles. This was true as well during Elizabethan times. In Japanese Noh theater, masks were worn to portray emperors and women, or beasts such as dragons. Unit Ten of this book includes a Noh drama by Zeami and a play set during the early 1600s written by Michael Mathias. In both of these plays, masks are worn on stage.

MASKS FOR RITES OF PASSAGE

Masks were worn by many primitive civilizations. Many tribal groups, even today, wear masks during religious ceremonies and for different "rites of passage" events—including the marriage ceremony—and ceremonies signifying entry into adulthood. Masks were worn by Native Americans during rituals for the induction of young braves as warriors. Ritualistic dances around campfires took place before "going on the warpath." Masks, as well as painted faces, were used to frighten off the evil spirits and the enemy once they were encountered.

Masks in the shape of ferocious animals—lions, tigers, and other beasts—were worn by African warriors. Witch doctors often participated and wore masks during these rituals to ward off ill health or potential harm that could befall these warriors.

Masks were worn in some cultures by families to protect themselves from vengeful spirits of the dead. Ancient and modern cultures often created death masks, molded from the actual face of an individual, to help send the soul of a loved one to the afterlife without fear of interference from some demon god.

The West African poet and essayist, Leopold Sedar Senghor's poem "Prayer to Masks" describes how people of his African culture wear masks to pray to the dead:

Masks of the four points from which the Spirit blows
. . .
Nor you the beast, the Lion-headed Ancestor . . .

In this poem, the African poet, Senghor describes his family's emblem or mask, which is in the shape of a lion with black and red, and white and black markings. This poem also points out how superstitious different cultures can be about death. Such masks are worn to bring the family closer to their dead ancestors. Others wear masks to scare away the evil spirits or demons sent by the dead.

5

MASKS FOR DISGUISES

Throughout the ages, evildoers, thieves, murderers, and villains wore masks to conceal themselves from the law or from their victims. Members of the Klu Klux Klan (KKK), a secret society that terrorizes African Americans and other minorities as targets of bigotry, wear masks made from sheets.

In contrast, characters such as the Lone Ranger, Batman, and Robin Hood use masks to conceal their identity so that after fighting crime, they can return to a life of normalcy. A half-mask worn by the Phantom of the Opera, on the other hand, was worn by this character to conceal his ugly face in order to woo a beautiful, young opera singer.

MASKS FOR CARNIVALS AND FESTIVALS

Carnival Masks are also worn during Mardi Gras in New Orleans, signifying the festival of Shrove Tuesday which is the last day before Lent. Similar carnivals, featuring masks, are celebrated in the Bahamas, in Latin America, in Europe, and elsewhere.

On Corpus Christi Day in June, Mexicans wear masks to frighten the evil spirits way and keep their families and neighbors safe from harm. Masks of great distinction are also worn during religious ceremonies and festivals in India, Java, China, Japan, by the Maoris of New Zealand, and by the aborigines of Australia.

The activities that follow will enable you to compare literature to the wearing of masks, and to relate different cultural perspectives to your own culture. You will also be given the opportunity to create your own masks, as well as poetry, drama, stories, and myths. You are encouraged to delve further into the research on masks to learn more about this fascinating art form.

© 1996 by The Center for Applied Research in Education

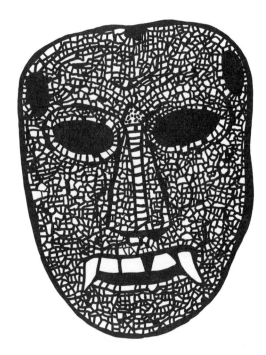

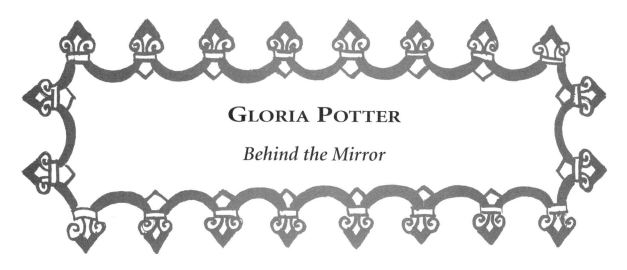

GLORIA POTTER

Behind the Mirror

FOCUS

Gloria Potter's poem, "Behind the Mirror" first appeared in *BRAVO, The Poet's Magazine* edited by José Garcia Villa. She was the featured poet; fifteen of her poems were published. Ms. Potter is an artist and a poet whose poems display exquisite craft and unusual language. Several of her poems also appeared in *The Atavist,* edited by Robert Dorset. One of her concrete poems was featured on the cover of the second number of this small-press poetry magazine. As you read "Behind the Mirror," you may want to think of it in the context of John Edwin Cowen's poem "Ask Nothing from Masks," in this unit.

Behind the Mirror

behind the mirror, to
          one side, also
upon the mirror frame
         and to one side

   the masks

   all smile.

because no mouths, all
        frown because no
eyes: alas-good morning
        borrows from them

   masks can

   ask much.

H.O.T. RESPONSES

1. The image of the mirror occurs in Gloria Potter's poem as it does in John Edwin Cowen's poem, "Ask Nothing from Masks." Compare and contrast the use of the mirror in these two poems.

2. Can you explain why "the masks/all smile" in the first part of the poem, but later, in the poem, they "frown"?

3. Explain Gloria Potter's final two lines: "Masks can/ask much."

4. Explain the contrasting views of Potter's last two lines with Cowen's line: "Ask Nothing from Masks . . ."

CREATIVE PRODUCT

1. Make a pencil drawing of a mask that, like Potter's, can smile and frown at the same time.

2. Briefly write, in prose, how animals may appear to be smiling and frowning simultaneously.

© 1996 by The Center for Applied Research in Education

CLARIBEL ALEGRIA

Time of Love
from LUISA IN REALITY LAND, A NOVEL

FOCUS

Claribel Alegria has received international acclaim as one of Central America's leading poetic voices. Señora Alegria is also a novelist, and an excerpt of her prose from *Luisa in Reality Land* is included in Unit Three of this book. She was born in Esteli, Nicaragua, and has lived most of her adult years in Santa Ana, El Salvador. In 1978 her book of poems, *Sobrevivo*, won the Casa de las Americas Prize of Cuba. As you read her poem, "Time of Love," think about the introduction to Unit One.

A student in your group should read the poem aloud after you have read it over carefully to yourself. It is important to read a poem silently two or three times to get a feel for the poem, and then to get a sense of what it means. Poetry is not written as concretely or explicitly as prose, and is, therefore, more difficult to comprehend at first. As you read the poem over and discuss it, however, it begins to reveal itself, much as a collage of different pictures on a single theme comes into clearer focus to reveal itself to you, if you are patient.

Reading the poem aloud also helps you hear the music and the rhythm of the poem. The dramatization of the poem sometimes helps clarify the sound and sense for you. This is a love poem, but it is deeply philosophical at the same time.

Time of Love
from Reality Land, a Novel

When you love me
I drop my polished mask
my smile becomes my own
the moon becomes the moon
and these very trees
of this instant
the sky
the light
presences that open
into vertigo
and are newly born
and are eternal
and your eyes as well
are born with them
your lips that in naming
discover me.
When I love you
I am sure I don't end here
and that life is transitory
and death a transit
and time a blazing carbuncle
with no worn-out yesterdays
with no future.

H.O.T. RESPONSES

1. The first line, "When you love me," creates a series of images that unfold. What are they? Can you explain how they are related?

2. There is no stanza break, but which line signifies a change of direction or intensity in the poem?

3. Explain why the poet says: "I drop my polished mask"

4. Why is the mask "polished" do you think?

5. Why do you think the poet chooses to use such an ugly word as *carbuncle* at the end of this poem? (Note: a carbuncle is a nasty, huge pimple or boil.)

   . . . and time a blazing carbuncle
   with no worn-out yesterdays
   with no future.

6. Discuss this poem with your group, and try to picture what kind of person this is. What kind of love is she describing? What emotions do you feel after reading this poem?

CREATIVE PRODUCT

1. It is often said that anyone who can write, writes at least one love poem in a life time. This is your chance, if you haven't done so already! A mask of some kind must appear in this poem, however. It can be a love poem to a potential loved one, to a past loved one, or to a current loved one (share it only if you want to).

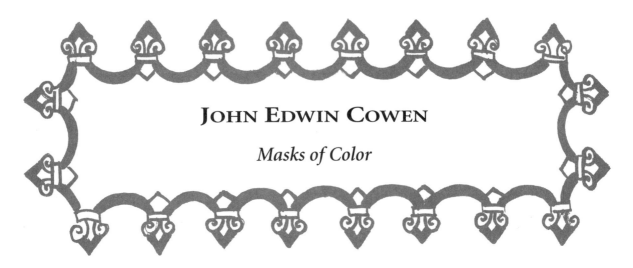

FOCUS

John Edwin Cowen, poet, is the author and compiler of the multicultural litera-ture for this book. Of northern European descent, he writes: " I come from a very multiethnic and diverse cultural environment. I was born and raised in Jersey City, New Jersey, and have lived most of my adult years in Teaneck, New Jersey. Both places are very diverse communities—ethnically and racially. Also, my mother's blood lines are Irish, Dutch, and German, and my father's are Russian and Austrian. My family's religious backgrounds are also diverse, including Judaism, Catholicism, and Protestantism. Through marriage, this diversity grew, adding Turkish and Italian to the rich cultural mix. Growing up in this multicultural environment, and then, living and working as a teacher and as an administrator in Teaneck, a microcosm of America, I often find myself thinking and writing about these differences. I believe that is why so many of my poems celebrate diversity and often take the point of view of ethnically and racially oppressed groups."

Read the following poem, "Masks of Color," and keep in mind how the poet's background may have influenced its creation.

Masks of Color

little less white
than black
from masks of the same
mind:

and traces of
holes to blur
deeper than smiles given
gold

from masks to
mirror the world
to blend softer, swifter
reds,

yellow heads
haught and eyes
fixed in curves of fire
moons:

hatchets halt.
witch doctors chant:
more color on white
mask!

H.O.T. RESPONSES

Read the poem, "Masks of Color," silently, then select a volunteer reader from your cooperative group. The volunteer should read the poem aloud with feeling. Then discuss the following questions in your group and have one student record the group's responses:

1. What is your group's interpretation of the first two lines in stanza 3?

> *. . . from masks to*
> *mirror the world . . .*

2. Which geocultural groups are included in "Masks of Color"?

3. Write the key words or phrases that support your answer for question 2.

4. Whose point of view is the poet taking? (Note: The irony and the humor of the last three lines of this poem provide a clue to question 4.)

5. Discuss the rhythms of this poem. Can you explain how these rhythms and sounds convey meaning in this poem? The introduction to this unit, Masks Around the World, indicates that different cultures have worn masks for different reasons. Which of these reasons for wearing masks best illustrates "Masks of Color?"

CREATIVE PRODUCT

1. On a blank sheet of paper, paper bag, or on a sheet of oak tag, illustrate stanzas 2 and 4 by creating your own mask. It is necessary to design your mask according to the description of the poem (stanzas 2 and 4), and to color your mask in like manner. Use crayons, color markers, or watercolor paints, if available.

   Note: Work independently on this product in class. You must share your mask with members of your own group, and with other groups in the class. (Keep your product in your portfolio.)

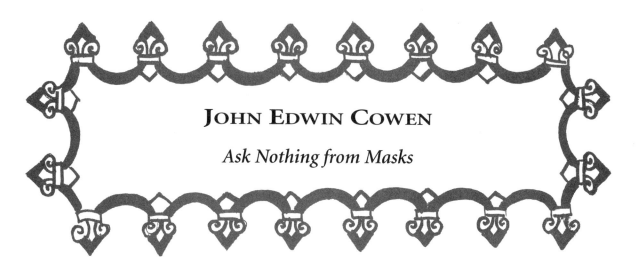

FOCUS

"Ask Nothing from Masks" is a poem about wearing masks. Read it carefully to yourself, then a student in the cooperative group should read it aloud with feeling.

Ask Nothing from Masks

Masked from this side
　　to fool fools!
　　　　Fooled enough?
Time, time to unmask!

Unwise or uncertain
　　whose mirror
　　　　fills with lies,
We—who trust their

Eyes—glinting without
　　shame—Ask nothing
　　　　from masks . . .
WEAR ONE—*yourself!*

H.O.T. RESPONSES

1. Explain who is wearing the mask in stanza 1.

2. What does the "mirror" in stanza 2 have to do with the mask? Explain.

3. T.S. Eliot, the poet of "Love Song of J. Alfred Prufrock," is discussed in the introduction to Unit One. Compare how Eliot's two quoted lines in this poem are similar in meaning to "Ask Nothing from Masks."

   . . . there will be time, there will be time
   to prepare a face to meet the faces that you meet . . .

4. Do you think the poet is being serious when he writes

   . . . Ask nothing/from Masks . . . WEAR ONE—Yourself!

5. Why does the poet tell the reader to "ask nothing from masks"?

6. Why do you think the poet recommends that the reader wear a mask?

   WEAR ONE—Yourself!

16

7. Which of the following reasons for wearing masks, given in the introduction to "Masks Around the World," is best illustrated by this poem? Explain your choice:

> Masks for Deceiving
> Masks for the Stage
> Masks for the Rites of Passage
> Masks for Disguises
> Masks for Carnival and Festivals

CREATIVE PRODUCT

1. Write a dramatic scene for two characters. Have one or both characters wear and interchange several masks to become different characters or personalities, or to express different points of view.

2. Using the above format, your cooperative group can create a debate or role-play different social issues. Different cultural perspectives can be presented on an issue such as prejudice, or bias. Each individual can role-play someone from another race or ethnic group.

3. Have each cooperative group or teacher select the best dramatic scene to be acted out before the class. Later, discuss the production and write a review as if you were a drama critic.

CREATING PAPER MASKS

FOCUS

The making of masks has been an art form performed throughout the ages. Masks were made of clay, plaster of Paris, papier mâché, bronze, animal hair, and bones. Masks have been shaped from the bark of trees, whittled from wood, or stitched on cloth.

Less ambitious masks can be made from paper, paper bags, and oak tag. See if you can create interesting "shopping bag masks" by following the directions below.

CREATIVE PRODUCT

Materials:

(Caution: Never use a plastic bag; it could cause suffocation.)

Paper shopping bag
Scissors
Pencil or felt-tip pen
Drawing colored markers
      or crayons
      or watercolor paints
      or acrylic paints
Art brushes
      And/or paint applicator

1. Cut half-moon circles at the bottom two sides of the bag so that the bag exposes your shoulders as shown in the example below.

2. With the paper shopping bag still on; feel for your eyes and draw a circle and place a dot. Do the same for your nose and mouth.

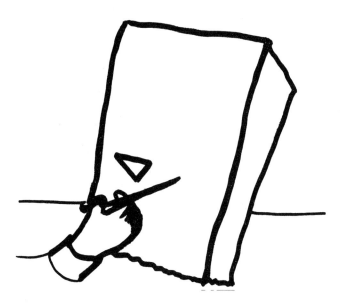

3. Take off the shopping bag and begin to create your own design. Look through this book for examples of mask designs. You may also want to look up other designs for masks in the library, to serve as models.

4. The design you make should serve as an outline for coloring the mask. Therefore, use a light pencil or fine-line pen to outline your design so that you can color within the lines as shown below.

5. Use your scissors to cut out small areas for seeing and cut out the mouth and nose.

6. Select the colors you want to use and apply the media (crayons, paint, markers). Enjoy wearing your mask. Use your mask to create skits with members of your cooperative group. Try to create impromptu skits, or create dialogues inspired by the different masks. Let the masks help dictate the story or scene you wish to create. Once you have perfected your scene, share it with the other members of the class.

CREATING CLAY MASKS

FOCUS

Throughout the ages, masks have endured as art forms through the medium of clay. These art forms can be worn or hung on the wall as you would a painting. The mask art form can also be displayed on a stand, similar to the way decorative plates are displayed.

Follow the directions below to create your own clay mask. You may work as a team in class, in art class, or you can complete this as a homework project. Your teacher will decide which option to choose. (If an art teacher is available to work within the English classroom, this exercise and other more complex mask projects can be explored.)

CREATIVE PRODUCT

Clay Masks

Materials:

Permanent pliable clay
Acrylic or tempera paints
Newspaper strips
Colored paper strips
Paste or water liquid glue
Vaseline

Optional ornaments:
Colored beads
Shells
Raw vegetables
(dry beans, peas, rice, noodles-shells)

Option I: Clay Masks

1. Before beginning to mold your clay form, it is advisable to sketch a design on paper.

2. Shape your permanent, pliable clay form in the shape of a face, making holes for eyes and mouth. The mask can be larger than the actual face, and it can take on a shape that is round, oval, pointed, square, or triangular. It may even take the shape of an animal's face.

3. Let your mask dry out in the sun. Lay it on a window sill. Be sure to place rolled up paper, or crumpled newspaper under your clay shape so it does not collapse.

4. Create your design by applying your acrylic or tempera colors.

5. When it has dried, add decorations as desired.

Option II: Peel-Away Masks

1. Follow steps 1 and 2 from Option I.

2. Cover the outside of the mask with vaseline so the peel-away mask comes off without sticking.

3. To create a peel-away mask, you must add moistened strips of newspaper or colored paper to the clay model.

4. Dip the strips of paper in paste and water liquid and smooth onto the clay form, working around the cut out areas.

5. When you have placed several layers of paper strips about 1/8″ to 1/4″ thick, let the mask dry out. Lay the mask on a window sill to get direct sunlight.

6. Color your mask design using acrylic or tempera paint.

7. You may glue on ornaments, and if you wish, add string, straw, rope, grass, or leaves to create hair for the mask.

8. Once the mask is completely dry, peel away gently (the vaseline backing should enable this process to work smoothly).

Share your finished product with your group and other classmates. Perhaps some of these masks can be displayed in the classroom or in your school's display case.

Option III

Write a poem, inspired by your own mask, or by masks made by others.

© 1996 by The Center for Applied Research in Education

Unit Two

THEME:
AWAKENING THE IMAGINATION

INTRODUCTION

This unit focuses on awakening the imagination by reading and writing poetry. Poets, more than any other writers, are interested in the magical sound of words and how these words and sounds interplay with rhythm, perhaps more than they are interested in meaning. As a matter of fact, it is rare that an outstanding poem can be read only once by the reader to fully comprehend its meaning. There may be many interpretations to a poem; from some, an exact meaning cannot be derived.

The poems in this unit have been chosen to invite you to learn how the poet's imagination is at play. In several cases, the poet actually provides us with his or her own definition of poetry. These definitions, however, are unique in that they are unlike any definition you might find in a dictionary. In fact, they are more like metaphors than definitions; that is, they compare unlike things to form an impression about what poetry is.

By following the suggestions that appear in this unit, you should find reading poetry an easier task compared with your earlier experiences. The poets selected represent the five major geocultural groups with which this text is concerned. Not only will you get a chance to learn about poetry, but you will be able to compare how poets from different cultural backgrounds use their imaginations to express themselves.

Imagination enables you to express yourself freely and uniquely. Instead of seeing a plain, white sheet of paper, for instance, you may feel its grain, or the pulsating skin of an animal, or the warmth of the touch of someone you love. Like the poet, José Garcia Villa, you may invite a tiger for a weekend, or imagine two lovely giraffes, a white one and a golden one, kneeling before you. Through the magic of imagination, you may explore past memories and write about them, bringing to life experiences that have been dormant for many years. Or, like a fortune teller, you may predict future events and create a world where artificial intelligence gives life to robots who rule like unkind monsters. By awakening your imagination, you will be able to explore many new possibilities, and learn more about yourself, and others, and you will be able to create a magical world of your own unlike any other.

HOW TO READ A POEM

Step 1

The first time you start to read a poem you must relax and read it once through without concentrating on its meaning. This first reading should be very much the way you would size up someone whom you are meeting for the first time. You will just get a first impression. You will observe this individual and listen to his or her voice, and you might enjoy just looking at or noticing his or her shape or movement. You may form some ideas about this person, but you should not think you really know or understand what he or she is all about. This metaphor or analogy is similar to reading a poem for the first time. You may enjoy the sound, rhythms, or description of the words, and you might form some general impressions about the poem, but you will want to learn more about it after each reading.

Step 2

On your second or third reading, you should concentrate a bit more closely on the general meaning or meanings in the poem. It is still too early to think about each specific line or word; stop, however, to think about a particular line that strikes you. It may be a certain phrase, or a word that is unfamiliar to you. You might ask a classmate in your group about this phrase, or look up the word in a dictionary. You will by now want to compare your feelings about the poem after reading it the second or third time with how you felt about it when you encountered it for the first time. Are your feelings the same? Are they similar? What is different and why?

Step 3

Any additional readings of the poem should be used to think more specifically about the words, phrases, or images you have read. It is now time to think more specifically about what the poem means. Once again, use the example given before about meeting someone. After you have seen this person on different occasions, do you still have the same first impressions? Or is this individual somewhat different now that you have gotten to know more personal details about his or her experiences, values, or beliefs?

Step 4

Poems usually are written to describe something that the poet sees differently, or is eager to convey uniquely. The poet may want to paint a picture or image with words for the reader, or to express a point of view so that the reader will think about it from a different perspective or meaning. These are some of the possibilities to keep in mind as you search for a clearer understanding of the poem.

Step 5

The more you become familiar with the poem, the better you should understand it. One helpful approach to understanding it is to try to summarize, or to put into your own words, the different interpretations you have about individual lines or stanzas in the poem. Compare your views with those of others in your group, and listen to how other students form opinions about the poem. Remember, however, that there is generally no exact or right meaning for a poem. Poets will often confess that they are not exactly sure what they meant when they wrote certain lines or phrases; they have even been heard to say on occasion that sometimes words seem to "drop from heaven" and land on the page. That is what awakening the imagination is all about. If you are lucky, and if you practice enough, magical things may happen when you write and you may be able to produce a beautiful poem or other work of art yourself.

H.O.T. RESPONSES

1. Choose a favorite poem to read to your group.

2. What metaphors or similes does it contain?

3. Describe unique sounds or rhythms in the poem.

4. Does it have unfamiliar or unusual words?

5. What meaning or image is the poet trying to convey?

CREATIVE PRODUCT

1. Write your own poem using metaphors and similes with unique sounds and rhythms.

JOSÉ GARCIA VILLA

Lyric 17

FOCUS

José Garcia Villa was born in Manila, Philippines. He came to the United States in 1930 and has resided here ever since. Villa has established an international reputation as a short story writer and as a poet, and was awarded the National Artist Award for Literature by the Philippine government. His first book of poems, *Have Come, Am Here* (1942), was hailed by American critics such as Marianne Moore and Mark Van Doren. This book received the poetry award of the American Academy of Arts and Letters.

"Lyric 17" is an excellent example of the use of the metaphor to create a better understanding of poetry. As you read "Lyric 17" think about the way this poem describes how a lyrical poem should be written. Be sure to use the five steps for reading poetry discussed in the introduction to this unit.

Lyric 17

First, a poem must be magical,
Then musical as a sea-gull.
It must be a brightness moving
And hold secret a bird's flowering.
It must be slender as a bell,
And it must hold fire as well.
It must have the wisdom of bows
And it must kneel like a rose.
It must be able to hear
The luminance of dove and deer.
It must be able to hide
What it seeks, like a bride.
And over all I would like to hover
God, smiling from the poem's cover.

H.O.T. RESPONSES

1. Explain how using the five steps for reading a poem helped you understand "Lyric 17."

2. When you read "Lyric 17," did you observe that every two lines rhyme? What else did you learn?

3. To show how well you understood this poem, summarize each couplet, every two lines, beginning with the first two lines:

   First, a poem must be magical
   then musical as a sea-gull.

   By the time you complete this activity, you should have written seven statements that explain what Villa's definition of a good poem is.

4. When you are finished, compare your summaries with other student summaries in your cooperative group.

CREATIVE PRODUCT

1. Create your own definition of poetry. (You may agree or disagree with Villa's view.) You may write your definition in prose, or if you like, in poetry form.

AN INTERVIEW WITH JOSÉ GARCIA VILLA

FOCUS

The following excerpt is an interview with the poet, José Garcia Villa. In this interview, he is asked to explain "Lyric 17." You should find it very interesting to compare your interpretation of each of the seven couplets to the poet's personal interpretations.

If you find that your interpretations differ from Villa's, do not feel that your ideas were necessarily incorrect. Note how both the interviewer and the poet admit that it is not an easy task to give an exact prose interpretation of a poetic expression, particularly because poems are not explicitly stated; the interviewer, at one point, admits: "I have always found the next lines difficult to comprehend":

It must have the wisdom of bows
And it must kneel like a rose.

Focus here on the poet's response: "You must remember," Villa said, "some lines and some poems cannot be explained. But let me try . . ."

Once you have finished reading the interview, compare his interpretations with your own and with the interpretations made by members of your cooperative group.

THE INTERVIEW

Villa's lyrical and exquisitely crafted poem, "First, a Poem Must Be Magical" (Villa, 1942), can serve as the basis for discussing his techniques of poetry. Although the poet did not set out to achieve this end, he does so, gracefully and economically. As you shall see, this beautiful poem leads to a unique definition of what a poem should be:

In a taped interview, Villa provided me with an explication of this poem. Of the first two lines,

> *First, a poem must be magical*
> *Then musical as a sea-gull.*

Villa said, "These lines mean exactly what they say: That a poem must have magic, and it must be musical."

I asked the poet, "What meaning would you ascribe to the next lines?"

> *It must be a brightness moving*
> *And hold secret a bird's flowering.*

Villa explained, "There are some brightnesses which are stationary and static, but a poem, like a bird, must fly. This is the difference between prose and poetry. Prose is flatfooted and stationary; poetry soars, flies like a bird. The stationary bird, when first seen, appears like a rosebud. When it begins to fly, it opens up and spreads its wings and blooms like a flower."

I asked him to explain the images in the fifth and sixth lines,

> *It must be slender as a bell*
> *And it must hold fire as well.*

To these lines, Villa responded, "A poem is economical; it's slender as a bell, it has no adipose tissue; it's lean and clean. Poorly written poems should, of necessity, go on a diet, to rid them-selves of excess verbiage and adjectives. And by 'fire' in the next line, I simply mean that a poem must have a spirit."

"I have always found the next lines difficult to comprehend," I confessed:

> *It must have the wisdom of bows*
> *And it must kneel like a rose.*

"You must remember," Villa said, "some lines and some poems cannot be explained. But let me try. I am speaking of the archer's bow. A good bow is one that knows when to shoot, and one that directs the arrow to its mark. Just as a good poem, it never goes astray. To 'kneel like a rose' is a metaphor for humili-ty. All fine people are humble and a poem should also be humble, however beautiful it is."

For the seventh and eighth lines,

> *It must be able to hear*
> *The luminance of dove and deer.*

"There's a good man behind every fine poem. A good poet is usually a good person. "Luminance' naturally means brightness. When I see a good face, it's a good face and I respond. When I see a bad face, it is the face full of crime, even though he doesn't proclaim his crime. His face proclaims it out loud."

"In other words," I asked, "the poet knows things instinctively?"

"Yes, naturally," Villa answered.

And for the meaning of the next couplet, I prodded Villa to discuss,

> *It must be able to hide*
> *What it seeks, like a bride.*

Villa, without hesitation, began, "A poem must *not explicitly* state meaning. The reader is supposed to sense it out, feel it. The language itself doesn't tell you, but the substructure behind that language is the real meaning. It is not explicit and declarative. That's why when I say, 'It must have the wisdom of bows,' you must guess at what I mean, and children love to guess at meaning. That's why they love riddles. I used to love riddles as a child."

The final couplet of this rather unorthodox sonnet,

> *And over all I would like to hover*
> *God, smiling from the poem's cover.*

is possibly one of the most beautiful ever written. "The last line has a masterfully dramatic effect. At the same time, this couplet is, to me, the most mystifying one in the poem," I commented.

Villa nodded and offered this explanation: "When you see a blessed creature, God shines and hovers over that saintly creature. The poem itself creates a God-hood, and the poem radiates Godness. At the same time, God is hovering over it, acknowledging the Godness radiating from the poem, itself, which embodies the spirituality existing in a poem and, at the same time, radiates it to others."

Indeed, there is a Godness to this poem; and there is a God-hood within this poet. Poet Richard Eberhardt understood this, too, evidenced in a review of Villa's work in which he states:

> *A pure, startling, and resounding body of poetry, informed with so much legerity and fire, remarkably consistent in its devotion to spiritual reality. The subject matter is formidable, the author a God-driven poet. He arrives at peaks without showing the strenuous effort of climbing; the personal is lost in a blaze of linguistic glories . . . . (Villa, 1958)*

The poet concludes that reading poetry might be compared to enjoying riddles, and that children enjoy solving riddles. Since poetry is neither explicit nor declarative, children must be taught through sheer joy to sense out and feel the meaning. Is there not much of this that goes on when we are "sensing" or drawing conclusions, or making an inference? Perhaps we should become more concerned about providing children with joyous language experiences that will enable them to better understand poetry.

H.O.T. RESPONSES

1. Compare and contrast your interpretations of "Lyric 17" to Villa's.

2. Discuss Villa's comments with your cooperative group to explore other interpretations.

3. Were you surprised by any of Villa's explanations? Explain.

CREATIVE PRODUCT

1. Interview one of the students in your cooperative group about his or her definition of poetry. Write down these views and follow the same interview format as that used with Villa.

HILARIO S. FRANCIA

To an Artist with a Beard

FOCUS

Hilario S. Francia is considered one of the finest poets, artists, and book designers in the Philippines. He has won a number of prestigious awards including the Palanca Award for Poetry. He is the author of four books of poetry; the latest entitled, *A Beacon in the Dark, and Other Poems* (1992), is written in English and Tagalog. Hilario S. Francia's art has been exhibited throughout the world, including art shows in New York and San Francisco.

The poem that follows combines visual as well as auditory effects to awaken the reader's imagination. It is not at all surprising that this poet is also an artist, especially when one considers his use of visual design in the poem presented here. It is dedicated to Filipino artist Armando Manalo, and poet Cirilo F. Bautista, whose poetry appears in Unit Nine of this book.

"To an Artist with a Beard" is a "concrete" poem that also has a lyrical quality in that its rhythm and sound are carefully interwoven into the form. The words, therefore, are not chosen solely to fit the visual, concrete form of the poem. Their main function is to sing, whereas their secondary function is to create the desired image or dramatic visual effect.

As you read Francia's poem, try to understand how the poet's choice of words and concrete shape create a harmony of sound, sense, and form.

To an Artist with a Beard
(For Armando Manalo & Cirilo Bautista)

As
you have
fire and height
which is only what
is elegant and light;
so are you most bright
when you are very right!
As your garden and high
walls serve only to guard
and beautify; so will com-
mendations be received;
which your tongue cannot
admit. As your mustache
and beard attend only
your mouth and chin,
so from ceremony
and rite: retain
only what is
pure and
white.

H.O.T. RESPONSES

1. Hilario S. Francia's poem, "To an Artist with a Beard," can be referred to as a "concrete" poem because of its visual shape. Identify what this poem and its shape have in common. Once you have done so, attempt to define what a "concrete poem" is in your own words.

2. In "To an Artist with a Beard" compare the lines, "As your garden and high/walls serve only to guard/and beautify . . ." to the parallel lines in this poem. In doing so, you will have identified the key words that form and extend the metaphor that unifies this poem.

35

3. Explain the meaning of this "extended metaphor."

CREATIVE PRODUCT

1. Write a concrete poem that forms a shape, that is, a circle, a diamond, a candle, a pyramid, and so on. Be sure that your choice of words and the shape they produce are similar in both form and sense.

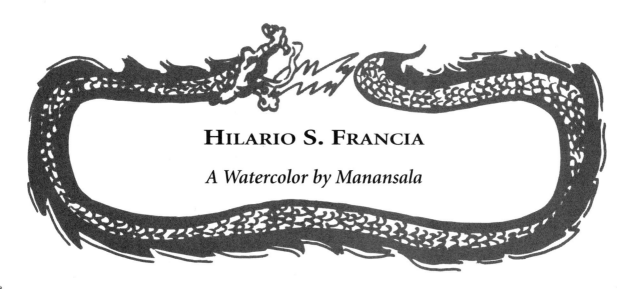

HILARIO S. FRANCIA

A Watercolor by Manansala

FOCUS

"A Watercolor by Manansala" is similar to Hilario S. Francia's preceding poem in that it combines visual and auditory effects to awaken the reader's imagination. In this poem, it is obvious that the poet is responding to a watercolor painting by the Filipino artist, Manansala, in which the color and light are so intense the poet imagines ". . . the Cold and the Heat are trying to destroy each other . . ." The poet uses dramatic, visual imagery to heighten the reader's imagination—a new technique or form created by poet José Garcia Villa, which he labels "Duo-Technique."

As you read this fascinating, beautiful poem, try to understand how the form of the poem helps to create a sense of tension in the movement of the words, which also heightens your sense of the meaning of the poem.

A Watercolor by Manansala

Something extra	ordinary
has hap	pened here
(in this water	color by
Manan	sala):
the *Cold*	and the *Heat*
are trying	to destroy
each	other.
But	both
the Water-issues	and the Fire-issues
are alive	and their beauty
becomes even	more brilliant—
like the	tiger
who has just	changed his stripes—
stripes that	are right
and possessing	inner strength:
passing through the cen	ter and leaving
through the mouths	of light.

37

H.O.T. RESPONSES

1. Observe the form used by Francia in "A Watercolor by Manansala." Explain why you think the poet created a gulf down the center of the poem.

2. The poet José Garcia Villa created this technique or form, which he labels "Duo-Technique." How would you define "Duo-Technique" in your own words?

3. Select key phrases or lines in this poem to illustrate how they are magnified or set into motion by the form. Also, discuss in your cooperative group how the form and language work together to create sense or meaning in this poem.

4. Summarize the meaning of this poem in your own words, then compare it with those of students in your cooperative group.

CREATIVE PRODUCT

1. Write a poem using "Duo-Technique." Use the space down the center of the poem to create a tension in the movement of your words, and see how you can use the form to heighten your use of language.

© 1996 by The Center for Applied Research in Education

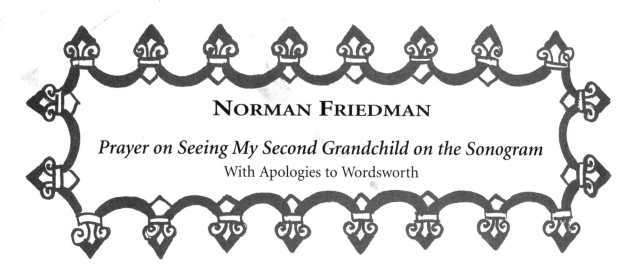

NORMAN FRIEDMAN

Prayer on Seeing My Second Grandchild on the Sonogram
With Apologies to Wordsworth

FOCUS

Norman Friedman is the author of two books of poetry: *The Intrusion of Love* (1992), and *The Magic Badge, poems 1953–1984*. Friedman has received a number of honors and awards, including a Phi Beta Kappa and a Bowdoin prize at Harvard, the *Northwest Review* annual poetry prize, a Fulbright, several Borestone Mountain poetry awards, and a prize in the All Nations Contest. He has published six academic books, including several on E.E. Cummings, and a study of fiction theory. Friedman also served as a sonar office on a Navy destroyer during World War II. Friedman is a Russian Jew who lives in New York.

As you read this poem, observe how the poet builds on the theme of technology and science to express his sense of awe. Also, note his use of the extended metaphor as you read and reread this beautiful poem.

Prayer on Seeing My Second Grandchild on the Sonogram

With Apologies to Wordswor*th*

Dear Lord, you see the baby in my
daughter's belly on the screen,
astronaut curled in his cockpit
upsidedown, lifesustaining equipment
attached to his navel, enfolded in
his pilot's bubble, hands fixed on
the controls, traveling on his trip
to life and to us, who have forgotten
You and this perilous journey from
wherever he came from, that unknown
planet, mysterious star and heat
of generation, assigned to enter our
atmospheres and climates here,

whatever weathers and conditions
he may find among us and our storms,
may his landing be gentle and safe,
and may he have been provisioned
against our viruses and tempers,
accomplishing his secret mission
to fill our hearts with such joy
that we will never again forget
the source and marvel of its fruit.

© 1996 by The Center for Applied Research in Education

H.O.T. RESPONSES

1. In your cooperative group, discuss why the term "extended metaphor" is used to describe Norman Friedman's poem.

2. Explain the metaphorical use of the "astronaut" in his poem. Do you think it is a good choice? Explain.

3. In your own words, describe how this poem progresses from the spiritual, to the scientific, to the human level.

4. What is the purpose of the astronaut's "secret mission," according to the poet? Discuss this point with your cooperative group.

CREATIVE PRODUCT

1. Write your own poem, making use of the extended metaphor. Use Friedman's poem as a model.

PABLO NERUDA

The Art of Poetry

Translated by Robert Bly

FOCUS

Pablo Neruda was born in 1904 in a small frontier town in southern Chile. At nineteen, he published *Twenty Poems of Love and One Ode of Desperation,* which is still loved in South America. By age twenty-three, he was recognized as a poet by the Chilean government and was given a post in the Far East. He later served in his country's senate. Later, in exile in Mexico, Neruda worked on *Canto General,* which Robert Bly calls "the greatest long poem written on the American continent since *Leaves of Grass* by Walt Whitman." Robert Bly, translator of this poem, poet, and critic writes of Neruda: "In Neruda's poems, the imagination drives forward, joining the entire poem in a rising flow of imaginative energy . . . His imagination sees the hidden connections between conscious and unconscious substances with such assurance that he hardly bothers with metaphors, he links them by typing their hidden tails."

Neruda's poem, "The Art of Poetry," is a poem that leaps from image to image, and may cause some difficulty at first in understanding; therefore, it is particularly important that you follow the five steps for reading a poem to help you understand this imaginative, elusive form. Then observe how Pablo Neruda uses contrasting images of light and dark in this intriguing and mysterious poem.

The Art of Poetry

Translated by Robert Bly

Between shadows and clearing, between defenses and young
    girls,
having inherited an original heart, and funereal imagination,
suddenly pale, something withered in my face,
in mourning like a desperate widower every day of my life,
for every drop of invisible water I drink
in my sleepy way, and for every sound I take in shivering,
I have the same chilly fever, and the same absent thirst,
an ear coming into the world, an oblique anxiety,
as though robbers were about to arrive, or ghosts,
inside a sea shell with great and unchangeable depths,
like a humiliated waiter, or a bell slightly hoarse,
or an aged mirror or the smell of an empty house
where the guests come in hopelessly drunk at night,
having an odor of clothes thrown on the floor, and no flowers,
—in another sense, possibly not as sad—
still, the truth is, the wind suddenly hitting my chest,
the nights with infinite substance fallen into my bedroom,
the crackling of a day hardly able to burn,
ask from me sadly whatever I have that is prophetic,
and there are objects that knock, and are never answered,
and something always moving, and a name that does not come
    clear.

H.O.T. RESPONSES

1. Study the contrasts in the words and phrases in Neruda's poem as listed below:

   "Between shadows and clearing, between defenses and young girls"
   "original heart, and funereal imagination"
   "suddenly pale, something withered in my face"
   "invisible water I drink"
   "chilly fever . . . absent thirst"
   "a bell slightly hoarse"
   "odor of clothes . . . and no flowers"
   "the crackling of a day hardly able to burn"
   "and there objects that knock, and are never answered"
   ". . . and a name that does not come clear"

Explain these contrasts within the context of the complete poem, and try to make some generalizations about how these images relate to "The Art of Poetry."

2. Discuss your views of this poem with students in your cooperative group.

3. How does this poem compare with the others you have read in this unit?

CREATIVE PRODUCT

1. Study the highly imaginative language used by Neruda in the following passage, and then summarize what you believe the poet is saying about the poetic process:

   An ear coming into the world, an oblique anxiety,
   as though robbers were about to arrive, or ghosts,
   inside a sea shell with great and unchangeable depths,
   like a humiliated waiter, or a bell slightly hoarse

2. Try to illustrate this eerie but imaginative poetry. Share it with your group.

3. Try to create your own leaping poetry, by letting your imagination "go wild"!

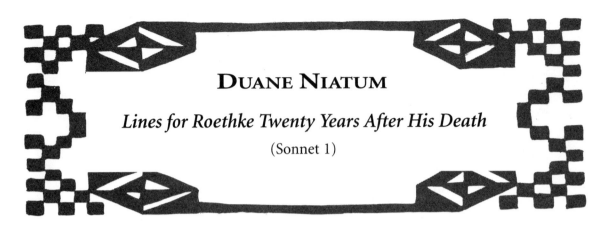

DUANE NIATUM

Lines for Roethke Twenty Years After His Death
(Sonnet 1)

FOCUS

Duane Niatum is a Native American and a member of the Klallam tribe, whose ancestral lands are on the Washington coast along the Strait of Juan de Fuca. Niatum's collections of poems include *After the Death of an Elder Klallam; Ascending Red Cellar Moon; Digging Out the Roots;* and *Songs for the Harvester of Dreams,* which won the highly prestigious National Book Award in 1982. He has also edited *Carriers of the Dream Wheel,* the most widely read and known book on Native American poetry (1975); and *Harper's Anthology of 20th Century Native American Poetry* (1988) in which "Lines for Roethke" appears. "Lines for Roethke" is written in sonnet form and is dedicated to one of America's most lyrical poets. As you read this poem, see if it echoes any of the other poets from this unit who have written on writing poetry.

Lines for Roethke Twenty Years After His Death
(Sonnet 1)

You asked us to hear the softest vocable of wind,
whether slow or swift, rising or falling to earth;
its fragments will drop in to place in the end.
You said, believe, endure, the ironies of birth!
If we succeeded in sleeping like thorns on a rose,
the nerves awake to the pulse, folklore of the sun,
the interior drifts may loosen, the nights freeze,
the passions whirl, not ramble until undone.
And no one colors the years black, but crow,
retouches the ruins, fakes the moon, pocks the beach.
Laugh right back, you sang, let it take hold,
it'll grow bored, forget whoever may be in reach.
Let your hand trace the riddle on the wave,
rejoice in the tale that leaves the ear a cave.

H.O.T. RESPONSES

1. Can you feel how sensually rich Duane Niatum's poem is? Which senses are addressed in his poem? Compare your list with those of students from your cooperative group.

2. Which sense is used prevalently in this poem? Why do you think this is so?

3. There is a play of words in the final couplet. Explain why the word, "riddle" in the phrase "riddle on the wave" is such a good choice. What other word would you have substituted for "riddle" if you were the poet?

CREATIVE PRODUCT

1. Write your own sonnet using Duane Niatum's sonnet form as a model. Share your completed sonnet with your cooperative group.

GWENDOLYN BROOKS

The Egg Boiler

FOCUS

Gwendolyn Brooks has a long established reputation as one of America's outstanding lyrical poets. Ms. Brooks is frequently compared to another great lyrical poet, Countee Cullen, who is also African American. Gwendolyn Brooks ranks high when compared with male poets or other female poets of any race or ethnic background; in fact, she is the recipient of the Pulitzer Prize, a prize bestowed upon only the greatest poets of our time. Previous books of poetry by Gwendolyn Brooks include *Annie Allen; A Sheet in Bronzeville;* and *Selected Poems.* She has also written a book of poems for children, entitled *Bronzeville Boys and Girls* and a book of fiction, *Maud Martha.* "The Egg Boiler" leads to a definition of poetry. Brooks uses the traditional sonnet form for this poem, a fourteen-line poem in which every other line rhymes. The poem ends in a couplet (the last two lines rhyme).

The Egg Boiler

Being you, you cut your poetry from wood.
The boiling of an egg is heavy art.
You come upon it as an artist should,
With rich-eyed passion, and with straining heart.
We fools, we cut our poems out of air,
Night color, wind soprano, and such stuff.
And sometimes weightlessness is much to bear.
You mock it, though, you name it Not Enough.
The egg, spooned gently to the avid pan,
And left the strict three minutes, or the four,
Is your Enough and art for any man.
We fools give courteous ear—then cut some more,
Shaping a gorgeous Nothingness from cloud.
You watch us, eat your egg, and laugh aloud.

H.O.T. RESPONSES

1. The use of contrast is employed by Gwendolyn Brooks in this poem. Explain who the "you" and the "we" represent. Discuss these contrasting views with your cooperative group.

2. Explain the use of the metaphors in this poem:

    "You cut your poetry from wood"
    "The boiling of an egg is heavy art"

3. Why does the poet refer to "we fools?" Are they really fools?

4. Explain the use of sarcasm or sardonic wit as it applies to this poem.

5. Summarize, in your own words, what Gwendolyn Brooks thinks good poetry should be.

CREATIVE PRODUCT

1. Select two other poems introduced in this unit and compare them with "The Egg Boiler" as a way of showing how three different poets use poetry to define their own taste in poetry. Do you agree with them?

   Explain your view.

THEME:
LEARNING FROM CONFLICT

INTRODUCTION

Conflict takes many forms. There are aggressors who initiate conflict, and there are those who are the recipients of such aggressive acts, who respond differently to them. Conflict often inflicts anxiety and suffering on innocent bystanders. In other ways, conflict stirs hatred and causes acts of retaliation by individuals and by groups which, in turn, may escalate a small conflict into a serious encounter producing violence, murder or war.

This unit addresses many such forms of conflict, and from these literary or vicarious experiences, the reader may be able to analyze the causes and responses to conflict, and learn how to cope with them in a more rational and reasonable way.

One thing is certain, conflict occurs in all societies and cultures, and unfortunately conflicts often repeat themselves on many levels. The innocent bystander becomes the recipient of aggressive, taunting, and violent acts in two short stories: "'Agua Viva,' a Sculpture" by Jack Agüeros; and "The Man Who Looked Like Rizal" by José Garcia Villa. Wook Lee is a Vietnamese civilian, victimized by cruelty and bias in Bart Edelman's poem, "They Shot Wook Kim."

War is major conflict; it has devastated people and nations for centuries. In this unit, stories are told from the point of view of the vanquished as in the case of the Nez Perce Native American, Chief Joseph. We learn about a Filipino soldier, who fights valiantly with his resistance troops, only to lose to the Americans, described in a moving chapter from Nick Joaquin's *The Woman Who Had Two Navels*. "Granny and the Bridge" is a story of guerrilla warfare, led by a seemingly mad grandmother. Finally, an ancient antiwar poem, written in 500 B.C. by the ancient Chinese poet, Li Po, tells about the futility of war.

From these multicultural readings, much can be learned about conflict. Whether acts of conflict will ever end is another matter. After reading these works, you will be able to judge for yourself.

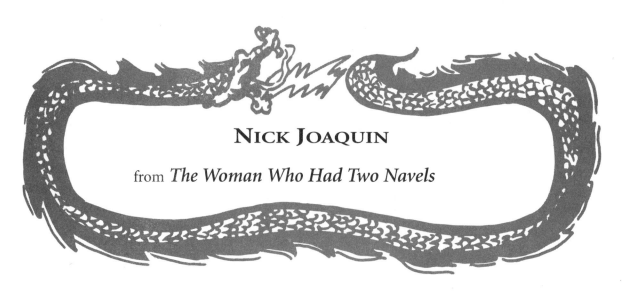

NICK JOAQUIN

from *The Woman Who Had Two Navels*

FOCUS

In recognition of his distinguished contribution to literature, the Philippine government conferred on Nick Joaquin in 1976 the award of National Artist. Joaquin's first book in 1952, *Prose and Poems,* met with instant acclaim. His play, *Portrait of the Artist as Filipino* was staged in Manila and New York, and was later made into a film. Nick Joaquin and José Garcia Villa are recognized as the two most important literary figures in the history of the Philippines.

The following excerpt was selected from Joaquin's novelette reprinted in the *Partisan Review* in the United States; it won the first Stonehill award for the novel (1960). This excerpt depicts a brutal battle staged in the Philippines when it went to war with the United States. Although the Filipino revolutionaries fought valiantly, they were overcome and occupied by the Americans until 1945 when they regained independence. In his book, *A Question of Heroes,* Nick Joaquin gives another perspective of how the conquered Filipinos really felt: "The fond cliché is of a people swiftly and wholeheartedly falling in love with America. The submerged evidence is of a bitter, stubborn, quite wide-spread resistance. The American lovers won in the end, and so thoroughly that we could forget there was even a struggle. The memory would have embarrassed our American passion when that passion was still a love affair."

As you read Nick Joaquin's story below, it is important to keep this perspective in mind. Dr. Monson did not die on the battlefield but the scars of that battle lingered with him until his death. In an earlier chapter, his daughter remembers and gives this account:

—But these hardheaded young men flung at the Yanquis their gesture, perhaps, and a futile one—but a beautiful, beautiful gesture nevertheless— and during those days that saw the failure of the Revolution and the establishment of new masters; when her father went about tight-lipped and stern-eyed, and her mother wept continually and put on black, and wailing people peeping through cracks in shut windows beheld what was left of their armies being led into prison camps by the Yanquis . . . the conquering Yanquis might jeer at the quaint architecture, the primitive plumbing, the ceremonious manners; behind impassive faces, people shared a secret pride, a secret exultation, and a lengthening litany of names.

from *The Woman Who Had Two Navels*

The wonderful silence followed them into the bedroom, where, in his huge old-fashioned canopy bed, Doctor Monson lay dying. He lay with the white sheet up to his chin and his hands were restless under the sheets. The eyes were still closed but the lips moved and the small wasted face was trying to rise from the pillow. The white hair and the dew on his brow glittered vividly in the shaded light. Standing on either side of the bed, his sons bent down to hear what he was saying but could make out no words. The thin lips continued to move, to speak; the bones stood out in his neck as he strove to lift his head in vain. Stooping lower, Pepe slipped an arm around the old man's shoulders and raised his head from the pillow. The sunken eyes did not open, the lips were still quivering. Pepe approached his mouth to the dying man's ear.

"Father," he called softly, "Father, here we are.

But Doctor Monson was not there at all. He was on the mountain pass and in history, young and booted and uniformed; and the long day's duty was ending at last.

HE WAS on the mountain pass, it was late in the afternoon, and the stiff December wind that had been blowing all day had finally died down. The new quiet was as clammy as the cold that clung to his tired bones; he felt steeped in ice though bathed in sunshine and, glancing sideways, saw the shrunk sun poised yet a few suspenseful inches from the line of haze that was the faraway sea.

He stood on the neck of the pass—a brief ledge the mountain tribes had cut from the steep hillside—and his nerves of a lowlander tensed in distrust of the floating height, the sky's tremendous closeness. To his right rose the wall of the cliff, matted with moss and topped with pines; to his left yawned the sheer drop into the valley. Behind him, the path ascended, widening, and disappeared into the

pinewoods; before him, the pass curved round the face of the cliff to join the trail down to the valley. It was twilight now in the valley, because of the encircling mountain ranges, but he could discern the stream below and the brown roofs of the village where the Americans were camped and the wrecked bridge at the foot of the hill. Three times this windy day, the Americans had come swarming up the trail; three times they had sought to storm the pass; and three times they had been driven back. He glanced up at the tall pines overhead, so finely golddusted with sunshine, so still and peaceful-looking; but in the dusk that showed behind the foremost boles were men waiting, squatted on the ferny ground; peasant warriors, barefoot and wrapped in gaudy blankets, cradling rifles on their laps—the twenty-odd defenders that remained of the fifty that had sworn to plug this pass with their bodies, to keep it closed and to hold it, if only for a day, so that up and across the wild mountains might be carried, sick and exhausted, into the most desperate of a hundred desperate refuges, the hunted man who was now, in person, the Republic, and all that was left of the Republic.

He had followed that hapless man in his violent retreat from the coast, where American ships now commanded the waters, and across embattled plain after plain in the lowlands—a track of fire, a trail of blood, that had now brought them, tragic remnants of an army, to the edge of the land, into the wilderness, up the cold soggy mountains of the north. And here on this mountain pass he had yesterday parted at last from his General; here he had promised to make a stand, while the fugitive Republic was carried deeper into the wilderness. Hardly a moment after the parting, he had heard cannon announcing that the Americans were already in the valley, battling the ghost village at the foot of the hill. He had been shocked to realize how fast the chase was narrowing: the hunted were only a few minutes, only a crucial mountain pass away from the hunters—and he had promised to hold that pass for a day.

Well, he had kept his word. The day was ending now, though not as rapidly as he would have wished. Troubled by the stillness in the valley, he yearned for the night, for darkness, but the shrunk sun seemed to have halted in the west. He lifted his field-glasses and trained them along the stream but saw no soldiers wading across the torrent or moving on the banks; even the sentries that had been posted at either end of the ruined bridge had vanished. He did not doubt that the Americans were waiting down there on the hillside—but not for the night; they would not attack during the night; and he dared not hope that they had desisted for the day, that this lull, this inactivity, signified merely a resting for the morrow. Hardening, he read his fate in the margin between the sun and the sea.

He turned and walked back up the path, into the pinewoods. In the damp green darkness sparsely striped with light, someone stopped strumming a guitar, faces peered out from behind the pine boles. He walked towards the camp clearing, where a steaming clay pot sat on three stumps of rock over flaming coals. Boiled rice was being simmered dry in the uncovered pot; strips of deer meat blackened among the coals, filling the woods with the smell of hunger. As he stood warming his hands at the fire the men silently gathered behind him; he glanced over his shoulder and saw them waiting, shrouded in their colorful blankets, hugging their rifles to their breasts as they leaned forward to drink the delicate steam, the homely smell of cooked rice.

Briskly facing them: "My friends," he said, "our day is not yet over. I think we may expect another visit. They will not wait until tomorrow, they will try again before the night falls. Come and fetch your supper, and then everyone back to his post. Let us eat, but eat quickly. We do not want our visitors to interrupt our meal."

Grinning, they crept round the fire; he returned to his place at the cliff's edge.

Sprawled on his belly along the brink he could watch the pass below, and the wooded hillside beyond, where the Americans hid, as well as the interior of the pinewoods. The bright space between the sun and the horizon seemed undiminished; there could be an hour more of daylight. A soldier crawled up to bring him supper: a bowl heaped with hot rice and a dish in which two strips of meat and a poached tomato swam in vinegar. He retreated behind a tree and sat up to eat, crushing the tomato into the rice and scooping up the rice to his mouth with his fingers, between bites of the hard salty meat.

It would be evening now in Manila but the skies would still be stained with sunset—the extravagant sunset of his city. The bells would be ringing for the angelus, ringing for supper, and the streets would be deserted, save for the vendors of the evening bread and the vivid presence of the night-blooming flowers. The house lizards would be climbing down to touch their heads to the silent, now darkening earth. But after supper the streets crowded up again, came to life with children playing water games on the cobbles, lovers whispering across grilled windows, carriages rolling past on their way to the seaside paseo. At candlelit stalls on street corners, chestnuts and young ears of corn would be roasting over coals, and he smelled the hot crust of rice cakes fresh from the fire, wrapped in banana leaves, studded with country cheese, smothered with grated coconut, and consumed with great bowls of tea. These first evenings of December would find the old folks making lanterns for Christmas. In his borough of Binondo the evening ended when the parish confraternity passed by in its nightly procession, with lights and banners, chanting the rosary through the streets. This was like a second angelus, and meant bedtime. Then down the deserted street came the watchman with his lantern, crying out the hours. You fell asleep to his long cry and woke up thinking you were still hearing it, but hearing now the cry of the fisherfolk as they rowed up the canal behind the houses, offering the night's catch for breakfast.

He followed the canal through the brightening city, pushing his mind past the mossy backs of old houses where, on waterfront azoteas, boys were stripping for a morning dip and hallooing at each other; past the great square of Binondo with its tall palms and its tobacco factory, lacy as a Moorish palace, its bookshops and printing shops and funeral-wreath shops, and its black-veiled women moving towards the vast cavern of a church, the darkest in the city and the most bat-haunted; the canal widening as it curved round the square and entered the Chinese quarter, but flowing more sluggishly now, clogged with water-lilies and the low bridges over which the pigtailed Chinese were swarming; the pagoda roofs overhead, and red candles burning in the sunshine at innumerable sidewalk shrines to the Holy Cross; the air humming more and more loudly as the dusty glare intensified about him, for he was now in the heart of the city, in Santa Cruz, borough of the merchants, of the goldsmiths and the silversmiths, and of the vainest folk in the city; there stood its grimy church, wild weeds dripping from its belltower, and the small noisy plaza where, during the October fiestas, the haughty women paraded, clustered with jewels; here to his right was the Escolta, with its bright little elegant shops and its stream of fashionable carriages; and ahead was the canal's mouth and the river, the city's river, the Pasig, where dwelt the enchantress whose golden cups and plates one often saw glittering under the water; and he was on those waters again, the brown waters of this, the dearest of native rivers, spanned here by three bridges and crowded with shipping, and flowing seaward past the old city that stood on the other bank, at the river's mouth: the walled city, "the noble and ever loyal," Intramuros; its legendary gates and bastions and belltowers sliding past like emotions through the heart, dazzling in the sunshine as he rode out into the bay, into the violet sea, the mountains before him and the Sleeping Woman in the sky, and behind him now, like smoky flames in the noon sun, the whole beautiful beloved city, the city that he guarded even now, here on this mountain pass, and for which he had come so far away to die—to the edge of the land, into the wilderness, up the cold soggy mountains of the north—and he told himself that, finally, one discovered that one had been fighting, not for a flag or a people, but for just one town, one street, one house—for the sound of a canal in the morning, the look of some roofs in the noon sun, and the fragrance of a certain evening flower.

He told himself that, finally, one found oneself willing to die, not for a great public future, but a small private past; and he picked up his pistol, having finished eating, and crawled back to the cliff's edge. The sun now stood on the horizon; the bright pass below him banked a rising flood of dusk. He trained his glasses on the lower hillside; the sunny treetops, pale green and fat as cabbages, stood still, thickly crowded together, but the darkness beneath them steadily rippled and he saw dust filming the air above the woods. The hillside was moving.

He beckoned to the trees behind him; faces appeared from behind the boles, quickly nodded, and vanished. He crept closer to the brink, pistol in hand, keeping his eyes on the edge of the woods below. The sun was sinking into the sea; in the silence he heard the pinewoods purring like clocks overhead. He waited, sprawled on the cliff's edge, lips pressed to the butt of his pistol, praying for darkness.

And then a shot rent the silence—a shot that froze his blood with horror, for it came, not from below, but from behind him. Springing around as more shots came singing from back there, he saw one of his men stagger up from behind a tree and collapse to the ground and a strange tall figure coming up running from the interior of the pinewoods and he lifted his pistol and fired and the American fell. Below, the Americans had emerged and were swarming up the bare upper shelf of the hillside, where the rocks danced to the cannonade. "Keep the pass! Keep the pass!" he cried to his men as he rose and ran into the pinewoods, for he had seen another figure moving in there, darting from tree to tree. He flung himself to the ground as a bullet whipped through the air but sprang up at once and fired as the American peered out to fire again and he saw the American flinging his arms round the pine bole, passionately embracing it as he sank to the ground. Deep in the dark forest he heard a babble of foreign voices and he crouched down and crawled desperately towards the noise. Behind him, the battle was raging on the mountain pass; ahead was the shallow murmur of the mountain brook and a sound of running. He squatted up against a tree and peered into the darkness. Nothing stirred for a moment; then some trees deep in the darkness seemed to divide and to be walking; the dusk moved, and he waited, flattened against the tree, watching the great stealthy shadows approaching. When the crackling of the undergrowth sounded like thunder in his ears, he leaned forward and began firing—firing steadily, deliberately, and in desperation; knowing, even as he resolved to die fighting, that all courage and heroism had now become useless. The pass and his men were lost and he was battling in vain with the forest. The dusk rattled with bullets but the trees kept on moving, unkilled, and as he rose in despair to fling himself upon them he felt his belly rent open, felt a large fire eating through his innards, and heard, as he tottered and crashed to the ground, the whole victorious forest loudly stampeding by.

The sounds of battle receded, grew fainter and fainter, until he could hear only the humming of insects and the murmur of the brook. The noise of the water obsessed him with thirst. He opened his eyes but saw only darkness and a vision of water. He groped about and touched the base of a tree. Clawing at the tree, he dragged himself up and staggered towards the sound of water. He saw the brook sparkling in the distance and began to run, tripped against a root, and fell on his face. Instantly the pain in his belly sprang afire. Moaning and writhing, he rolled over on the ground then fell mute to see stars glinting among the pine boughs. He stared up at the stars with astonishment, with delight: the night had come at last and his task was over. Up and across the wild mountains, the Republic had been carried to safety.

Smiling rapturously, he closed his eyes, folded his hands on his breast, and started to say:

"Nunc dimittis . . ."

But the words choked in his throat as a current of pain flashed through his body, and opening his eyes he saw, not stars or pine branches, but the canopy of a bed and the faces of his two sons hovering over him; seeing suddenly in their faces all the years of foreign wandering, the years of exile, but knowing suddenly now that the exile had, after all, been more than a vain gesture, that his task had not ended with that other death in the pinewoods, that he had stood on guard, all these years, as on the mountain pass, while something precious was carried to safety. For there it was now in the faces of his sons—the mountain pass, and the pinewoods, and the shapes of the men who had died there. There it was now in their faces—the Revolution and the Republic, and that small private past for which he had come so far away to die. It had not been lost; he had been foolish to think it could ever be lost; there was no need to cross the sea to find it. Here it was before him (and he strove to rise to salute it) in the faces of his sons. He had saved it and it was now in the present, alive now everywhere in the present, and the hovering faces brightened and blurred about him, became the sound of a canal in the morning, the look of some roofs in the noon sun, and the fragrance of a certain evening flower. Here he was, home at last. Behind him were the mountains and the Sleeping Woman in the sky, and before him, like smoky flames in the sunset, the whole beautiful beloved city.

"*Nunc dimittis servum tuum, Domine!*" he rapturously whispered, and as they, his sons, bent down together to sustain him, lifting him up with their arms and sharing his body in their arms, he smiled, closed his eyes, folded his hands on his breast, and died.

AFTERWARDS, in the living room, they wondered over that dying rapture.

"All the time I was trying to get him to wake up," said Pepe, "I dreaded the moment when he would open his eyes."

"Me, too," said Father Tony. "I could feel him coming back from somewhere deep in the past. And there we were, waiting, the horrible present. Our faces were bound to be a shock."

"But he was delighted to see you," said Rita. "Oh, I'll never forget how his face lighted up when he saw you."

"Maybe it wasn't us he saw," said Pepe. "Maybe he was never really conscious at all."

"No, he did recognize us," said Father Tony. "There was recognition in his eyes—and a sort of salutation."

"And he spoke the Nunc dimittis," said Pepe, "as though to reassure us, to make us happy . . ."

"And as though to inform us," said Father Tony, "that he had made his peace with the present . . ."

H.O.T. RESPONSES

1. Discuss with your group the meaning or sensitivity of the passage: ". . .and he told himself that, finally, one discovered that one had been fighting, not for a flag or people, but for just one town, one street, one house—for the sound of a canal in the morning, the look of some roofs in the noon sun, and the fragrance of a certain evening flower."

2. Explain your feelings when the Filipino soldier describes the Americans ". . . swarming up the bare upper shelf of the hillside . . ."

3. Explain why the passage quoted in question 1 is repeated again at the end of this story.

CREATIVE PRODUCT

1. Write a story about war. Write from the perspective of the enemy. Recall how you, the reader, felt when the Americans were ambushing Dr. Monson; capture this reversal of emotions.

   Option: Research this period (1890–1945) in Philippine-American-Spanish history. Check to see if the historical account you research glosses over the points made by author-historian Nick Joaquin.

59

LI PO

Fighting South of the Ramparts

FOCUS

Li Po is one of China's greatest poets; he lived from 701–762 B.C. Li Po was a court poet of the emperor of China. In his later years, he experienced civil war and "Fighting South of the Ramparts" is, in a sense, an antiwar poem. This poem is also a philosophical poem sympathetic to Taoism. A Taoist believes that the value of human life is all important. Conquest is not; it leads you always from heaven. This Taoist view can be seen in the last two lines of the poem.

Fighting South of the Ramparts

Last year we were fighting at the source of the Sang-kan;
This year we are fighting on the Onion River road.
We have washed our swords in the surf of Parthian seas;
We have pastured our horses among the snows of the T'ien Shan.
The King's armies have grown grey and old
Fighting ten thousand leagues away from home.
The Huns have no trade but battle and carnage;
They have no fields or ploughlands,
But only wastes where white bones lie among yellow sands.
Where the House of Ch'in built the Great Wall that was to keep
    away the Tartars,
There, in its turn, the House of Han lit beacons of war.
The beacons are always alight, fighting and marching never stop.
Men die in the field, slashing sword to sword;
The horses of the conquered neigh piteously to Heaven.
Crows and hawks peck for human guts,

Carry them in their beaks and hang them on the branches of
    withered trees.
Captains and soldiers are smeared on the bushes and grass;
The general schemed in vain.
Know therefore that the sword is a cursed thing
Which the wise man uses only if he must.

© 1996 by The Center for Applied Research in Education

H.O.T. RESPONSES

1. Compare this poem with the views of war in Nick Joaquin's story.

2. Discuss the poet's view of the Huns.

3. What is the Taoist's view of war?

4. The Great Wall of China stands to this day. What does it symbolize?

5. Describe the images and the mood created in this poem.

CREATIVE PRODUCT

1. Based upon this poem, write your own proverb about war from a Taoist perspective.

2. Write a poem about your own view of war.

CLARIBEL ALEGRIA

Granny and the Golden Bridge
from *Luisa in Reality Land, a Novel*

FOCUS

Earlier we read Claribel Alegria's poem, "Time of Love" (Unit One), which also appears in her novel, *Luisa in Reality Land*. Claribel Alegria has been an outspoken advocate of the liberation struggle in her home, El Salvador, as well as in Central America. She has also published ten volumes of poetry, three short novels, and a book of children's stories. Alegria's interest in the liberation struggle is evident in her amusing character study in "Granny and the Golden Bridge."

GRANNY AND THE GOLDEN BRIDGE
from *Luisa in Reality Land, a Novel*

Manuel had an endless store of anecdotes about his crazy grandmother who owned a small hut on a strip of ground half a kilometer from the Golden Bridge.

"She was crazy, but a very active old lady," he grinned reminiscently, "and terribly proud of her huge bridge spanning the Lempa River. 'My little bridge,' she used to call it."

Everybody else in El Salvador called it the "Golden Bridge," because with contractors' kickbacks to high government officials and inflated materials and labor estimates, it had cost the Salvadoran taxpayers three or four times as much as it should have.

Manuel was the leader of the Salvadoran peasant organization, who had been invited to Europe on a speaking tour.

"Why do you say she was crazy?" Luisa asked.

"After the civil war started, the army stationed troop units at either end of the bridge to protect it and to control traffic crossing it. It occurred to Granny that she could make her fortune by cooking for the troops. She'd get up every morning at 4 A.M. to cook beans, make tortillas and prepare a huge kettle of rice. She'd load everything into her handcart and push it down the highway to serve breakfast to the soldiers on the near side. Then she'd push it across the bridge—almost two kilometers, imagine!—to serve the troops on the far side. She'd get back to her hut in time to start preparing their lunch, and off she'd go again, pushing her cart."

"Very energetic, as you say, but she doesn't sound crazy."

"She was crazy," Manuel insisted, "because she only charged them for the cost of the food she cooked, and she didn't earn a penny for all that work."

"Patriotic, maybe?" Luisa ventured.

"Maybe," Manuel lifted a shoulder, "but as if that weren't enough, what did it occur to her to do after the *compas* blew up her bridge? She went out and dyed her hair red, that's what."

"Why, for heaven's sake?"

"There was a surprise attack before they blew up the bridge. The *compas* has to take out the guards at both ends so the demolition team could place the charges. But one of the *compas* was killed in the shootout, and he was carrying a plan of the defen-

sive trenches, the location of the machinegun nests and the exact number of troops on both ends.

"A few days later a market lady warned Granny that the Guards were looking for the woman who cooked for the troops. So the dear old lady bought a packet of henna, a tube of lipstick, and went back to her ranch.

"A pair of Guards showed up the next day, asking for her. Without turning a single red hair, Granny said to them: 'Ah, that must be the old woman I rented this *finca* from last week. She threw a fit when they blew up the bridge, and she told me she was moving to San Vincente to live with her daughter.'

"'And who are you?' the Guards asked her.

"Granny drew herself up. 'I'm the respectable owner of a house of pleasure in Suchitoto,' she replied, 'but what with all these subversives shooting up the Guard barracks every other day, I ran out of clients and had to retire. That's the war for you,' she sighed."

The two of them broke out laughing.

"But that's not the end of the story," Manuel continued. "A few weeks later I was visiting a guerrilla camp near the banks of the Lempa, when whom should I see but my redheaded grandmother paddling strongly upstream in a dugout canoe filled with baskets.

"'I'm selling *jocotes,* papaya, lemons, sweet oranges, mangoes. Who'll buy from me? she chanted in her street hawker's call.

"'Hello, Mama Tancho,' the camp commander called out. Not knowing she was my grandmother, he told me: 'This is the old lady who gave us the plans for the attack on the Golden Bridge.'

"We helped her tie up the canoe under a tree, and she started complaining as soon as she hugged me:

"'Ay, Memito,' she signed, 'these kids are making my life more difficult all the time. Ever since they blew up my bridge, I have to paddle all the way up here every day.'

"The guerrilla chief grinned and asked her: 'And what else have you brought us, Mama Tancho?'

"She removed a layer of mangoes from one of the baskets and started chanting in her streetseller's voice:

"'Fragmentation grenades, G-3 cartridges, 81-millimeter mortar rounds. Who'll buy from me?'"

H.O.T. RESPONSES

1. Discuss how the author combines humor in a story that is about civil war.

2. Explain why "The Golden Bridge" is symbolic of the struggle for freedom.

3. Manuel is the grandson who talks about his crazy grandmother. In your opinion, does he really think she is crazy?

4. Why is Granny only charging the cost of the food she sells without caring to make any profit?

5. Are there any comparisons that you can make with the previous story by Nick Joaquin?

CREATIVE PRODUCT

1. Describe, in writing, someone you know, or have heard about, who appears to be crazy, but is not.

2. Write a brief character sketch, using dialogue. Use Claribel Alegria's style as a model for your own work.

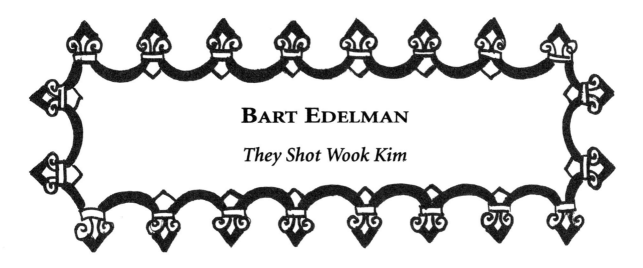

FOCUS

Bart Edelman is a young Jewish American poet who was born in Paterson, New Jersey, grew up in Teaneck, and is living and teaching in California at Glendale College. He is the editor of *Eclipse,* a literary journal. This selected poem appears in Edelman's first book of poems, *Crossing the Hackensack,* which received the following praise in *Steel and Ivy,* Chapman University: "Edelman bridges the two worlds of scholarly poetry and the oral traditions of street poetry to create a rich work of art which touches the reader on many levels . . ."

They Shot Wook Kim

One
                         Two
Three
        Four
                             Five
                    Six
       Seven
Eight

Times
For thirty dollars,
His only crime
Working at the Texaco down the boulevard,
A long, long way from
Korean fields he fled,
But not far enough, it seems:
For man is always
At the mercy of other men,
Sentenced by the absence of laughter and love,
All the race has to give.

65

They Shot Wook Kim

(cont'd)

But he could laugh
When something struck him,
Strange American customs
Brought it on.
He often laughed at himself,
Wondering how and why
He'd ended up here,
"Complex cultures thrown into chaos,"
He'd mutter, shaking his head.

As for love,
There was family back home
He was determined to send for,
He owed them everything,
And a brother, here in town,
But the "special love" he hoped for
Had not found him.
"Perhaps, she's just around the corner," he joked.
A matter of time.

Neither laughter, nor love,
Hung in the air
Over the petroleum morgue that night.
Only a strong wretched odor—
Powder burns and blood,
Vomit and urine.

They

Shot

Wook Kim

H.O.T. RESPONSES

1. In Unit Two, the term "concrete" poetry was used to describe Hilario S. Francia's poems. How can you compare "They Shot Wook Kim" to a concrete poem? Explain your views to your cooperative group.

2. What does the poet imply as the "real cause" of Wook Kim's death?

3. In the context of the entire poem, discuss the line "complex cultures thrown into chaos."

4. The visual shape of the opening line "one, two, three, four, five, six, seven, eight" forms a large question mark. It also shows the directions the bullets took. Explain the symbolic use of this concrete image.

5. Racism and bias are serious evils that confront people every day. Why is it that people cannot tolerate differences? Discuss this question in your cooperative group, but do so with the following lines from the poem in mind:

    . . . *For man is always*
    At the mercy of other men,
    Sentenced by the absence of laughter and love,
    All the race has to give.

CREATIVE PRODUCT

1. As a cooperative group project: Give your advice as to how we can help solve racism and bias. Write a position statement or poem, or create a poster that best promotes your views.

JOSÉ GARCIA VILLA

The Man Who Looked Like Rizal

FOCUS

José Garcia Villa began his creative artistic career as an artist, then was a short story writer and later a poet, and now is writing aphorisms. In his words, each time he moved to a new medium or genre, he graduated to a higher art form. José Garcia Villa was born in Manila and moved to America at the age of eighteen, with the prize money he earned from a short story contest.

The following story was printed in a volume entitled *Footnote to Youth* (1933), of which the highly regarded critic, J. O'Brien writes: "It places him among the half-dozen short story writers in America who count . . . Mr. Villa's tradition is an ancient one. It goes back to and is deeply rooted in the country life of the Philippine Islands. Blended with his Filipino sense of race is a strong Spanish sense of form and color."

THE MAN WHO LOOKED LIKE RIZAL

(Author's Note: Doctor José Rizal is the national hero of the Philippines. Educated in Europe he became doctor, linguist, painter, sculptor, poet, and novelist. Upon his return to his native land, then under the sovereignty of Spain, he was accused of sedition against the mother country. He was arrested, deported, imprisoned, and finally shot. The day of his death is observed annually in the Philippines as an official holiday.)

Once there was a man who looked like Rizal. His face had a sad geometry and his eyes were always sad even when he was happy. His hair was black and it was perched on his head like a black mother hen; the hen had one wing spread and it waved like a suspended cloud over his right forehead. He was puny and his dark skin, which was wrinkled as if he had been dipped in glue and the glue had dried, clothed him tightly. When he got angry he remained quiet but his half-decayed, yellow, square teeth chattered.

He was an insignificant person but for his face that resembled Rizal's. He was reticent and restrained and his life beat a dull tempo. Too, he was always sentient of things about him, but whether he liked them or not he assented to them quietly. Sometimes, when he was bathing and he stood naked, he looked at his body and flexed his arms to try his muscles, and when he found that he was weak he cried softly. Then he stood still while he mastered himself and then continued his bathing.

He had narrow, quick-sloping shoulders and his neck was too thin to keep it in good proportion with the rest of his body. His chest had a deep groove along the middle and sometimes he imagined it was a long river that deposited sediment of unrest in him. But if the river between his breasts deposited such sediment at all, it was latent, for he was a very quiescent, innocuous person.

To his wife he was loyal and he loved her as well as the two children she had borne him. They were longitudinal, gluttonous children and he knew they were not good-looking but still he loved them. He thought of them when there was nothing else to think of and it made his heart feel big and generous.

His wife was a short, young woman with a little black mole on the nape of her neck. He loved that mole and sometimes he felt he wanted to touch it to see how it would feel. He thought that maybe if he pressed his little finger to it his wife would be tickled and she would titter. But he was undemonstrative and afraid to be called silly, so he never dared to touch it and his wife never learned his little secret desire.

He had married her young but he himself had been her senior by half her age on her bridal day. It had been a simple marriage, he recalled, for they were poor. There had been no feasting and the day had passed dully but in the night they had slept together. She was still young now although not so light-bodied. She dressed often in green and he liked it for it reminded him of trees. He was a carpenter and he loved trees because they yielded good, fragrant, strong wood. Once he had even told her he wished they lived in the country where the greens were abundant and inspiriting. Here in the city, he said, the greens were expressionless and left a gap in the souls of people.

He told her such things for he was poetic-minded and he had desires that he knew physicalities could not quench. Sometimes he had beautiful thoughts but he lacked the words with which to express them. When he could not say them he touched his hands to his temples and closed his eyes and his lips trembled. At such times his wife looked at him silently, for she did not understand and even thought he was a little crazy.

He said, "If I were not a carpenter and poor, my hands would be beautiful." He said this looking at his work-deformed hands by the gaslight while his wife spread the mat on the floor for them to sleep on. His wife who did not understand him looked at him with compassional eyes and he thought as he looked back at her that she was beautiful and that she understood his meaning.

One day accident befell this simple quiet man. He was a carpenter and he worked with nails, hammers, and chisels. While chiselling a board the chisel slid suddenly and landed transversely on his one toe. The instrument struck deep and much blood flowed. He felt great pain and fainted and the foreman of the laborers ordered somebody to call for an emergency ambulance. When the ambulance arrived he was put in it and taken to the hospital. There they severed his cut toe completely.

When he returned home his wife blamed him for being careless. She said this weeping but at the same time her voice was chiding. "You had to cut your toe off as if you had too many toes," she said.

"But I didn't want to cut if off," he said earnestly, as if he were pleading with her not to be so hard on him.

When his foot healed he had a slight limp in his gait and his wife told it to him satirically. "You have learned to dance," she said. But he did not mind her, thinking she was joking him.

When his daughter reached school age he enrolled her in the district school. He was a proud father and each morning before she left for class he gave her centavos with which to buy little things she liked. Sometimes she asked for more and he gave it to her, foregoing his cigarettes for the day.

One day she squeezed herself in playfully between his legs and talked to him about the things they did in class. She said the teacher was a woman who had thin arms but she seemed to know much for she knew every word in the book they studied. How did she know all those, she asked, and he said because

she did much studying. "Teachers study for many years and then they teach," he said.

Then his daughter recited to him that c-a-t spelled cat and meant *pusa,* and b-o-y, boy, meant a male *bata,* and that Juan, the little brother, was a boy. To explain herself further she said, "When you were young, Father, you were a boy," and he nodded to tell her he understood. She was happy and ebullient and she said she liked going to school.

Then she told him she had almost forgotten the most interesting thing she had to say. "In our classroom," she said, "there are three pictures on the wall behind the teacher. The middle one is big, but it is not very big," she said, "and the man in the picture looks like you, *itay.* His name is Rizal, the teacher said."

Then because he made no reply she said again, "You look like him, *itay.*"

Now he gazed at his daughter from the sad observatory of his eyes and she thought she saw a puzzling light in them, so she moved quietly away, turning to look back every two steps or three. When she reached the end of the room she continued gazing at him but still he did not move and she began to have a queer feeling so that she cried.

When his daughter told him that he looked like Rizal the man's mind began to have strange thoughts. He was a weak puny man and his daughter had compared him to Rizal. In his mind the thought started by his daughter created a catena of thoughts. He imagined he was really Rizal and forgot his ugly reality. He became a great man, noble, loved by everybody. "I am a hero," he thought, "and people love me. I am immortal, I shall not die. In dying for my country I have learned to live forever. I am the resurrection and the life." He was a tower of love and from the top he scattered seeds to his people below. The seeds were light and soft and the winds made love to them; they fell tenderly, flower-soft, onto the bosoms of his countrymen. "They take root, my seeds, and I myself become a seed again. I would be a seed and sprout with my children-seeds for I love them so." As he thought these he realized he had become a poet and he grew excited. "I am a poet," he said with trembling lips.

He was no longer the carpenter but a different man. He was Rizal and he felt big as the soul of the man who was shot at Bagumbayan field. He was in a cell and on the morrow he would be shot. "I shall be shot," he said "I shall be shot and my body shall give forth blood. The blood of my body shall be many rivers of color . . . . Make the pale flower of my country's soul beautiful. Take me. I am the color and I give myself to you."

He was Rizal and he was a poet. "I shall write poems," he said. His one rough hand clutched fervently an imaginary pen and began moving across his lap. He was writing a poem. He had many songs in his being and he wanted to let them out. "I am a man of many songs and because I have many songs I am a woman. My many songs have made me a woman." How freely his hand that was writing the poems moved! "I am the womb of song and I am filled with music. My songs are only half-born, they are struggling to come out of the womb."

He wrote many poems and when he grew tired he laid his head on the windowsill and thought nothing. He pretended that he had no life now, he was only a mass of flesh and what happened round him did not matter. He was tired and all he wanted to do was to rest.

After he had rested he looked for the poems he had written. But he could find none, not even the pen he had used. And he felt a deep void in him that hurt. He was disappointed that his poems, written when he was a great man, were lost. He wept softly.

He was the carpenter once more but he was sentient that a few minutes before he had been Rizal, a great man. He had written poems while he was Rizal but now that he was the carpenter again he could not find these poems—the beautiful thoughts that lived in his mind and for which he had had no words, but which as Rizal he had been able to express. They were his songs and now they were lost. "I was a poet and I wrote poems. First they were seeds in the house of my mind, later they became stalks, then flowers. I made them beautiful and they ran away from me. They ran away from me and I cannot find them."

Later, when he got over his disappointment, he touched his hands to his breast and knocked lightly. "Open," he said. "You are a soil, Rizal is a tree and he grows in you. His roots are strong and because his roots are in you you are strong too. You are a soil that is black and coarse but because there is a tree living in you you are become beautiful."

He felt tender and compassionate with himself after he had said this and he told himself he was not sorry he was not Rizal.

About a week after, his wife ran away with another man, leaving her children behind. He did not know his wife had run away, he was so latent he came to know of it only when his daughter came crying to him. She told him between little sobs that she had heard their neighbors say her mother had left them for another man. She said she didn't want another man to be her father. "You are my father," she said.

And he took it calmly. He was always passive on the outside but really his wife's desertion made an hiatus in his existence. He loved her and she had run away from him. "She ran away from me but I cannot run away from her. It is because I am breathless, I am breathless with love and I cannot run away. I love her, I love her."

He learned the name of the man with whom she had run away. He was a vicinal acquaintance, a big massive fellow with a quadrate face and pileous arms and chest. Pedrong Sabong the people appellated him. And he was a plumber but he made his money in cockfighting. He was a better and he gambled on the sly. On Sundays he dressed himself gaudily and the women rested their eyes on him. He liked women to look at him.

For a time the man whose wife had left him had the desire to meet Pedrong Sabong face to face. He would get angry, mad, hurl incisive words, use his fists. He would be so angry he would not feel any counterblows. "I shall be like a fortress and I shall not feel anything. As I lick him I shall be a giant. I shall pound him to a pulp. Pulp. Pulp. Pulp." He said, "Pulp. Pulp. Pulp," and he repeated it three times because the sound pleased him.

Then he thought of his wife. She had been good to him and she did her housework well. She cooked with taste and took good care of the children. He wondered why she had left them behind, but after all he was glad the children remained with him. "I love my children," he said, "and I suppose they love me too."

He had not been aware of any carrying-on between his wife and Pedrong Sabong. Why did she leave him? She had never complained to him of their life. He had thought her faithful and he was himself faithful to her. She had a little beauty and was still young, around twenty-five was she, and she had a shy, fluctuant voice. Whenever he heard her voice with its little dancing notes, he had prided himself that she was his. "I own her—her and her body and her voice. Her arms are my lovers and they are not afraid of me. It is because they are woman lovers and they know how to love."

As he thought of her he suddenly rose from his seat and closed all the windows of the house. "She ran away from me and now I am alone. I am dangling in the wind and if the windows are open I shall sail away with the wind. It may be that if I sail away with the wind, out of the windows of this house, into infinity, I shall be running away too, like my wife. I shall be guilty like her and I shall have run away from myself. How am I to find myself again?"

Then because the room was dark and the children began to cry, he himself opened the windows he had shut. He looked at his children and asked them why should they cry. "You are young and do not understand, why should you cry?" ran the question in his mind. "You are young, my children, and you should not cry. It is all right for me to cry because I am old and I love her, you see." And he wept silently.

He became tender and his thoughts of revenge fled. If he met Pedrong Sabong he would not get mad as he had planned. He would understand. "She ran away from me because she liked you better. It was not your fault. A woman likes one man better than her husband and she leaves her husband for him. Don't I understand?" He would shake Pedrong Sabong's hands and then there would be no

more hurt feelings. "I shall tell him further . . . to be good to her," and he felt big as his heart. "I am strong and big. Lord, I am strong and big," and his eyes moistened.

The months passed and things began to grow fit again. His children became used to him, eating with him, sleeping beside him, and he bathing them. He became their mother and a happy thought lighted his mind. "I have become a mother," he said. "I, a man, have become a mother and I am proud. I did not think I could become a mother."

His children loved him and he knew it and it made him happy. His daughter who went to school combed his hair for him and taught him the few English words she learned in school. To her he talked about his work and on Sundays they three, he, his daughter and the little brother, went to the district *cine* together. Before they entered they bought boiled maize, or sometimes peanuts, which they ate inside. He did not know how to read and when his daughter asked him to explain the subtitles of the film he felt embarrassed. He told her they were written in Spanish and in English and he did not understand any of these tongues, so he could not explain them to her. She believed him and said never mind.

They lived in so harmonious a filiation that their neighbors said to each other it was indeed a pity such a good man should have been left by his wife. They said his wife had been senseless to abandon him, him so quiet, so reposed, and who knew if now she was not repenting her behavior. "She will not come to a good end. Restless woman!"

One day it came to pass that the man who looked like Rizal went to a Chinese store in a near corner to buy cigarettes. He was accompanied by his young daughter and he held her little brown hand in his as they crossed the street. He told her to make her strides big, for look, there was a big blue automobile coming and he told her automobiles ran over children and the poor children either died or became humpbacks or lame or lost their limbs. "I do not want you to get run over by it," he said.

So they crossed hurriedly and went into the cube-like affair that was the Chinese store. On

© 1996 by The Center for Applied Research in Education

the walls there were nailed tin advertisements of American cigarettes and soaps and they were in colors that glistened and attracted. She looked at these while her father bought his cigarettes.

Her father asked for a match and she turned her attention to him to see how he would light the cigarette between his lips. He struck a matchstick against a sulphured side of the box and a pale flame sprang.

He was about to raise it to the tip of the cigarette in his mouth when he lowered it abruptly and looked at his daughter and said, "Did you see? Did you see?" He was pale and the cigarette dropped from between his lips and he stepped limply out of the store.

He had seen a man pass by and suddenly he could not light the cigarette. The man had passed by with his face not very visible from the angle at which the carpenter stood, but he had recognized the wide heavy shoulders and the way the long feet touched the ground.

Pedrong Sabong it was and the man who looked like Rizal remembered the story of his life. There had been a wife with a shy, fluctuant voice and Pedrong Sabong had run away with her, the wife he loved, the mother of his children. Suddenly he recalled his resolve, that he would not be angry, that he would be big enough to forgive. He felt soft and tender and a great well of good-will rose in him. He wanted to follow and call the man. He had things to tell to Pedrong Sabong. "Be good to my wife. She is not my wife any more for she has gone to you . . . but she is the mother of my children. Love her and do not scold her. I never scolded her yet, Pedrong Sabong. And tell her I . . . understand. Tell her I am sorry I was . . . not good enough for her . . ."

As he thought his message his eyes became clouded and he saw in a hazy blur. And groping for the hand of his daughter he hurried to catch up with the man who was luckier than he.

Together they ran after Pedrong Sabong and when they were already only a few metres distant from him the man who looked like Rizal called, "Pedro!"

Pedrong Sabong turned and seeing them his knees weakened. He wavered and a nervous

pounding troubled his chest. He felt guilty all at once and he blamed himself for passing through this street. But he determined to grow bold. If this aggrieved husband desired vengeance, well, let him see. He wanted to resume running but the man and his daughter were already so near him.

Undecided for a moment Pedrong Sabong rushed toward the man and struck him blows. The man who looked like Rizal gazed with poignant eyes at his aggressor as he curled down and fell helpless to the street. He was silent—not a moan left his lips but they trembled. His face rasped against the stony ground and bled and his lips cracked under the force of his teeth. He did not rise and his daughter wailed with all the lust of her lungs.

A crowd had gathered round them when the man who looked like Rizal was able to lift himself up. Little sharp stones clung to a side of his face and thin lines of blood flowed from his mouth.

"He attacked me from behind," Pedrong Sabong was declaring to the crowd, "and I turned around and beat him down. I had to protect myself." He stood tall and big and his words rang with vibrant force. "Imagine trying to attack me from behind. It's treacherous!" he said and looked at his adversary with flinty, lying eyes.

The man who looked like Rizal gazed at him with his sad impotent eyes while his daughter beside him continued crying. He was a weak, shriveled figure and he saw the eyes of the people around looking on him with scathing pity. He felt a revolt in him, he wanted to tell them no, he was not so mean as that, that what Pedrong Sabong said was not true. "I am not treacherous, I could not be. I ran after him because I wanted him to know I had forgiven. I wanted to tell him to be good to her . . ." But the intensity of his feeling choked him down, left him powerless.

"If he were not so helpless I would have given him . . . a more thorough beating," Pedrong Sabong told the crowd.

Then, the heart of this puny man rising above all ill feeling, noble enough to rise above the dolor in his soul, he waved a pathetic hand and commanded all to hear:

"You have heard him—you have heard Pedrong Sabong," he said. "Yes, all is . . . true."

And then he clutched his daughter by one thin hand and they walked slowly away. The crowd followed them with their eyes and some one laughed derisively. Pedrong Sabong stood still but when he heard the man's laugh he could not control the lump that had risen in his throat and his thick arm described a swing that sent the man who laughed down. Pedrong Sabong did not look at the fallen man for his eyes kept following the figure of the shriveled man whom he had not treated fair—and somehow his very masculine lips trembled.

When the man and his daughter reached home, he sat his daughter on a chair and he knelt contritely before her, as if she were a little precious goddess that he treasured and loved infinitely, as if he were a penitent sinner and he wanted to confess himself to her, to purge the bad blood out of him. He wept and explained himself nervously to her, holding her little hands tightly.

"I was not afraid of him, daughter. No, I was not afraid." He appealed to the little girl with his little wet eyes that were like sick little cats. "It takes a big, strong man to admit he is wrong," he said, sniffing softly, not removing his entreating gaze from her. "And it takes a bigger, stronger man to admit he is wrong . . . when he is right . . . and apologize. You see, daughter, I am . . . a big, strong fellow," and he knelt straight and put out his narrow thin chest, his shaking lips essaying a conceited smile. "It is because I look like Rizal," he added bravely. "It is because I am like Rizal, daughter, and he was . . . great . . . a great, noble man. It is because Rizal is in me . . ."

His little goddess did not move but looked at him with helpless, wet, un-understanding eyes.

"Did you understand me? Did you understand me, daughter!" he pleaded, kissing her little frightened hands.

And the little daughter looked on.

H.O.T. RESPONSES

1. In Villa's story, underline the passages that are very poetic, that is, where the language is very rhythmic and musical, and makes use of the metaphor and simile.

2. Villa uses similes and metaphors to describe his main character: "Once there was a man who looked *like* Rizal." (Similes are comparisons that use "like" or "as.") "His face had a sad geometry . . ." is a wonderful metaphor. Even when this man was happy "his eyes were always sad."

Study your classmates' faces by looking at the "geometry" of their faces. Select a classmate whose face is most similar to that of Villa's main character. Write a paragraph explaining why you chose this classmate's face.

© 1996 by The Center for Applied Research in Education

3. Another striking simile is Villa's description of this character's hair: "His hair was black and it was perched on his head like a black mother hen; the hen had one wing spread and it waved like a suspended cloud over his right forehead." Explain why the author goes to this length to describe the character's face and hair as he does.

4. Discuss the behaviors of the husband and the wife. Do you favor one over the other? Explain your views.

5. There are cultural values that are discussed in this story that may seem offensive to you today. What are they? Are these differences more cultural or are they more reflective of the time that this story was written? Explain your views:

6. Do you think you might have behaved the way Pedrong Sabong did in a similar situation? Explain.

7. Why do you think the man who looked like Rizal, after being beaten down, says:
    "You have heard him—
    you have heard Pedrong Sabong . . .
    Yes, all is . . . true."?

Discuss your views with your cooperative group.

8. Does the father's explanation to his daughter regarding his actions enable her to understand them any better? Do you understand his actions?

9. Finally, explain the "inner conflict" in the man who looked like Rizal. Speculate on the probable causes of this conflict.

CREATIVE PRODUCT

1. First, sketch the face of one of your classmates. (It is important that you concentrate more on the "geometry" of the face than on the actual features.)

2. Now, describe this same person's face as you have drawn it. Describe the person's hair, using a simile like Villa's, when he compared the character's hair to a black hen. (Share your products with your group.)

JACK AGÜEROS

"Agua Viva," a Sculpture by Alfredo Gonzalez

from Dominoes and Other Stories from the Puerto Rican

FOCUS

Jack Agüeros' story, "'Agua Viva,' a Sculpture by Alfredo Gonzalez," is printed in his collection, entitled *Dominoes and Other Stories from the Puerto Rican.* Jack Agüeros was born in New York City in 1934 and has been the recipient of numerous awards. He is a poet, a playwright, and an author of children's stories, and he has written for television's "Sesame Street" and WNBC-TV. He has also been the director of the Museo del Barrio in East Harlem, the only Puerto Rican museum in the United States. Jack Agüeros has said of his writing "I don't like the way Latinos often get portrayed. The lives of working people are unheard from because it's hard to write about them. But those lives are frequently heroic and have their drama, too. I'm also interested in what happens to them."

"Aqua Viva," a Sculpture by Alfredo Gonzalez

The knuckles ached as did the hands of the man who had been dragging chain and handling heavy iron pieces for years. His greasy hands, hair follicles and pores super-saturated with oils, grime and ferrous particles caught and caked in them, no longer felt the long, sharp, and shallow cuts, or the multiple punctures that scalpeled edges on cams and cogs of highly polished steel and burrs on poorly finished cast iron inflict on human skin.

He had never liked work gloves.

He had not washed his hands for five years.

He tugged at the tangle of chains, of pulleys, of polished parts, of alternately painted and rusty parts that lay scrambled on the concrete driveway next to his house and midway between the street and his garage. He was pulling the mass toward the garage when it occurred to him that it would make a very beautiful sculpture. He would have to affix one end to the top of an A-frame, arrange the chains like runners of Virginia Creeper and then tie weights at the bottom of each of the chains so that they would hang taut. He could call it *Agua Viva* because it would remind him of the jellyfish that inhabit the waters off Puerto Rico.

There was a good A-frame in the shed. Too good in fact. He would have to cover part of the frame under plastic while he hosed the A-frame down to induce some rust, and he would probably have to distress the A-frame with the peen side of one of his hammers to chip away the industrially baked-on enamel paint.

You had to transform the A-frame to make the whole piece harmonious. Otherwise it would be two separate elements—one of pretty painted parts and one of junk. The A-frame had to be distressed, yes. Distress can turn the dull to beauty.

Iron and steel do not tangle like thread, cord or rope. Perhaps chain tangles like logs, and

words like jam or snag would be better to describe what happens when links twist out of line and chains of different gauge twine like tresses. Wood has water, or better said, logs have water to propel them part of their way. Professional handlers have winches and pulleys and special vehicles to transport piles like the one the man now dragged up the slightly inclining driveway.

Something hit his face, and he realized that something had hit his body twice before. He looked up to see three boys throwing things at him that he could not immediately identify. Nor could he recognize the boys. Were they his son's friends? Where was his son?

"Filthy Fredo, filthy Fredo, ya ya ya-ya-ya," they shouted.

Were they talking to him? Who was "filthy Fredo?" He dropped the mass of chains and took up one of the thrown things. It was a clod of soil with tufts of grass and grass roots holding it together.

"Dirt for the dirty, dirt for the dirty, filth for filthy Fredo," chanted the boys, nearby.

In his hand the sod felt like a pearl compared to the usual objects he handled. He threw it and hit one of the boys squarely on the face, striking both the nose and lips. The boy, perhaps eleven, started to cry and bleed at the same time. None ran. The man started forward and the boy, perhaps fourteen years old, decided to run. But the man caught him and clamped one hand on the boy's shoulder at the same time that he brought his other hand open across the boy's head. With a dull "whup," the boy twirled, and the man then shove-kicked the boy down the driveway. The third boy, the youngest of all, was long ago gone.

From across the street a man hollered "Good for you Gonzalez. Welcome back to earth."

What the man across the street knew, and the boys had known, was that the man they all called "filthy Fredo" had never retaliated, had never even chased the taunting teenagers or the ya-ya-yaing younger boys. No wonder they were caught off guard. In fact, before this moment he had never reacted at all, not for five and maybe seven years.

To anything.

Except iron and steel.

Wheels and manhole covers, and grates and wrenches and gaggers and rods and gears, and discs and platens and gates, and chucks and clutches and grills, and spools and bobbins, locks and keys, pinions and racks and gaffles, and meat-hooks and ball-joints and shuttles and flycocks and gaffers, and dividers and rasps, and gyroscopes, graters, and gymbals, grab-hooks, and a thousand parts too small or too complex or too divorced from their origin or context or too specialized and thus identifiable only by their creator, cluttered the length and breadth of the walls of his house, of the walls of his garage, of the walls of his shed, and finally, having displaced length and breadth, the pieces also piled and accumulated in corners and centers, so that finally, finally, they even displaced the girth, the very girth of his abode.

His house had become the lair of the iron woodchuck, the hive of the iron bee, the storeroom of the iron squirrel, the complex of chambers of the iron ant.

From wall to wall, from floor to ceiling the mountain of metal was broken only by a thin corridor that was wide enough for the passage of one man at a time and which changed direction as often as a young river in the mountain.

In the beginning—not in the very beginning of his life when he was named Alfredo after months and months of arguing between his mother and father. In that beginning he had been the first son, and his parents had spent a considerable amount of their waking hours, perhaps of their sleeping hours also, in consideration of an appropriate name. By the seventh child, selecting names was less of a problem. In the beginning, "Alfredo" had been agreed to after eight and one half months of arguing, and just fourteen hours before he was born. As soon as he was brought home, his father looked at

him all swaddled against the winter and said, "If we were still in Puerto Rico, he would not wear so much clothing, and oddly, I would find him bigger. Now he looks so small that I, I think I shall call him Fredo."

The boys were cruel and called him filthy Fredo, thus facing a creature they only partly recognized and did not understand. The scientists created chains of *-noias* and *-phrenias* and complicated sprockets of interlocking phrases to describe Fredo. In the end—after a year—they released him as "traumatized" but "harmless," and on the cover of the file folder that contained his dossier there was a number, a date, and the simple phrase "returned to community." There was no name on the face of the folder, but perhaps the letters GON were an abbreviation for "Gonzalez" rather than an abbreviation for "Gone."

But in the beginning of the iron collecting, he had brought the pieces home after much thinking, hesitation, selection and bartering. Then he would spend hours removing paint or rust, applying naval jelly or a torch and wire brush depending on the need. And he would hang the pieces, leaving "air" around each piece so that it could "breathe" and be seen both in the beauty of its form, composition and harmony, its exquisite proportions, or in its indivisible simplicity, in its own beauty, and in relation to the other members of the displayed collection. And he kept notebooks, assigning a number, noting measurements, weights, a description of the object, what metal it was, its uses or purpose, if he knew it, and its provenance, if he knew that. A price and date would be entered if it was a purchase, and if it had been found or given to him, the place found, or the name of the giver. Finally, if any appeared, the maker's mark, and if known, who that mark belonged to. There generally was a drawing or a photograph as well.

Thus in the beginning, the interest in collecting had been a pleasure and a hobby and even a science—sometimes the avid amateur can be more thorough than the museum professional. And the iron had occupied a portion of his life space, his time, his psyche, his physical space. Now it was iron and steel wall to wall—one of a kind decaying next to scrap, art under decoration under function under technology under dross, all in an incubator—no, a compost. And parallel to this total displacement of his physical space iron had totally replaced his time or blocked or separated him from time. As if time in its rigid tick tock trajectory were thwarted by the crumpled metallic maze. Or perhaps the magnetic mass was so great it created a false true north for time. Or perhaps time entering the irrational dimension of this prodigious pile was bent the way sun rays refract through angled glass and then cannot escape the greenhouse.

Alfredo Gonzalez, mostly known as Fredo, also known as "filthy Fredo," entered his house and was shocked at the disorder. It was as if he had entered a tight stack section of a library with a minimum walk space between the stacks. But there were neither books nor shelves, just piles of metal objects—from clockworks to the flywheel of a tractor, to the cap piece of a massive boiler. There was barely a path among the piles of objects. He switched on a lamp that was made from a cast-iron newel post that he had assembled in 1959, but it would not light. Neither would any others when he could reach around the mountains of objects to try switches.

Had it not been for the newel post he would not have believed he was in his own home.

He worked his way to the telephone, which buried under dirt and grease, did not work. Neither was there water or gas in the kitchen and the windows were opaque. The meager grey light that filtered through was further defeated by the piles and piles of objects on the available counter space and leaning in rows against the cabinets on the floors. He could not locate the refrigerator.

He remembered that his hallway bathroom had two windows. But even there the light was insufficient to illuminate his image in the mirror. He opened one half of one window with a small pry bar that lay behind the commode. And he turned and gazed in the mirror—what he saw there stopped his heart.

In the mirror was the head and shoulders of a man who had not bathed, shaven, or shorn his hair for five or more years and who had not seen himself in that time either.

He reacted by looking at his hands, one of which still held the pry bar. In disbelief, he raised his hands and looked again in the mirror. The hands matched, and then there was an explosion. The hand holding the pry bar had come down on the mirror creating everything from glass dust to splinters to large chunks which still held the bizarre face.

Fredo gasped, and his breath came short and with difficulty, as if he had been running. His head whirled with fear, with incomprehension with loathing with disorientation with dread. He was about to pass out when he saw the figure of the teenage boy go up the driveway.

The boy was spraying gasoline over the shed, the garage, and even on the pile of chains still at the upper end of the driveway as Fredo came around the house. When the boy saw filthy Fredo he panicked and quickly lit the book of matches which at once ignited the boy's hands and one of his trouser legs.

Fredo pushed the boy down to the ground and away from the gasoline. He was less concerned with the boy than with keeping the gasoline from igniting, although when he contemplated the shed and garage they were crammed solid containers of spare parts with very little to burn—a bit of residue of grease or oil. The structures themselves were of wood as one would expect from a man who loved iron and would have nothing but contempt for aluminum siding or pre-fab metal panels. He remembered now that he had read in one of his books on iron:

One would expect to find few samples of ancient iron works, and many of brass and bronze. However the reverse is true, for nothing is as destructive as man, and while time has a ferocious effect on badly cured and maintained forged or cast iron, man has an even more pernicious effect on brass and bronze. Because they are more precious and often employed by men of war, ornate baptistry doors and colossal cannons are subject to remelting and reworking. Works of art become works of war, in turn plain shields are converted to decorative serving platters. Iron, properly forged and cured, watches inplacably resisting wave after wave of heat and cold, army after army.

The neighbor from across the street was spraying the boy on the ground with a huge fire extinguisher. "Serves 'm right," the neighbor was saying, then turning his extinguisher onto the non-burning gasoline and the yet to be assembled sculpture called *"Agua Viva"* and winking "just in case, you never know." He seemed to be enjoying the steady rope of white foam uncoiling from the extinguisher.

"What do you want to do with this boy?"

Fredo wanted to say "nothing" but no sound came from him. When he tried again a very guttural noise that sounded like "teen" came out.

He had not spoken in over five years.

"Nothing? You wanna do nothing?"

Fredo shook his head yes.

The neighbor helped the boy up and said to him, "Don't ever come in this block again and I won't tell your father the details of this accident. Let's just say one of your jerky friends sprayed you with a fire extinguisher after you lit up a can of lighter fluid. And for god's sake leave this man alone."

"Tell me Fredo, have you looked at yourself in a mirror today? Because you are not the man in the mirror. I know you Fredo—come over to my house I'll give you a haircut, a shave, a cold beer, you can take a bath—two baths, and I'll tell you what I think happened to you. Do you hear me Fredo? Do you understand?"

Fredo shook his head and made a sound like a hack saw on cast iron. It was "yes."

H.O.T. RESPONSES

1. In your cooperative group, try to explain why the boys were so cruel to Gonzalez. Have you ever seen this kind of taunting before? How is this a kind of bias?

2. Do you think Gonzalez was justified in retaliating as the man from across the street seemed to think, hollering: "Good for you Gonzalez. Welcome back to earth."

3. Explain the author's play on the letters "GON" on his medical folder.

4. Compare Fredo Gonzalez to Granny, the character in "Granny and the Golden Bridge."

5. Explain the use of the metaphor of "time" and how it relates to the "magnetic mass" of iron collected in Gonzalez's house.

6. Explain the irony in the neighbor's question to Fredo: "Tell me Fredo, have you looked at yourself in a mirror today?"

7. Why does Fredo agree to go with the neighbor to get cleaned up?

8. What do you think his future will be like?

CREATIVE PRODUCT

1. Write an essay on violence. Explain how and why people are so ready to inflict great harm on one another just because they are different.

2. You may want to look up "junk sculpture"—an art form that became popular in the 1950s and 1960s as part of the "pop art" craze—to get a better idea of what the "Agua Viva" sculpture was to become. Give an oral report on "junk sculpture."

3. Create your own scaled-down version of "junk art" using tin cans, bottle caps, aluminum foil, paper clips, pins, nails, screws, nuts, and washers.

CHIEF JOSEPH

Bear's Paw Battleground Speech

FOCUS

Chief Joseph was the leader of the Nez Perce Native American tribe. His band and other nontreaty Nez Perce were retreating, with families intact, when ambushed at Bear's Paw, Montana, by the United States Army at General O.O. Howard's orders to Colonel Miles. The Nez Perce were outstanding marksmen, however, and as a result, the battle ended in a deadlock. Unfortunately, Chief Joseph's band was greatly battered; it was freezing cold and the wounded lay dying, and the women and children were cold and hungry. Rather than abandon the dying and the women and children, Chief Joseph was finally forced to surrender, but not before more than 200 of his warriors escaped into Canada. In this speech following his surrender, Chief Joseph speaks with dignity, but also with anger and with grief over the loss of so many loved ones, including women and children who were victims of a cruel and relentless army. This speech is just as it was given on the battlefield, written down by a U.S. Army interpreter. Many historians compare its form, its poetry, and its simplicity to Lincoln's Gettysburg Address. Consider this as you read Chief Joseph's sad words, uttered at one of the last major battles of the Native American Wars.

Bear's Paw Battleground Speech

Tell General Howard I know his heart. What he told me before I have it in my heart. I am tired of fighting. Looking Glass is dead. Toohoolhoolzote is dead. The old men are all dead. It is the young men who say yes or no. He who led the young men is dead. It is cold and we have no blankets. The little children are freezing to death. My people, some of them, have run away to the hills, and have no blankets, no food; no one knows where they are—perhaps freezing to death. I want to have time to look for my children and see how many of them I can find. Maybe I shall find them among the dead. Hear me, my chiefs. I am tired; my heart is sick and sad. From where the sun now stands I will fight no more forever.

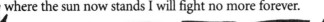

H.O.T. RESPONSES

1. When Chief Joseph says: ". . . I know his heart . . . I have it in my heart," what is he acknowledging?

2. Appreciate the power of the last two lines of this desolate speech. Why is the statement so profound?

3. The Western Movement had a disastrous effect on the Native Americans; they were under constant attack and forced to flee the old life and to find new land or end up on reservations. Discuss this moment in history with your cooperative group, and see if you have understood this perspective from previous readings or from what you have learned in history about the Western Movement.

4. Compare Chief Joseph's speech to Lincoln's Gettysburg Address. (The Gettysburg Address should be found in your school library.)

CREATIVE PRODUCT

1. You and your cooperative group can write to the Nez Perce National Historical Park in Montana to ask for information about the Bear's Paw Battleground. (This battleground was dedicated October, 1993, one hundred years after the Bear's Paw Battle.)

2. Write a poem or statement about how you felt after reading Chief Joseph's speech.

Unit Four

THEME:
DREAMS DEFERRED

INTRODUCTION

The American dream is about freedom, equality, and the pursuit of happiness. To some, this dream of happiness includes riches and opportunities. Peoples from around the world have left their homelands in search of this American dream, only to find that the dream is not as fruitful as it once seemed, and as Langston Hughes' poem, "A Dream Deferred" questions: "Does it dry up like a raisin in the sun?"

For so many immigrants and minorities, their dreams, too, have been deferred, or put off for awhile. Perhaps their dreams will never be realized. In this unit, heartache is a recurring theme. Like Langston Hughes, Lorraine Hansberry has experienced this heartache described in *To Be Young, Gifted, and Black,* and to further give testimony to her feelings, she uses Hughes' line for the title of her play, *A Raisin in the Sun.* African American authors Countee Cullen and Lottie E. Porch each write about this derailment of happiness, as does Robin F. Brancato in *White Chocolate.* Chief Big Eagle, a Native American, tells of the never-ending struggle of his people in *Quarter Acre of Heartache.*

Bart Edelman expresses a certain self-consciousness about being a Jew in today's biased climate, and Yun Wang is reminded of injustices back in her own homeland, in China.

The voices of these authors, however, never dim; instead, they seem to prod at the conscience of America reminding us, just as Martin Luther King once reminded us in his "I Have a Dream" speech:

So I say to you, my friends, that even though we must face the difficulties of today and tomorrow, I still have a dream. It is a dream deeply rooted in the American dream that one day this nation will rise up and live out the true meaning of its creed—we hold these truths to be self-evident, that all men are created equal.

LORRAINE HANSBERRY

from *To Be Young, Gifted, and Black*

© 1996 by The Center for Applied Research in Education

FOCUS

Lorraine Hansberry is most famous for her first play, *A Raisin in the Sun,* for which she became the first African American playwright to win the New York Drama Critics' Best Play of the year award. She wrote several more plays before she died from cancer at age thirty-four. Her title for her famous play is an allusion to Langston Hughes' line from, "A Dream Deferred," in which the poet asks: "Does it dry up like *a raisin in the sun?*" As the title of this selected essay suggests, Lorraine Hansberry was, indeed young, gifted, and black and was the victim of threatening bias from neighbors and students in an all-white neighborhood to which her prosperous real estate broker family moved. As you read Lorraine Hansberry's essay, keep this perspective of bias in mind.

from *To Be Young, Gifted, and Black*

O, the things that we have learned in this unkind house that we have to tell the world about!

Despair? Did someone say despair was a question in the world? Well then, listen to the sons of those who have known little else if you wish to know the resiliency of this thing you would so quickly resign to mythhood, this thing called the human spirit . . . .

Life? Ask those who have tasted of it in pieces rationed out by enemies.

Love? Ah, ask the troubadours who come from those who have loved when all reason pointed to the uselessness and foolhardiness of love. Perhaps we shall be the teachers when it is done. Out of the depths of pain we have thought to be our sole heritage in this world—O, we know about love!

And that is why I say to *you* that, though it be a thrilling and marvelous thing to be merely young and gifted in such times, it is doubly so, doubly dynamic—to be young, gifted, *and black.*

Look at the work that awaits you!

Write if you will: but write about the world as it is and as you think it *ought* to be and must be—if there is to be a world.

Write about all the things that men have written about since the beginning of writing and talking—but write *to a point.* Work hard at it, *care* about it.

Write about *our people:* tell their story. You have something glorious to draw on begging for attention. Don't pass it up. *Use* it.

Good luck to you. This Nation needs your gifts.

Perfect them!

H.O.T. RESPONSES

1. Lorraine Hansberry addresses the hard issues of living in this world: Despair? Life? and Love? What does she believe is the plight of young people? Explain.

2. To be young and gifted in such times, she says is "thrilling" and "marvelous." Why do you think Hansberry writes this, when, on the other hand, she speaks of prejudice?

3. Why does she say ". . . it is doubly so, doubly dynamic—to be young, gifted, *and black*"?

4. Why does Hansberry encourage her readers to:

   Write about our people: tell their story. You have something glorious to draw on begging for attention. Don't pass it up. Use it. !

CREATIVE PRODUCT

1. Follow Lorraine Hansberry's imperative and: "write about the world as it is and as you think it *ought* to be and must be—if there is to be a world." Use this point of view to write a prose essay about your own culture or race.

FOCUS

Countee Cullen is one of the greatest lyrical poets of the twentieth century. He was one of the major writers of a period referred to as "The Harlem Renaissance," which gave rise to other major African American writers that included Langston Hughes, Anna Bontemps, and Jean Toomer. After graduating from New York University, Cullen earned a master's degree at Harvard. He also wrote two books for children and a play with Anna Bontemps.

Countee Cullen's poem, "Tableau," addresses race as an issue, but the poet is not embittered nor pessimistic in his outlook. As you read "Tableau," ask yourself what clues in this poem provide hope for the future.

It is critical to know why the title of this poem adds to the significance of both its mood and meaning. A *tableau* is a scene presented onstage by costumed actors who remain silent and motionless as if in a picture.

Tableau

(For Donald Duff)

Locked arm in arm they cross the way,
  The black boy and the white,
The golden splendor of the day,
  The sable pride of night.

From lowered blinds the dark folk stare,
  And here the fair folk talk,
Indignant that these two should dare
  In unison to walk.

Oblivious to look and word
  They pass, and see no wonder
That lightning brilliant as a sword
  Should blaze the path of thunder.

H.O.T. RESPONSES

Work in teams of two from your cooperative group:

1. The contrast of color is a theme in this poem. In your cooperative group, discuss how the various shades of color and light are used in this poem to accentuate bias and prejudice.

2. If this is as it should be, that is, black and white friends walking arm and arm, what's all the fuss?

3. Explain the significance of the following two poignant lines:

   Oblivious to look and word
   . . . They pass, and see no wonder

4. Explain the meaning of the last two lines of "Tableau."

5. Relate this poem to Lorraine Hansberry's essay.

6. Why is this poem entitled "Tableau" ?

7. Why do you think the poet has the *dark folk* "stare" from lowered blinds and the *fair folk* "talk"?

CREATIVE PRODUCT

1. Write about different kinds of prejudice you have observed—particularly when the offenders were not aware you were watching them. Compare your observations with Cullen's line:

   And here the fair folk talk,
   Indignant that these two should dare
   In unison to walk.

2. Write a poem or story that makes a positive statement about race relations in spite of adversity.

CLAUDE CLAYTON SMITH

from *Quarter-Acre of Heartache*
(The Story of Chief Big Eagle)

FOCUS

Claude Clayton Smith wrote three books prior to *Quarter-Acre of Heartache*. As a matter of fact, he was researching a historical novel for young adults, *The Stratford Devil,* when he realized the sad truth about our Native Americans' struggles that continue to this day. Claude Clayton Smith writes: "I have chosen to write in the first person, in the voice of Chief Big Eagle as I have come to know it, to let the Chief speak for himself . . ." As you read, consider the warning of Native American Leslie Mormon Silko of the Laguna Pueblo: ". . . The American Public has difficulty in believing that injustice continues to be inflicted upon Indian people because Americans assume that the sympathy or tolerance they feel towards Indians is somehow 'felt or transferred to the government policy that deals with the Indians.' This is not the case."

from QUARTER-ACRE OF HEARTACHE
(The Story of Chief Big Eagle)

So the war for this quarter-acre is over. That heartache, at least, is in the past. But the heartache continues, because an invisible war is being fought every day—by the Golden Hill people and Indians all over America. The war is being fought because Indians still have many grievances.

Indians want their tribes to be recognized. Indians want terminated tribes returned to tribal status. Indians want sacred tribal lands returned. Indians want to end archaeological digs that disturb our burial grounds, because it is disrespectful and sacrilegious to treat human remains as museum exhibits.

Indians want mission churches removed from the reservations because we have our own church—the Native American Church. Indians want the Environmental Protection Agency to become a separate department of the United States government, so that economic programs can be developed, so reservation resources can be properly maintained.

And Indians want an Indian university.

The invisible war continues because, when people think of Indians, they still think of John Wayne and his Comancheros on TV. They think of Indians in war bonnets. But only the Plains Indians wear bonnets. You'd look like a fool running through the woods with a bonnet on your head.

Not all Indians wear bonnets or wear their hair in the same way. The Hopi wear their hair to the side. The Apache wear their hair shoulder length. The Navajo wear their hair in a bun. Only the Plains Indians wear bonnets full of feathers.

Such misconceptions continue the invisible war. People still think that western Indians are western Indians. But most of the western Indians were originally from the east—the Creek, the Chickasaw, the Pawnee, the Sioux, the Cherokee—all of those tribes were originally from the east.

Years ago, when the Paugussett nation broke up, many of our people joined the Iroquois in New York. It was the Iroquois who ran the Sioux out of New York. The Huron ran them further, and the United States Army ran them out of Minnesota to the Plains. That's how the Sioux went west.

Or take the Cherokee. In 1838, President Andrew Jackson used the army to enforce an illegal treaty that required the Cherokee to move out of Tennessee. They were driven all the way to Oklahoma. Four thousand Indians died on that march. It was known as "The Trail of Tears." Some of the Cherokee hid out in the Smoky Mountains and stayed in the east. Only recently, in the spring of 1984, have they had a council with their brothers in the west, as they try to reunite their divided nation.

Reservations for many of these eastern tribes were set up out west in the 1800s, after the Constitution of the United States came into being. But the Golden Hill Reservation was set up in 1659, not long after the white man came to America.

The invisible war continues each time an Indian child is born. Let me give you an example.

I have eighteen children. And many grandchildren. I have been married four times. It is difficult for a woman to marry an Indian chief, because she marries his tribe. She marries his ancestors and his responsibilities.

My youngest child is a boy. His name is *I-Hahm-Tet*. It means *Little Eagle*. His name is Little Eagle because I am Big Eagle.

Little Eagle was born in 1983. And when he was born, the woman at the hospital put his

© 1996 by The Center for Applied Research in Education

name on the birth certificate in his manner: First name, *Little*; Middle name, *Eagle.*

And my wife told this woman, "His name is 'Little Eagle.' No middle name."

"But that doesn't fit the form," the woman said.

Indians never fit the form, because the form is made by a white man.

So I went to the hospital administrator and asked if the birth certificate shouldn't be changed. "I suppose so," she said. So the record was changed at the hospital, but not at the Bureau of Vital Statistics in Bridgeport. The hospital would not send a corrected form to the Bureau of Vital Statistics.

So I went to the Bureau of Vital Statistics, and the person there promptly crossed out Little Eagle's middle name and wrote in *at request of father.* That puts the blame on me. But I made no mistake.

And let me tell you why this is so important. There was a man at the hospital who had worked on the land claims of the native Alaskans. He said, "Any birth certificate with any mark on it does not go." It's invalid.

I know of a Schaghticoke Indian who was refused her Indian status here in Connecticut because someone had written in "Schaghticoke Tribe" on her birth certificate. It had been "tampered with." So it was not a valid document.

So my son Little Eagle has two strikes against him already in his life. First, he's an Indian. Second, his birth certificate has been tampered with. At request of father.

And yet changes *are* made on birth certificates. When a woman has a baby and doesn't know who the father is, she can come in a year or two later and add the father's name. So why can't changes be made for Indians? Why are there two standards?

My youngest daughter lives here on the reservation, too. She is three years old. Her name is *Waup Athoo Kwey.* It means *White Fawn.* Her first name is not White. Her middle name is not Fawn. Her name is Waup Athoo Kwey. *White Fawn.*

The invisible war continues wherever the schools do not teach the truth. I'm sure that most people around here—despite all the noise of the war for this quarter-acre—aren't even aware that this is an Indian reservation. Because schools don't teach anything about the local Indians. They don't know much about the local Indians. That is why I have agreed to tell my story.

It is in the greatest interests of history that the truth be told. That we teach the truth. So that future generations will walk in truth.

H.O.T. RESPONSES

1. It is one hundred years after Chief Joseph gave his famous battleground speech, and yet it is strange to learn that the "invisible war continues." Why do you suppose this continues? Discuss this issue with your cooperative group.

2. Reread the paragraph that describes how "President Andrew Jackson used the army to enforce an illegal treaty." Compare these events with the points made in Chief Joseph's speech (Unit Three).

3. The personal struggles described by Chief Big Eagle are reminiscent of other struggles by other minority groups. Explain how.

4. Do you think it is important to learn about the literature, the problems, and the triumphs of other racial and ethnic groups? Discuss your responses to this question with your cooperative group.

CREATIVE PRODUCT

1. Oral history is a way to pass down important information. Ask your parents, grandparents, neighbors, or teachers to share any stories or history that were passed down. Record and share. Compile a class *Oral History Newsletter.*

YUN WANG

The Carp

FOCUS

Yun Wang, a Chinese American author, was born in China to an educator and a political dissident. Her father was imprisoned for making political statements in favor of human rights. This autobiographical piece by Yun Wang is written in the form of a "tale" or "parable," which teaches a lesson. This excerpt, another example of human conflict, is the opening piece of a very lyrical and charming book entitled *The Carp*.

The Carp

My father was the school principal. The day I was born, he caught a twenty pound carp. He gave it to the school kitchen. All the teachers and boarding students tasted it.

Around us, there were waves of mountains. I grew up yearning for the ocean. Smoke arose from the ever green mountains to form clouds each morning. My father named me Cloud.

When a son was born to Confucius, the king of Lu sent over a carp as present. Confucius named his son Carp.

The wise say a carp leaping over the dragon gate is a very lucky sign. My father says he named me Cloud because I was born in the year of the dragon, and there are always clouds following a dragon. Confucius' son died an early death. My father has only three daughters.

When I was three, I wandered all over the campus. A stray cat in a haunted town. My mother says I passed the room where my father was imprisoned.

The Carp
(cont'd)

He whispered to me, hid a message in my little pocket. It was his will that I should grow up a strong woman, and find justice for him.

They caught me. My father was nearly beaten to death. Some of them were students, whose parents were peasants. Some of them were teachers, who used to be his best friends. They had tasted the carp.

It has been recorded that Confucius could not tell the difference between millet and wheat, and was thus mocked by a peasant. This peasant became a big hero, representing the wisdom of the people, thousands of years after Confucius' death.

My father still goes fishing, the only thing that seems to calm him. The mountains are still sleeping waves. My father catches very small fish. My mother eats them. My friends laugh at me, when I tell them that once upon a time, my father caught a carp weighing twenty pounds.

H.O.T. RESPONSES

1. What is the parallel example made between Confucius, the Chinese philosopher, and Yun Wang's father? Discuss this point with your cooperative group.

2. What kind of person did Yun Wang grow up to become?

3. Discuss the significance of the following passage:

   They caught me. My father was nearly beaten to death. Some of them were students, whose parents were peasants. Some of them were teachers, who used to be his best friends. They had tasted the carp.

4. Discuss the irony and significance of the following passage to the parallel drawn between the giving of "lucky" gifts:

   It has been recorded that Confucius could not tell the difference between millet and wheat . . .

5. What do you know about the students' fight for human rights and the government's suppression and treatment of these students at Tiananmen Square? Can you draw any comparison between Wang's story and this conflict in modern Chinese history?

CREATIVE PRODUCT

1. Write an autobiographical or biographical parable that shows a particular form of rebellion that you or someone else had engaged in. Describe its outcome as a "dream deferred."

ROBIN F. BRANCATO

White Chocolate

FOCUS

Robin F. Brancato has written several novels, short stories, and a play for young adults. She has won two highly coveted American Library Awards for two of her seven novels: *Sitting Under the Apple Tree* (Knopf) and *Winning*. Her novel *Blinded by the Light* later became a featured television film for National Broadcasting Company (NBC), starring Khristie McNichols. Robin F. Brancato is also a creative writing teacher at Teaneck High School, which comprises a racially and ethnically diverse student body in Teaneck, New Jersey, acclaimed for being the first public school system in the nation to voluntarily bus its students to integrate its schools. Although Ms. Brancato's heritage is German American, an interracial marriage in her family and her experience as a teacher in a multiracial high school may have been drawn upon to create this powerful and dramatic story.

WHITE CHOCOLATE

I'm telling straight out who I am. Not like in this certain story *she* made us read, where you didn't know for ten pages who the teller was. You were thinking it was a guy, and then it turned out to be a tomboy girl. Wally is my name, which I'm not crazy about, but it's better than being called Walter, like my father. And I may as well tell this right off, too, so you aren't picturing me as some blond-headed, surfing-movie type: one of my parents is black and one is white. If you think I'm going to tell which is which, and how they got together in the first place, and what they're like now, and how I feel about it, *forget* it. Those are the kinds of questions *she'd* be asking, if I went in and talked to her. *What are you angry about, Wally?* she sometimes asks me right in front of everybody. *Something wrong, Wally? What's bothering you?*

"You!" I tell her right out. This ridiculous English class!"

It really gets to her when I talk like that. The other kids start laughing and snorting. They're all thinking the same as I am, but they're too chicken to say it out loud. Meanwhile, she tries to act so calm and cool, but her mouth gets tight, and she repeats something she already said, and a pink line creeps up her neck to her white cheeks. And then she gets herself in deeper. Instead of just yelling, "Shut your mandibles, Keating!" like my health teacher would, she says. "I'm curious, Wally. What would be your idea of a fascinating English class?"

Oh, man, is she *asking* for it! I feel like saying something really crude and lewd, but I don't. All I say is "A class where we *learned* something. Where we read something *interesting.* Where we didn't do all this *useless* stuff."

Then her face gets redder, the way it can only when somebody has white, white skin,

and I see I've hit her on the right weak spot, as usual. She *can't stand* hearing that she isn't teaching us anything, because she's such a serious, trying-to-be-so-good person. Practically every day she comes in with different books, or magazines, or stories she's copied on a machine. Stuff that is supposed to get us all excited but never does. Sometimes Tim the Gook talks to her about the papers she hands out, because he's as serious as she is, but the other kids—Ribs, Mr. Clean, Sherlene, and the Preacher—think just the same as I do: why don't this lady go off and be a librarian on a desert island?

You might be wondering why I'm taking Themes English, which is the lowest level there is. It's not as if I'm illiterate, like Mr. Clean and a couple of the others. It's because I do lousy in school, which is because I'm not interested in most things they try to teach us, and *especially* not in stories about girls who start off being tomboys, and guys and girls who fall in love even though their families hate each other, and mixed-up teenagers who run away from home. Half the stores we've read in her class are about kids running away from home, and in all of them the kid "wises up" and comes back. If I ever take off, which I might, the way things are going right now, at least I'll follow through with it and stay gone, not like these gutless wonders, who supposedly come to their senses on the last page of the story.

And what's pushing me into thinking about getting the hell out of here? This latest thing with *her,* Mrs. Loring. It's been building since the beginning of school. Right off, the first English period, I knew we'd be enemies, but it's taken till now, the end of March, for the battle to get really bad. Teachers. I can't take any of them, but the worst are the so-called understanding ones. I can't take people like Loring

103

and my grandmother—my father's mother— people who think that whatever goes wrong, you can fix it by *talking* about it *calmly*. I hate talk. I'm not talking again, especially to either of them.

Let me tell you how I knew right away that Loring and I were going to be enemies. I had been running a little wild last summer, and my mom practically dragged me to the first day of school. "You got the brains, Wally," she was saying as she dropped me off. "Don't let these troubles between me and your daddy affect you. Your daddy was *always* looking for something different in his life, and now he's *gone off* to find it. Don't give me trouble this year. Go in there and act right!"

So I walked into first period, annoyed to begin with, and who did I see in front of the class but this teacher who looks a lot like my grandmother I mentioned before. My grandmother is older, naturally, but they both have these blue, blue eyes, and besides that they both sound the same. They're both cool, in the sense of acting a little *above* everyone else. Not snobby, exactly, but *proper*. "Watch your manners, Wally dear!"

I wasn't in the mood for that watch-your-step stuff. I had spent some summers at my grandmother's and had had enough of learning how to be polite. She was always trying to *teach* me things. So was my father. And now here was Loring sounding just like my Grandma Keating. "Oh, isn't this wonderful, brand new books!"

Loring had taught in a different school before, she said, but she was glad to be here, supposedly. *Sure* she was. Then why did she look at us as if we were from outer space? She was trying not to stare at Mr. Clean's white skinhead and hula-hoop earring, and her expression when she saw Ribsy Johnson was *Help! call the narcs!* Okay, so skinny Ribsy is something else, with his gold tooth and jewelry, but she acted like she'd never seen a kid who's a drug runner before. Sherlene Lovering upset Loring, too, by showing pictures of her new baby. I naturally said, "Who were you lovering, Sherlene, to end up with that?"

And there were more of us aliens, nine or ten others, including the Preacher, this sophomore about three feet tall, who always talks like a minister. "Mornin', brothuhs," he said when he walked in. "Mornin', sister," he said to Loring. "So glad you could find in your souls to attend this A.M." Most teachers would have done something, either answered him smart or put him down. Not her. Soft and sweet, as if she thought that would turn us polite. Everyone took advantage. When she asked us about what kinds of things we liked, we gave stupid answers. And right away I decided to show her that marshmallows end up getting burnt.

My fellow classmates, as they say, were more than willing to help me. You could say there was a fine spirit of cooperation between Mr. Clean and Ribsy and me. Still, they left it to me to be leader, because those two care about passing. I used to care, too, back when we learned stuff that mattered. Anyway, everyone was happy that I took the initiative by winging a paper airplane over her head.

From then on it was downhill for her, mainly because, instead of yelling like a normal teacher, she kept on trying so hard to be patient and *nice*. It didn't help that her voice was shaky, or that she kept repeating certain dumb expressions. Soon the whole class was saying things like "People, I wish I could hear myself!"

She made us write almost every day, and a lot of the topics were personal. If I did the assignments at all, I just made up lies, and she was so easy, all she said was "You're very creative, Wally." My biggest creativity was thinking up ways to mess up her lessons.

"Where's your book today, Wally?" she asked me once. "Close your eyes," I said. She actually did it, and while her eyes were closed I walked out and cut class. After that, though, she laid down a rule. "Anyone who comes without a book goes to the principal." So I'd trick her, pretending I had no book, and then I'd pull it out of hiding at the last minute.

Once she actually sent a pink slip on me down to the office to Bird-doo. That's the principal, Mr. Berdew, who called me in for a weekly conference.

104

"What's up *now?*" Bird-doo asked me. "I shouldn't be having to see you so often. You're a smart kid. Get your act together. You should be a *leader* in that class."

"I am," I told him.

"That's not what I hear," Bird-doo said. "Hey, look, I don't want to have to call your father."

"He's away—on business."

"Your mother, then."

"Nah don't." I actually broke down and pleaded, "she's got a lot on her mind. I'll be a leader, I will." And then I said something else I knew that Bird-doo would listen to. He's white, Mr. Berdew (like bird-doo), but half the kids in the school are black. "Hey, Mr. Berdew, can't you find a better Themes teacher?"

"What are you talking about?" He came on impatient at first. "Who put you in charge of teacher evaluations? Mrs. Loring came here from Warrensville, the top school in the country."

"Warrensville?" I smiled and looked at him shrewd-like. "I guess that explains it. She must not be used to . . . students like us.

Bird-doo gave me a deep look. "You're not saying she discriminates, are you?"

I shrugged. "She *acts* like she thinks we belong in a zoo."

He clammed up and got rid of me fast, but soon after that he observed our Themes class. Naturally I kept all the flying objects grounded that day and answered Loring's questions left and right. Her voice was shakier than usual, and she repeated herself and blushed a lot, and if you ask me, we came off a lot better than she did. That was my main aim, let's face it, to get Loring out of the picture.

Anyway, I'm pretty sure that Bird-doo criticized her somehow, because after that she quit sending down pink slips on me. Instead, whenever I drove her nuts she made silly threats, like "How would you like to keep me company until five o'clock today?"

"I wouldn't like it," I'd tell her. "I'd rather hang out with Mrs. Dracula." Or else "I'd love it, but at four o'clock my father is taking me up in his private plane." She never carried out a threat and I knew she never would, but what she did do was to keep asking me to come in *voluntarily* to discuss what was bothering me.

"You've got to be kidding," I'd say to her.

"Then I'm going to have to speak to your parents."

"Go ahead." Let her waste her time, just like my grandmother, who keeps calling once a week to see if I'll come visit her, like I used to do. She'd like to talk with me about family matters, she says. As if I could *talk* my dad back from Alaska, when even the letter I sent up there he still hasn't answered!

Dodging my grandmother is a pain (my mom doesn't feel like seeing her either), but I wasn't worried at all about Loring calling my house. The only number I had given at school was the one to my dad's old business phone that is still there but we haven't answered since he left last May.

So that's how it went for a while, with me as the chief toaster at the marshmallow roast. Every day, as soon as Loring would start her lesson, I'd stir up something.

"Brothuh Keating," the Preacher would say, "give Sistuh Loring yo' full attention."

"I'm giving it." I'd smirk. "She's got my attention, *full time.*"

We would probably have gone on like that, with me annoying her constantly and her passing me at the end of the year with a D, just to get rid of me. But then she made a mistake. She brought in this certain story, and I had a hunch right from the beginning that she had brought it in to get at *me*. "White Chocolate," it was called, and when she handed it out, she looked at me.

"I'm curious what you'll think of it," she said.

"Curiosity killed the cat."

"I'm not a cat." She was blushing as usual. "Start reading, please, Wally."

She was always having us read out loud, with Mr. Clean spitting out one syllable per hour and the Preacher shouting "Amen!" at the end of each sentence. Sometimes I refused, but other times I read so fast that everyone would start yelling, "Hey, we can't understand what he's saying!"

This time I began fast, but right away she said, "Wait, please, Wally. This is one story I want everyone to hear every word of, particularly you."

"Why me?" I snapped back at her.

"Because I think you might be interested."

"Fat chance," I said. "What's it about?"

She was cool as usual. "Go on reading."

I should have quit then and there, I should have refused to continue, but I figured I'd ham it up and she'd have somebody else go on. I did ham it up somewhat, but she had me read anyway. I should have known. It was about a white girl going out with a guy who was black. "What makes you think I'm interested in this?" I boomed out at Loring.

"I've gotten the impression that you're interested in race relations."

"Wrong again," I informed her. "I'm definitely not."

Loring looked as if she was going to ask me to read further, but then she said, "Would you continue, please, Sherlene?"

I tried to make her laugh, but Sherlene went on with "White Chocolate." The story was the worst. It shouldn't be allowed in print. It's about this white girl who meets a black guy in college. They fall in love, but their families don't want them to get hitched. They won't give up, though. They *love* each other too much, and they want to *prove* something. So they work on their families real slow, and they take a lot of abuse, and finally—this is the worst part, I almost threw up all over the copies of the story—finally their families come to see things their way and they all plan the wedding together. And you can probably guess by now where the idiot title comes in. The icing on their wedding cake is—wow, so *symbolic*—made of *white chocolate.*

At some point in the reading I started humming pretty loudly, but fortunately not loud enough to drown the thing out. Loring gave me one of her hurt looks, which made me hum more. And at the end, when she asked, "Well, what do you think?" I let out a deep belch.

Nobody laughed. What was *wrong* with them? Sherlene said, "It's a real nice story." I couldn't believe my ears. "Nice!" I yelled. "There's nothing I hate more than *nice!*" If Ribsy had been there, he'd probably have cheered me on, but he was away on a business trip, and all the Preacher had to say was "True love is the greatest, amen!"

Loring looked at me, so serious. "So, what do you think, Wally? What are the chances for people from different backgrounds working things out?"

I went crazy at that point. I got up and headed straight for her. "Quit bugging me, lady! Why are you picking on *me* about that?"

She thought I was going to hit her, and I was. My arms were raised, ready to pound her, so that the Preacher came rushing up and yelled, "Now now, no *vi*-lence!"

The bell rang at the exact moment. Usually Loring blocks the doorway and doesn't let us leave the room until we've picked up our mess. This time she pushed everyone else out and blocked only me.

"You're talking to me right now." She stood with her arms folded.

"Can't," I said, nastily, "I got a class."

"*Forget it,* as you love to say." Her arm shot out. "Sit down."

I sat, but slowly, so she would know I wasn't jumping at her command.

"There's too much to say to say it all now." She stood over my desk and looked at me with those icy blue eyes. "All I'm saying for the moment is, *Don't lose control like that again.* If I ever ask you something that makes you angry, it's only because *I don't know any better,* and if I don't, it's your fault, because you want it that way. I can't make you tell me what's bothering you. I don't necessarily want to know your personal problems. If you want me to know, I'll do what I can to help. If you don't want me to know your business, follow this rule: Don't show me you're hurting. Fake it. Pretend you're a model kid.

"One more thing," she babbled on, "it's ironic that you refuse to talk—talk seriously, I mean. I know you're willing to talk to put people down. Don't you know how good you are with words? Don't you know the *power* that could give you? Getting through to other people with words is our only hope in this world!

"*Go,*" she told me all of a sudden. "Enough for one lecture. Get moving to your class, so I won't have to write a note. I'd like to really talk sometime, I mean a two-way conversation. If that's not possible for you, remember what I said, *lose control again and you're out.*"

106

I took off without saying beans. Not like these kids in her stupid stories, who hear some wise-as-an-owl speech and it changes their teenage hearts. In fact, if she knew the effect, she would have kept her precious *words* to herself. The effect is, I'm probably not going back to her class ever again. Who needs credits? Both my parents went all the way through college and their lives aren't that great. What I'll probably do is go away, and like I said, I'll stay

gone. I'm thinking about Alaska. I'm going to actually look at a map tonight.

Meanwhile, I hope I don't see Loring anymore in the hall today. She probably thinks, now that I listened to her for two seconds, that I'll be like Silly Putty in her hands. She probably thinks she'll eventually get me to show her the stuff I write, that I've never shown anybody. Just let her *try* pressing me into shape, and let her see how sticky I'll be.

H.O.T. RESPONSES

Discuss the following with your cooperative group:

1. Do you think Wally detests Mrs. Loring, his English teacher, as much as he protests that he does?

2. Explain the irony of Wally's statement:

   I can't take people like Loring and my grandmother—and my father's mother—people who think that whatever goes wrong, you can fix it by talking about it calmly. I hate talk. I'm not talking again, especially to either of them.

3. What do you suppose are the underlying causes of Wally's frustration and anger?

4. In your own words, explain the author's metaphor:

   And right away I decided to show her that marshmallows end up getting burnt.

5. Discuss some of the characters in this story, particularly Wally, Preacher, and Mr. Clean. Are these believable personalities? Explain.

6. What do you think about the final confrontation Mrs. Loring has with Wally? Did she finally get through to him or will he run away to Alaska? Explain.

7. Why is it that only Wally detests the story, "White Chocolate?" Why does he nearly become violent and ridicule the story so:

> *And you can probably guess by now where the idiot title comes in. The icing on their wedding cake is—wow, so symbolic—made of white chocolate.*

Explain the "symbolism" of the title as you describe Wally's anger.

CREATIVE PRODUCT

1. Robin Brancato's success as a short story writer stems from her ability to create dialogue that is real. Write a story based upon an incident in class in which one of your teacher's has a "verbal conflict" with you or one of your classmates. Use Brancato's style as a model for creating dialogue for your main characters.

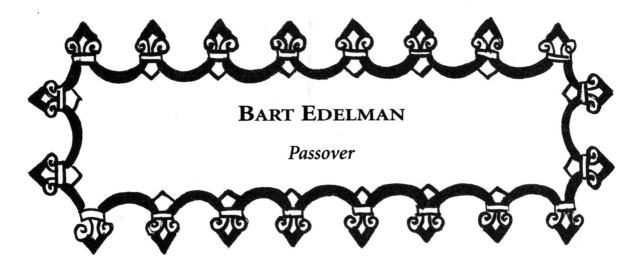

BART EDELMAN

Passover

© 1996 by The Center for Applied Research in Education

FOCUS

Bart Edelman draws on his Jewish American heritage in creating his poem, "Passover." In Unit Three, Activity Four, you may remember reading Bart Edelman's poem, "They Shot Wook Kim." "Passover" deals more with the nostalgia of past experiences, related to cultural as well as religious responses to today's society. As you read this poem, see how remembrances build to frustration, a dream that is unrealized. Several cultural and religious words and expressions are listed in the glossary on the next page. Study these terms before reading the poem, and return to them after you have reread the poem to better understand the meaning of these words in context.

GLOSSARY

YARMULKE	(Yarmuku)	Religious skull cap
CHUPAH	(Cupä)	Wedding canopy
NACHAS	(Nakus)	Joy
SEDER PLATES	(Sayder)	Plates used for serving the Passover meal.
HAGGADAHS	(Hägädäs)	Books that tell the story of Passover.
CHAROSETH	(Caroseth)	Red bricks (represented by apples, wine, and raisins) signifying the temples Jews were enslaved to build for the Pharaohs.
THE FOUR QUESTIONS		At the Passover ceremony, for example, "Why is this night different from all others?"
TEN PLAGUES		The Pharaohs brought ten plagues against the Jews. One plague dictated that every first-born would be killed.
UNLEAVENED BREAD		Matzoh is the flat, dry, crackerlike bread symbolic of the bread made by the Jews when they left Egypt in such a hurry that they forgot yeast to make the bread rise.
MORNING SH'MA		Prayer
TALLITH		Shawl with fringes worn by very religious Jews.
PHYLACTERIES		Leather cases holding scripture passages, worn for morning prayer.
KADDISH		A prayer said for the dead.

Passover

On Fairfax, near Farmer's Market,
I'm told I should marry.
To grow old is no bargain
They mutter in their long black coats
And nod beneath their yarmulkes,
Noticing how my hair thins:
This is a sure sign of worry.
A wife will calm my nerves,
A full head of hair will be mine
One year to the day
I stand under the chupah.
The holiday just tomorrow:
What am I doing with my life?
How can I pray alone on the Sabbath?
From whom shall I receive nachas?
If not now—when?
They offer to make inquiries for me.

Late evening,
I lie alone
Searching the darkened universe
For tiny Stars of David
Glittering in the sky.
I dream of endless Seder Plates,
Stacks of Haggadahs surround me,
I cannot reach the charoseth,
The cup I've filled for Elijah
Empties before my eyes,
The Four Questions become Five
And I behold the Ten Plagues
Spread upon the unleavened bread at my side.
I scream
Loud enough
To disturb a Pharoah's nap.

I wake the next day rested
And recite the morning sh'ma.
Dressed in a cobalt suit
I walk to synagogue,
Tallith and phylacteries clutched in hand.
Today's prayer is one of redemption,
God knows my affliction—
Reciting Kaddish,
I ask to be led
Out of bondage from Egypt
Into the land of Israel.

H.O.T. RESPONSES

Discuss in your cooperative group (record your responses; choose a leader).

1. Cite lines and phrases to support your responses: What is the poet's worry?

2. Why does the poet scream in stanza two?

3. Do you get the impression that the poet was always a religious observer? Explain.

4. What does the poet mean by: "God knows my affliction"?

5. How do the cultural and religious terms you have familiarized yourself with create still another layer of meaning in the poem?

6. Explain why the poet ends the poem praying:

   I ask to be led
   Out of bondage from Egypt
   Into the land of Israel.

CREATIVE PRODUCT

1. Write a poem or a story that relates to your own religious and cultural background. Use cultural or religious terms that will enhance the texture of your creative work.

FOCUS

Lottie E. Porch is a new African American playwright, short story writer, and poet. Her work has been anthologized by Globe Book Company, and her poetry appears in several literary magazines and journals. Lottie E. Porch is also an actress, and a director who has directed over thirty productions for children and young adults. Her specialty is writing and directing plays about the African American experience. Miss Porch holds a Master of Arts in Educational Theatre from New York University. She teaches at William Paterson College and for the Teaneck Public Schools. She is also enrolled in Temple University's Ph.D. program in African American Studies.

Her new play, *A Woman's Dance, Song, Cry!* sponsored by the African American Studies Center of Teaneck High School, explores phases of womanhood and the lives of Mahalia Jackson, Zora Neale Hurston, and Ella Baker.

Ms. Porch has received the Allen Ginsberg Poetry Award and the NANBP Black Heritage Award. Her poetry and writings have been published by the Haggerty Museum of Milwaukee and by the American Baptist Churches. Her first play, *Rhythms of Life: A Historical Journey,* was performed at the Harlem Abyssinian Church in New York City.

The following excerpts are from the first four chapters of her new novel, *The Year of LoriAnn.*

Chapter One
"She Came in June"

The new girl who moved in downstairs musta stole something or done something really bad 'cause she was getting the whupping of life! I heard her screaming up through the ceiling. She was begging her mom to stop and promising she wouldn't do it again.

The yelling started to make me feel nervous and jumpy like, so I went in the front room and turned on the TV. I figured maybe that would drown out the sound.

But the TV didn't help. I could still hear her yelling, running from room to room. So I turned the TV off and decided to just listen. She was screaming real loud now, "screaming bloody murder" as my mom would say. "Why is she being beat like that?" I thought, "Can't her mother hear how sorry she is?" My skin was starting to crawl.

Finally her yelling stopped, and I heard their back door slam. I went to the back bedroom window to peek into the yard and see what she was doing. She was sitting kinda hunched over like on the stoop sobbing and sniffling. "Man," I thought "her mom and dad must be the meanest people in the whole world."

I guess it was 'round two days later, I was out playing stick ball with my friends, Jamal and his brother. I saw her again. She musta been coming home from the store cause she had two big bags fulla groceries. As she walked past I felt myself wanting to say hello or something. But geez, I couldn't quite think of anything clever to say—you know so she wouldn't think I was weird or anything—so I just let her

go by. In a funny kinda way I thought she was pretty. I mean she wasn't beautiful like Janet Jackson. But there was something pretty about her. And something—well, how can I say it? Something sad—yeah, that's it, sad. I thought back to the other day when I heard her getting that beating—all that screaming and yelling came back into my mind like a flash. And her sadness seemed to wash over me. I felt like I wanted to help her, be real brave, you know like Indiana Jones does in all his movies.

Well after that, I didn't see her for almost two weeks. Although it was only the beginning of July, I was busy getting ready for school to start. Since I was going to military school, and it was my first time living away from home, I had tons of stuff to do. Each day mom made a list of things for me to pick up and folks to visit. My mom is real big on respecting elders and visiting relatives and friends. So each day, I had "my work cut out for me." That's another of my mom's favorite sayings. Anyway, like I said, I guess it was about two weeks later when I saw her.

I was just on my way out to pick up the clothes labels mom had ordered for me when someone rang the door bell. When I looked out the peep hole—something my mom insists that I do, whether she's home or not, even though we live in a good neighborhood and all. Anyways, it was her, staring right back at me not knowing I was looking at her. I opened the door.

"Hi" she said. "Are you Andre?"

"Yes."

"Well, my name is Lori." She stretched her hand out, and gave me a torn envelope. "Uh," she stammered, "I made a mistake and opened this letter of yours. It was in our mailbox. Sorry."

I glanced at the return address. It was from my pen pal out in Iowa, a kid named Dennis Keasing.

"Gee," I said "don't worry about it." I realized my palms were sweating. "Uh, you, I mean, anybody can make a mistake."

"Thanks," she said. "See Ya."

She turned and left.

I backed inside and as I closed the door I thought to myself, "Did I see a funny looking birthmark under her chin? How come I didn't notice it before?" Then again I thought, "You dummy, you never been that close up. How could you have noticed?" One thing for sure, she was real pretty and real sad too.

Chapter Two

"July's Letter"

Lori rushed back down the stairs. She didn't want to be caught out of the apartment if her aunt came home early. "What would a Black kid have in common with a kid from Iowa named Dennis Keasing?" she thought. "Shucks—I should of at least read the letter before I returned it." "I guess I wasn't thinking," she mumbled.

"Lori!" a voice yelled from inside as she stepped through the door, "Bring me a beer from the fridge."

"Okay!" The sound of her uncle's voice jarred her into action. She quickly went to the fridge, opened it, and pulled out a bottle. As she opened the cap with a "pop," the beer's white foam spilled out over the edges. The acrid smell insulted her nostrils. "I just don't see how anybody could enjoy drinking this nasty stuff," she thought. She wiped the bottle's edges and wrapped it in a paper towel the way Uncle Henry liked.

She delivered the beer, and went to her room and sat in front of her desk. "At least I have a pen pal who really understands me," she thought. She lifted the desk top and pulled out a notebook with lavender paper and hot pink lines.

July 7, 1988

Dear Mama Reynolds,

Hi! I bet you didn't expect to hear from me so soon. Well to tell you the truth, I was feeling kinda lonely and decided maybe writing would help. Actually, I was also hoping you'd be coming for a visit soon.

Anyway, guess what? Well, okay, don't guess. I bet you could tell by the return address of this letter. We moved! Yeah, we live in Englewood, New Jersey, now. It's much better than the Bronx in some ways and much worse in others. I mean it's much cleaner. And we live in a house, and we have a big backyard. We share the house with the family upstairs, but the backyard pretty much belongs to us. They call it a "two-family house." Makes sense I guess. Oh yeah, the house is cream colored with green trim. It's pretty.

Here's another guess what. There's a boy about 13 or 14 living upstairs with his mom. He's cute in a different sort of way. His skin is a really smooth golden brown. But what I really like are his eyes. His eyes are really kind looking, and his eyelashes are soooo long! Other than that he's average. A little taller than me. Since it's still summer, I don't know what grade

© 1996 by The Center for Applied Research in Education

117

he's in, but he has a pen pal all the way from Iowa. I had to look up Iowa in the encyclopedia 'cause it was too far away for me to remember exactly where it was. Anyway, his name is Andre.

Don't you think it's strange that he has a pen pal in Iowa? Doesn't that mean his pen pal is white? After all, his name is Dennis Keasing. There can't be any BLACK people in Iowa with names like that—can there?

Suddenly Lori heard a crash in the next room. She jumped thinking, "Oh God, what did Uncle Henry do now?" She put down her pen, and went quietly to the door of his room. He was picking himself up off the floor. The beer had spilt all over Aunt Mavis' new rug. "Boy! Aunt Mavis is gonna be pissed when she gets home and sees that," Lori thought as she crept back to her room. "Maybe he'll go right back to sleep and not bug me for another beer just yet." Sitting back at the desk, she hurried to finish the letter before her uncle woke up.

Oh yeah, there was something else I wanted to tell you. It happened again the other day, you know, a beating. It was bad too. I mean it hurt, hurt, hurt. I guess it was my fault though. I lost my house keys, and that made Aunt Mavis really mad. First Uncle Henry yelled at me, and then Aunt Mavis started. I tried to explain that it was an accident. She didn't want to hear it. Anyway I promised never to lose them again. They said if I did, I'd have to stay outside until they came home, no matter what time it was. Right now I don't have to worry too much 'cause Uncle Henry is on strike. He stays home all day drinking beer and sleeping. I hope I remember not to lose them again. Anyway, I just heard the front door open. Aunt Mavis is home from work. Got to go.

> Miss you sooo much,
> Your only God daughter,
>
> Lori Ann

P.S. Do you think it's a sin to hate someone even though they take care of you and buy you things?

Lori pulled the letter out of the notebook's spiral binding. She folded it carefully and hid it in a box with the others in the back of her closet.

"Lori" Aunt Mavis yelled.

"Coming" Lori replied.

Chapter Three
"August Prayers"

Sister Katie Reynolds was a big brown woman with a perpetual smile and eyes that danced. She always smelled good like the newest Avon perfume. And except for the bangs that framed her face, her mixed gray hair stood straight up on her head—giving you the feeling that she was always ready for action.

It was a steamy hot Friday afternoon, and she bustled about in the kitchen wanting to get her cooking done early. In spite of the heat, she fixed a huge meal of fried catfish, collard greens, potato salad, sliced tomatoes from the garden, and golden hush puppies. After turning the hush puppies to brown on the flip side, she set the table and yelled, "Come and get it

Deek." (Her husband, Campbell Reynolds, had been a deacon in the church for over 30 years, and everyone called him "Deek.") After seeing that Deek was settled down to the hearty meal, she went out on the front porch intending to catch the first breezes of the evening.

"Aren't you eating with me honey?" Deek piped questioningly.

"Naw, sweetheart. You go 'head and help yo'self. I'll wait till my food cools down some. 'Caint stand to eat a real hot meal on a real hot day. I'll be back in a bit."

Plopping down into the wicker rocker, she felt a sort of restlessness take over her. She wondered what it was. She knew she missed her friends in New York. Readjusting to country life after so many years was harder than she had imagined. But her mama was sick, so they had come back. Besides the fact that she absolutely didn't believe in nursing homes, things in New York were getting tougher. And she and Deek weren't spring chickens any more. Still, something nudged at the back of her mind. So she rocked back and forth to calm herself.

All at once, she thought of Lori Ann. She hadn't heard from her in quite some time. And the card she mailed Lori had been returned marked "undeliverable." An uneasy feeling took hold of her, so she uttered a flash prayer, "Lord, watch over her please." As she rose to go inside and join her husband for dinner, Katie Reynolds made a vow to ask about Lori at church as soon as they returned to New York for a visit. If not sooner.

Chapter Four
"September's Promise"

"Military school! Military school!" The words hovered in the air over my head. As the time came closer the promise of their meaning became clearer, filling up my days from the time I woke up till late in the evening. Getting uniforms, getting a physical, more tests. The C.A.T.'s and P.S.A.T.'s that I took last year weren't enough. Now there was a whole bunch of other ones whose names I can't even remember, don't wanna remember.

Mom says that they don't believe in telling kids the scores, but that I did well—real well. I was even getting a minority scholarship 'cause my grades and test scores were high. Mom said I was lucky to get it, especially since I missed a couple of deadlines.

"Andre," she said, "I could never afford to send you to this school without help—we're very lucky. And I'm so proud of you!" Geez, when Mom says stuff like that, I get embarrassed. I was glad none of my friends were over when she said it. But I was happy too. Ever since I was in about the third grade, I wanted to wear one of those deep blue uniforms with big brass buttons, and march in formation like the guys do in the 4th of July parade. And the marching bands, man they really got me going!

Still I couldn't quite understand what the big deal was about the scholarship, that is. Why'd I get a MINORITY scholarship? Not that I wasn't grateful—but I mean, why didn't I just get a scholarship? Still, minority or not, I got a scholarship and I'm glad. I'm glad I'm going.

It seems as if somebody or something wanted to interrupt my thoughts right then, 'cause suddenly I heard a big crash. Downstairs. Geez! I thought, what the heck is going on down there, World War III? There was more screaming and yelling and pleading. I felt myself getting hot under the collar. Boy oh boy, what is wrong with those people? Then I heard it again, sobbing. And I new it was her. Somehow I began to understand her sadness.

I knew it was none of my business. Mom always says people need to be minding their own affairs. But, I tip-toed to the back stairs door. It was always locked, but it had steps that led right into their apartment. So you could hear real good standing there.

Listening real carefully, I heard a man yelling, "Clean it up now!" Then a door slammed. Then came the sound of sweeping, tinkling glass, and a sob or two.

Shucks, I missed it—whatever it was. So I made a mental note to be quicker next time. I wanted to make sure I wasn't leaving Mom home alone in a house with a bunch of crazies. Even if they did live downstairs, who knows what could happen?

Just then, the picture of Indiana Jones on a rope swinging down and scooping up a terrified girl came to the front of my mind. And a strange feeling came over me. For a split second I saw her eyes.

119

H.O.T. RESPONSES

1. Write a brief character description of the two main characters, Andre and LoriAnn.

2. What impression do you get from Andre's allusion to his mom's sayings?

3. Lori has moved out of the Bronx into the suburbs of New Jersey, but has her life really changed for the better? Explain how LoriAnn copes with her situation.

4. In your cooperative group, discuss LoriAnn's comment and perception that she guessed the beatings were deserved because it was her fault for losing the house keys. Do you think her beatings are deserved? Explain.

5. Have you read about how abused children and how abused women often consider themselves to be at fault, and, therefore, remain in these abusive situations without seeking counseling or legal intervention? Why do you think this occurs? What would you have advised LoriAnn if you were Andre?

CREATIVE PRODUCT

1. Create a scene in which you or Andre counsel LoriAnn in dealing with her situation. You may want to seek out more information by contacting your community's local Division of Youth and Family Services organization.

Unit Five

THEME:
WHAT IF? SCENARIOS

INTRODUCTION

What If? Scenarios are a series of problem-solving situations presented here for you to consider and to try to resolve.

Some of these scenarios are based on events that have actually occurred, such as the Pepsi Cola contest fiasco written about by a journalist in the *Los Angeles Times*. Other scenarios are based upon real problems that society has seemingly been unable to face or, at least, has been unable to solve—escalating violence, the homeless situation, or inadequate schooling in poor, urban areas.

These scenarios or problems need creative solutions or they will remain unresolved, threatening social dilemmas that you will one day be facing as adults.

Here, then, is an opportunity for you to voice your opinions, to raise alternative solutions that may even be shared with government officials to let them know that the youth of this nation really does care and wants to contribute to making this a better society for future generations.

FOCUS

What if you won a million-dollar prize but were told the company refused to pay because of a marketing error? This actually happened in the Philippines. Pepsi said anyone holding a bottle cap marked 349 had won about $40,000 tax free. (At a 25-to-1 rate of exchange from dollars to pesos, $40,000 would be equivalent to one million pesos.) Read the *Los Angeles Times,* July 27, 1993, account of this unfortunate error that first raised and then dampened the hopes of thousands of poor Filipinos.

Mistake by Pepsi enrages Filipinos

❒ Pepsi said anyone holding a bottle cap marked 349 had won about $40,000. Problem is, up to 800,000 Filipinos have that number.

Los Angeles Times 7/27/93

MANILA, Philippines—Pepsi's advertisements, splashed for weeks all over Philippine newspapers, radio and TV, were hardly subtle: "Today, you could be a millionaire!"

From her tin-roofed shack in one of Manila's more squalid slums, Victoria Angelo couldn't resist. The unemployed mother of five, and her husband, Juanito, who pedals people about in his three-wheeled cab for about $4 a day, began drinking Pepsi with every meal and snack. Each morning, the family prayed for a specially marked bottle cap. And each night, they and their neighbors flocked around a small television to see if their prayers were answered.

And then, a miracle!

On May 25 last year, the nightly news announced that anyone holding a bottle cap marked 349 had won up to 1-million pesos—about $40,000, tax-free.

Spreading her collection of caps on a table, Victoria Angelo screamed, "We are a millionaire!"

Her voice ringing with excitement, she recalled that she turned to her family: "I tell my children you can finish school and go to college. I tell my husband he can buy a (passenger jeep). I tell myself we can buy a real house. Can you imagine? It is a dream come true!"

But her dream has become a nightmare for New York-based Pepsico Inc.

In a marketing mistake that surely must rank among the world's worst, Pepsi had announced the wrong number. Instead of a single 1-million-peso winner, up to 800,000 bottle caps marked 349 had been printed. And tens of thousands of Filipinos soon began demanding billions of dollars that Pepsi refuses to pay.

H.O.T. RESPONSES

Reflect and Discuss

1. How would you react if this had happened to you?

2. What course of action would you take, if any?

3. What do you think Pepsi's responsibility is?

4. Could you offer a solution to this problem that would be reasonable and satisfactory to Pepsi and to the people who hold the winning number—349?

CREATIVE PRODUCT

1. Develop a cooperative group short story or one-act play, using the facts from this article. Quite often, authors take real incidents such as this one, and allow their imaginations to run wild! Based upon this bit of truth, an author begins to weave a story or drama:

   a. Start your story a few weeks before the prize is actually discovered.

   b. Describe in detail the place where the Angelo family lives.

   c. Establish a story line showing this family to be in need.

   d. Describe the miracle in vivid detail, but embellish on a few of the sentences from the article.

   e. Using your own imagination, develop the characters and plot, taking the situation beyond the article you just read.

   f. Create a dramatic conclusion for your story or one-act play.

FOCUS

What if you were a young screenplay writer, and you were asked to collaborate on the writing of a film? This film would have to be exciting, have a great deal of action, and be entertaining, but at the same time, persuade a multicultural teenage generation to become more accepting of others' differences. The main character must fight against prejudice and violence and be a voice of reason in the midst of a horde of violent, angry hoodlums.

H.O.T. RESPONSES

1. Brainstorm with your cooperative group how such a film might be constructed.

CREATIVE PRODUCT

1. Write the first, second, and final scenes of this movie, establishing conflict between characters sharing opposing points of view.

2. Write a "Letter to the Editor" explaining the futility and despair that exists in today's society. Express what needs to be done to turn this seemingly hopeless situation around. Is there anything that we, as citizens, can do collectively to create a more peaceful, cooperative society?

FOCUS

What if you were a television film critic writing for a multicultural audience? You are assigned to review either the best or the worst film you've seen recently. (Each member of your cooperative group will work independently on this assignment.)

H.O.T. RESPONSES

1. Each member of the cooperative group should read his or her review aloud to the other members and then critique one another's reviews and TV presentations. If possible, videotape your reviews.

CREATIVE PRODUCT

1. Write your review, giving specific reasons why you liked or disliked the film. Be sure to write about how the film includes or excludes people of color. Be prepared to read it in a two- to three-minute time slot for television.

FOCUS

What if you and the members of your cooperative group were summoned by the President of the United States to create a plan for rebuilding America's cities? You are given total freedom to make recommendations to the President for dealing with such urban crises as (a) the homeless, (b) run-down housing conditions, (c) poverty, (d) crime, (e) drug trafficking, (f) health problems, (g) violence and poor achievement of African American and Latino students in urban schools.

H.O.T. RESPONSES

1. Brainstorm the causes for the seven listed problems.

2. Brainstorm ideas for making changes in each of the above areas. If your solutions require spending huge amounts of money, you must tell from where that money will come. (For example, huge sums of money have been diverted from the defense budget to pay back government loans, commonly referred to as the "budget deficit.") What money sources can be used? As you plan, give careful thought to alternatives and to setting different priorities.

CREATIVE PRODUCT

1. Create a plan that provides solutions to the seven key areas listed. Once you and your group are satisfied with your plan, commit it to writing. First, outline your plan.

2. Share your plan with your teacher, and perhaps you will be encouraged to write a letter to the President outlining your recommendations for urban renewal.

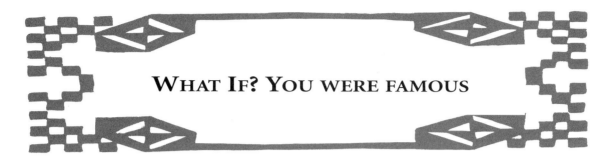

WHAT IF? YOU WERE FAMOUS

FOCUS

What if you were able to become a famous person representative of your own racial or cultural group? Choose the character that you would wish to be. Be sure to select a role model of whom you would be most proud.

H.O.T. RESPONSES

1. Be reflective and work independently on this assignment. In a paragraph or two, write down your choice and explain your decision. Share it with your cooperative group.

CREATIVE PRODUCT

Work independently on this creative product. Choose from among the following suggestions, or make your own choice. Having your chosen celebrity serve as the main character, do the following:

1. Write a fable.

2. Write a mystery story.

3. Develop a logo or an artistic representation of your chosen person.

4. Write a narrative poem that describes the person you've become.

WHAT IF? NO ONE EVER DIED

FOCUS

What if no one died from natural causes any more? Think about the global-multicultural problems this seemingly desirable situation would create. What would it be like to live in such a world? What creative solution(s) would you need to employ if you were a leader in such a world?

H.O.T. RESPONSES

1. First, discuss with your cooperative group the advantages of living in such a world. Then, discuss all of the resulting problems. Finally, offer possible solutions to counter these problems.

CREATIVE PRODUCT

1. Create a game that signifies both the problems and the solutions. Who wins? Who loses?

2. Develop a one-act play as a collaborative group activity. Prepare to act out your play for your classmates.

FOCUS

What if Richard Wright, the African American writer were correct in his view that: "The differences between black folk and white folk are not blood or color, and the ties that bind us are deeper than those that separate us. The common road of hope which we all traveled has brought us into a stronger kinship than any words, laws, or legal claims"? (Richard Wright, *12 Million Black Voices,* 1941)

H.O.T. RESPONSES

1. Choose a partner from your cooperative group and make a list of the *ties that bind us.* Compare your list with those of other teams from your cooperative group, and form one extensive list.

CREATIVE PRODUCT

1. From this list write an article, a poem, or an essay showing that we are more *alike* than *different.*

2. Make another list showing how different we are. Then, write a play, or a script for a television trial, showing that we are *more different* than we are *alike.*

WHAT IF? YOU WERE A WRITER

FOCUS

What if you were a writer for a newspaper or a magazine and your editor asked you to write about why so many African Americans, Latinos, and other minority men (and women) can be seen hanging out on street corners drinking from bottles wrapped in paper bags, or selling and using drugs? Burt Saxon, a teacher at Hillhouse High School in New Haven, Connecticut, recalled seeing such a scene in his youth and remembered hearing his father's and uncle's "stereotypical" remarks. The memory made him reflect recently on this social problem and to write an article, published in the *Harvard Educational Review*, February, 1991. An excerpt is shown below for you to read to help you write an article of your own.

> *Sam and Mike occasionally returned to Chicago, taking my cousin Bob and me to Comiskey Park a couple of times each year to see the White Sox play. As we drove through the South Side, we would see Negro men drinking from bottles wrapped in brown paper bags. My uncle would gaze out of his Lincoln Continental and announce, "They have to do what we did, Sam. They have to pull themselves up by their boot-straps." My father would nod weakly as his younger brother spoke, but say nothing. Sam seemed unsure that hard work always paid off. Uncle Mike used the bootstrap argument every few minutes, and my cousin and I would giggle nervously. We were not only giggling at him, however. The men on the corner made us nervous, and it was hard to imagine them becoming doctors and lawyers.*

H.O.T. RESPONSES

1. Can you recall hearing *biased, stereotypical* remarks such as those heard by Burt Saxon? If so, use these remarks to help you discuss social problems or issues that are prevalent in today's society.

CREATIVE PRODUCT

1. Use these biased remarks as a basis for writing your own views about current day problems and *real* situations, using Saxon's article as a model.

© 1996 by The Center for Applied Research in Education

FOCUS

What if you were an *anthropologist?* An anthropologist is someone who studies a specific group or culture and records notes about his or her observations. In anthropology, this notetaking is called *ethnography*. An anthropologist is mainly interested in observing and recording a certain group's or people's behavior, customs, or unique ways of communication. From this study, the observer learns a great deal more about a group's culture.

Anthropologists usually focus their observations on a few basic things such as (1) behaviors or rituals; (2) values; (3) speech patterns, gestures, and body language; (4) dress; (5) eating habits; and (6) family structures or organization. For instance, in some Native American tribes, the female plays a very dominant role. Other unique behaviors that may be of interest include hunting, dances; work habits; leadership; male and female roles; and the roles of children.

Some anthropologists record their observations in a diary or a journal. Others create a notebook or use forms that specify areas on which they wish to focus as shown below:

Entry date	Time	Place	Focus group		
Behavior (rituals)	Male/female roles	Unique communication (gestures, body language)	Unique dress	Eating habits	Other

H.O.T. RESPONSES

1. Identify an age group that you are interested in studying more closely—young children, adolescents, or adults. Decide in which setting or settings you will feel most comfortable observing their behaviors. (It is important to observe without letting those being observed become self-conscious about being studied.) You may have some hunches, or develop hypotheses about some of the behaviors you observe, but for the most part, you should remain open-minded and nonjudgmental. The best experiences occur when you are surprised by what you observe as a result of being so focused.

CREATIVE PRODUCT

1. First, observe a group from your own ethnic or racial group and record your observations using a data collection form similar to the one shown under "Focus." You may want to use a tape recorder to tape conversations and transcribe them at a later time. A minimum of two or three days of observations is needed to allow for patterns to be established. Some anthropologists spend weeks, months, and years compiling ethnographic notes before drawing conclusions and writing about their findings.

2. Study an ethnic or racial group different from your own. Select a special setting in which to observe your group. Some settings you may wish to consider are the classroom; the cafeteria; or a gathering place, for example, street corner, ice cream parlor, extracurricular activity, part-time job.

© 1996 by The Center for Applied Research in Education

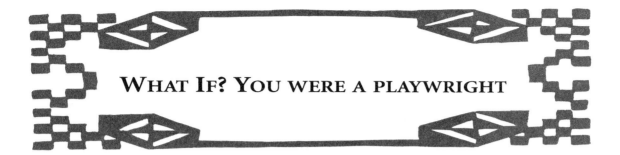

FOCUS

What if you were a playwright and a former anthropologist? You would have developed the skill of listening carefully to the speech of individuals from a variety of settings. Playwrights are also specialists when it comes to listening to speech patterns, and call upon their past experiences and memories in recreating dialogue. You can develop this skill by becoming a good listener, and by actually recording interesting comments made by particular groups of individuals to be utilized in helping you build dialogue for a play you may wish to write.

CREATIVE PRODUCT

1. Listen to your friends, parents, or other adults speaking, and record some of their interesting comments. Use this dialogue as a starting point to create your own play. Write a scene or one-act play from a multicultural point of view, based upon the dialogue that you have recorded from real life. Then allow your imagination to take over to establish characters, a setting, a plot, and a conclusion or climax to your play.

Unit Six

THEME:
CULTURAL PERSPECTIVES
THROUGH POETRY

INTRODUCTION

Reading multicultural literature enables the reader to learn about the many feelings and points of view from the perspective of the individual presenting his or her cultural experiences. These experiences often differ from those presented in most history books.

The *Western Movement,* for example, is viewed much differently from the Native American perspective. A Native American historian might refer to such a movement as the *Eastern Invasion.* Therefore, a more global, multicultural perspective helps the reader empathize or feel how others may perceive such events from their own experiences.

In this unit, Bly and Cowen address the cruelties of humankind as well as animalkind and in their poems they empathize with the oppressed. The African American poet, Countee Cullen, marvels about a God who dooms his people to endless struggle, like Sisyphus who must forever push a huge rock up a hill, and in "Tableau" he comments on how the young are corrupted by adult prejudice. Soon after migrating from his native Cuba, poet Noel Jardines travels to Kansas, where upon he *envisions ports* and *imagines* manatees.

We learn from Chinese-born Kuangchi C. Chang how difficult it was for him to run away from his homeland to escape communism. From Filipina Virginia R. Moreno, we learn about an ancient craft, and about idealized love.

Michael Mathias' spirituality and his poem to the Indian avatar Meher Baba, enables the reader to feel his devotion to this great avatar.

Finally, a song, written by the Mohawk Native American poet, Maurice Kenny, tells how his people struggled but continue to endure centuries of suffering.

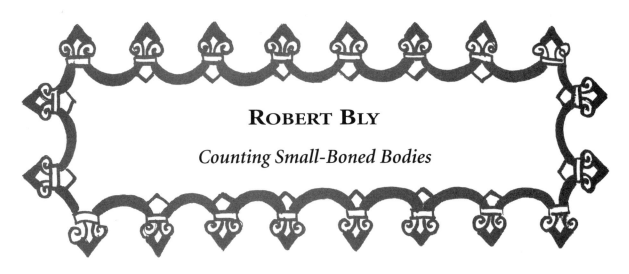

ROBERT BLY

Counting Small-Boned Bodies

© 1996 by The Center for Applied Research in Education

FOCUS

Robert Bly is an outstanding poet, critic, editor, storyteller, and translator. As early as 1950, he pioneered efforts in the area of multicultural literature—introducing a new poetry of imagination with such writers as Federico García Lorca, Pablo Neruda, Ibn Hazm, Juan Ramón Jiménez, Antonio Machado, Basho, Issa, Shiki, and Vallejo to name a few. His literary magazine, *The Fifties,* and later, *The Sixties* and *The Seventies,* provided a stage for writers to be heard from South America, Japan, and other parts of the globe. Bly is of Swedish American ancestry. Robert Bly is the author of several volumes of poetry; a book of criticism, *American Poetry: Wildness and Domesticity;* a prose work, *A Little Book on the Human Shadow;* and a full-length book of prose, *Iron John: A Book About Men.* Bly's poetry has won many awards, including the National Book Award. The poem, *"Counting Small-Boned Bodies,"* from *The Light Around the Body,* was written at the height of the Vietnam war by an enraged poet who was one of the earliest public critics of this most unpopular war in American History. Televised accounts of the bloody fighting were carried nightly on the evening news, and "body counts" were reported much like baseball scores. With this background in mind, read Robert Bly's poem below and reflect on his perspective, his anger, and his frustration.

Counting Small-Boned Bodies

Let's count the bodies over again.

If we could only make the bodies smaller,
The size of skulls,
We could make a whole plain white with skulls in the moon-
   light!

If we could only make the bodies smaller,
Maybe we could get
A whole year's kill in front of us on a desk!

If we could only make the bodies smaller,
We could fit
A body into a finger-ring, for a keepsake forever.

H.O.T. RESPONSES

Discuss the poem with your cooperative group:

1. What is your first response to this poem?

2. What tone is used throughout Robert Bly's poem?

3. Why does the poet repeat the line, "If we could only make the bodies smaller . . ."?

4. Is Bly writing from the average American perspective of the Vietnam war? Explain.

5. Do you think this poem is "un-American?" Explain your point of view.

6. The use of the metaphor is very effective throughout this poem, and particularly in the last line. What is the poet referring to with this rather bizarre image?

CREATIVE PRODUCT

1. Write a satirical poem from the point of view of the Native Americans that would express their perspective of the "Western Movement." This assignment may be done individually or as a collaborative effort.

2. Write your own antiwar poem based upon recent wars in which American troops fought.

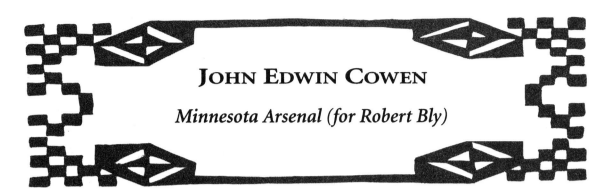

JOHN EDWIN COWEN

Minnesota Arsenal (for Robert Bly)

FOCUS

A newspaper article reported a story about a herd of deer that became victimized in their own habitat by the Army. The Army had set up a "mock war zone" in Minnesota to practice war games with real military machinery, including armored tanks. Unfortunately, the deer came to graze in this field, which disrupted the military maneuvers. The Army decided to round up the deer by shooting them with drug pellets. Unfortunately, the deer were not sedated as planned, but instead, ran helter-skelter, frantically throwing themselves into containment fences.

The Humane Society and animal lovers across the nation were appalled and consequently protested over this situation. The poem is dedicated to the poet, Robert Bly, who is a native of Minnesota. Read the poem, noting its economical use of words, with which it tells the same story, but with a rhythmic and poetic force.

Minnesota Arsenal (for Robert Bly)

the deer
are in the
way. their
innocent speed
is clogging the
military machines
and disrupting
war games
in Minnesota
today.

the army
is shooting
deer. early
to the
slaughter house
to be packed away
with old foes
like buffaloes
and men
with black hair.

147

H.O.T. RESPONSES

1. Aside from the fact that poet Robert Bly lives in Minnesota, why do you think this poem is dedicated to Bly? You may want to base your opinions on your previous reading of "Counting Small-Boned Bodies."

2. Study "Minnesota Arsenal" visually and describe how the two stanzas are similar.

3. In what ways are the two stanzas very different in tone and image?

4. Why are deer compared to buffaloes?

5. Who are the "men with black hair"? (You may want to compare this line to Bly's perspective in "Counting Small-Boned Bodies.")

6. How is this poem expressing a different multicultural perspective?

CREATIVE PRODUCT

1. Think of a news item that disturbed you greatly. Express your feelings in some creative way, by writing a poem, by making a collage, or by drawing a picture. Share your completed product with your cooperative group and explain the *source* or *inspiration* for your creation.

© 1996 by The Center for Applied Research in Education

FOCUS

The poem, "Dakotas" is composed as three distinct "concrete" stanzas; that is, the shape of the poem has to be considered within the context of the meaning of the poem. The title, *Dakotas,* is also significant and is alluded to in one of the stanzas. Once again, the poem expresses a particular perspective.

Read the following poem and reflect on your previous reading of "Minnesota Arsenal" as you respond to the meaning and point of view expressed in "Dakotas."

Dakotas

into untold light—
whose darkest stories
dispatched as
centuries
of rage
centered
in the eye
of a buffalo
(a carpet
once dried
by the
sun)

into cultures torn from
skins, like fibres and omens,
omens baked
like bread
turned to
stone, to
howls by
wolves,
lonely
in Da
kot
a

Dakotas
(cont'd)

out of darkness and steel
shines the first fist
or flint baked/by
centuries of
cruelties to
kill by the
sword, the
dagger or
knife, a
glint of
strength
like an
eye in
a bone
sharp
tooth
or n
ee
dl
e
.

H.O.T. RESPONSES

Discuss the following in your cooperative group:

1. How far back does this poem take the reader? Why does the poet have the reader reflect on so many "centuries of cruelties"?

2. What observations can you make about each stanza? The concrete shapes of the stanzas seem to be making a statement. What is their dual meaning, or purpose?

3. Explain how the word "eye" becomes a central focus, or symbol.

4. Do you see any similarity in Cowen's previous poem, "Minnesota Arsenal"—
   the crafting of the stanzas, the feeling and tone?

5. Note the repetition of the word "centuries" in stanzas 1 and 3. Can you compare and contrast the sense in each stanza?

6. What is the significance of the wolves howling?

7. What do you know about the Dakotas?

8. Explain the poet's multicultural perspective in this poem.

CREATIVE PRODUCT

1. Working independently, create your own "concrete poem," sharing your own
   multicultural perspective. Your sensitive form of expression may take the perspective of any minority group. Share your completed concrete poem with your
   cooperative group.

NOEL JARDINES

Kansas

Translated by Janice Dowd

FOCUS

Poet Noel Jardines was born in Santiago, Cuba, in 1957, and came to the United States at the age of thirteen. His family has lived in New York and New Jersey, and he presently teaches Spanish at Teaneck High School in New Jersey. Mr. Jardines writes in Spanish as well as English. While studying Spanish literature at Jersey City State College, he won the José Marti Poetry Contest. In addition, his book of poetry, *Pan Canibal,* in which this poem can be found, was awarded the "Letras de Oro" (Golden Letters) Prize for poetry.

Translator Janice Dowd received her doctorate from Teachers College, Columbia University. She is a foreign language teacher at Teaneck High School. She has presented lectures and demonstrations about language teaching at conferences throughout the United States and abroad. Mr. Jardines and Dr. Dowd collaborated on the translation of his poem, a process that resulted in fascinating discussions about the imagery, a deeper self-analysis on the part of the author, and a clearer understanding of the mind of the poet.

As you read the poem, "Kansas," keep in mind the birthplace of the poet. Think about the geographical differences between Jardines' native land and Kansas.

Kansas

in kansas we envision the ports
night comes
grimacing like a manatee
in the tongue of the calves
breathing between laps of water

the simplest way into immensity is this
enter the foggy keel
like the spider in the continent
of the missing

embrace the cows
in a modest friendly way
in the part of the faces
that have balanced us
in pieces
in a prone position
with an eye that finally envisions the fright

Translated by Janice Dowd in consultation with the author.

H.O.T. RESPONSES

Work as a team with one member from your cooperative group as you both analyze "Kansas."

1. Why do you think the poet, Noel Jardines, envisions ports in Kansas?

2. Explain how Jardines' simile in the first stanza can be compared to Carl Sandberg's lines: "The fog comes in/on little cat feet . . ."

© 1996 by The Center for Applied Research in Education

3. Why do you think the poet combines the images of two very different kinds of animals in the first stanza—the manatee and calves?

4. From the mood of this poem, can you imagine what "immensity" it is that the poet is referring to in the second stanza?

5. The poet introduces "cows" in the final stanza. What is meant by "balance us in pieces" ?

6. Note that the poet's final line ends with the phrase: "envisions the fright. "Why do you think the poet ends the poem using the word "envisions" and opens the poem with the phrase "envision the ports" ?

7. Explain the mood and images in this highly imaginative poem. How is the poem like a fantasy?

CREATIVE PRODUCT

1. Think about a place that you once visited. What was unusual about this place? To what might it be compared that would interest the reader? Write a poem, a short story, or a descriptive prose passage using your unique recollections.

2. Write a poem that uses metaphors and similes and that compares a geographical location to the shapes of animals.

FOCUS

Countee Cullen is one of the leading poets of the Harlem Renaissance of the 1920s, and his great lyrical poetry, children's books, plays, and novel are still being widely read all over the world. Countee Cullen was a scholar as well as a writer and graduated with Phi Beta Kappa honors from New York University; he received his master's degree from Harvard. His poetry received national acclaim during his short life (1903–1946), including the prestigious Witter Bynner Poetry Prize, the Harmon Foundation's first gold medal for literature, and a Guggenheim Fellowship Grant to study at the Sorbonne in Paris. *On These I Stand,* Cullen's selected best poems, was published after his death in 1947, from which the following poem appears.

Countee Cullen's poem, "Yet Do I Marvel," is a lyrical sonnet; that is, it is written in fourteen lines with a rhyme pattern. When you read the poem, it reads with ease and does not jump out and say, "I am a sonnet!" yet it has a wonderful artistic effect.

Yet Do I Marvel

I doubt not God is good, well-meaning, kind,
And did He stoop to quibble could tell why
The little buried mole continues blind,
Why flesh that mirrors Him must some day die.
Make plain the reason tortured Tantalus
Is baited by the fickle fruit, declare
If merely brute caprice dooms Sisyphus
To struggle up a never-ending stair.
Inscrutable His ways are, and immune

To catechism by a mind too strewn
With petty cares to slightly understand
What awful brain compels His awful hand.
Yet do I marvel at this curious thing:
To make a poet black, and bid him sing!

157

H.O.T. RESPONSES

1. In your cooperative group, study the sonnet form of this poem. Try to list all of the patterns that you discover. Treat the form the way a detective would a murder case, by searching for clues to solve the mystery.

   For example:

   a. What is the rhyme scheme?

   b. What can you determine about the rhythm and the syllables per line?

   c. What other unique and crafty patterns are employed?

2. Note how diplomatically Countee Cullen goes about questioning God's ways. Explain, therefore, why the last two lines of this poem have such a powerful dramatic effect.

3. Read the Greek myths of Sisyphus and Tantalus and explain why Cullen compares their struggles to the struggles of African Americans.

© 1996 by The Center for Applied Research in Education

CREATIVE PRODUCT

1. Once you have been able to answer the H.O.T. questions in activity 1, above, write a definition of a sonnet. Check with your teacher or a reference book that defines the sonnet, and compare your own discovery.

2. Try writing a sonnet of your own. Model it after Countee Cullen's.

KUANGCHI C. CHANG

Garden of My Childhood

FOCUS

The poet Kuangchi C. Chang was born in Shanghai, China, and fled the Communists by running away to America, a haven for refugees seeking political asylum. "Garden of My Childhood" is his poem about this traumatic decision to flee his homeland. Read Chang's poem, and feel the pain of his decision.

Garden of My Childhood

"Run, run, run,"
Whispered the vine.
"A horde is on the march no Great Wall can halt."
But in the garden of my childhood
The old maple was painting a sunset
And the crickets were singing a carol;
No, I had no wish to run.

"Run, run, run,"
Gasped the wind,
"The horde has entered the Wall."
Down the scorched plain rode the juggernaut
And crossed the Yangtse as if it were a ditch;
The proverbial rats had abandoned the ship
But I had no intention of abandoning
The garden of my childhood.

"Run, run, run,"
Roared the sea,
"Run before the bridge is drawn."
In the engulfed calm after the storm
The relentless tom-tom of the rice-sprout song

Finally ripped my armor,
And so I ran.

159

Garden of My Childhood
(cont'd)

I ran past the old maple by the terraced hall
And the singing crickets under the latticed wall,
And I kept on running down the walk
Paved with pebbles of memory big and small
Without turning to look until I was out of the gate
Through which there be no return at all.

Now eons later and worlds away,
The running is all done
For I am at my destination: Another garden.
Where the unpebbled walk awaits tomorrow's footprints.
Where my old maple will come with the sunset's glow
And my crickets will sing under the wakeful pillow.

H.O.T. RESPONSES

1. In your cooperative group, discuss Chang's first response to "Run, run, run." Explain the use of the metaphors, "Whispered the vine;" "Gasped the wind;" "Roared the sea."

2. What is meant by the metaphor:

   The relentless tom-tom of the rice-sprout song
   Finally ripped my armor,
   And so I ran...

3. Explain the line: "A horde is on the march no Great Wall can halt."

4. Discuss the last stanza, from the poet's perspective. Is he happy now? Is he content to be in his other garden?

CREATIVE PRODUCT

1. Have you ever had to face making a difficult choice or decision? How did it affect you? What did you finally decide, and what action did you take? Write about this action in any form you like, prose or poetry. Share this writing with your cooperative group.

VIRGINIA R. MORENO

Batik Maker

FOCUS

Virginia R. Moreno is one of the most lyrical female poets. She was born in Manila, Philippines. Currently she is the Directress of the University of the Philippines' Film Center, and she has received international acclaim as a playwright. Her poem, "Batik Maker," is the title poem of her exquisite book made of batik and rice paper, designed by artist, poet, book designer, Larry S. Francia.

Batik is an ancient Malayan art, still crafted in the Philippines, a dyeing process in which designs are made by covering fabric with removable wax. The famous English poet, John Keats, wrote the immortal poem, "Ode on a Grecian Urn," having been inspired by the painted wedding scene decorating an ancient Greek vase. Moreno's poem is similar in that the "batik maker," like the Greek artisan, has created a romantic scene that has, too, been immortalized by art.

Batik Maker

Tissue of no seam and skin
Of no scale she weaves this:
Dream of a huntsman pale
That in his antlered
Mangrove waits
Ensnared;

And I cannot touch him.

Lengths of the dumb and widths
Of the deaf are his hair
Where wild orchids thumb
Or his parted throat surprise
To elegiac screaming
Only birds of
Paradise;

And I cannot wake him.

Shades of the light and shapes
Of the rain on his palanquin
Stain what phantom panther
Sleeps in the cage of
His skin and immobile
Hands;

And I cannot bury him.

H.O.T. RESPONSES

In your cooperative group, discuss the following:

1. Virginia R. Moreno's startling first lines create what kind of magical image?

2. How can the "... lengths of the dumb and widths of the deaf ..." be "his hair"?

3. Why is the poet's choice of the word "mangrove" more alluring than "tree" or "tropical evergreen"?

4. Discuss the three refrains and the poet's use of drama and climax.

CREATIVE PRODUCT

1. Create your own artifact, or modern object, that can be designed so "beauti-fully" or "horrifically" that it might inspire a poet to write about it.

2. Ask one of the members of your group to be the poet and write about your artistic creation.

3. Think about a design on fabric or pottery, or a mural or fresco that captured your imagination, and write about it.

4. A lyrical song was written about van Gogh's famous painting "Starry Night." Do you know the song? Write about a famous piece of art that has inspired you. Poetry or prose can be used for this creative expression.

MICHAEL MATHIAS

from *The Divine Theme*

FOCUS

Michael Mathias is a mystic, poet, playwright, actor, and at his best, one of the handful of outstanding lyrical poets writing today. Mathias is author of two epics entitled *Vision from the Bridge of Fire: Ierlandis,* and *Vision from the Bridge of Fire: The Advent of Avatar Meher Baba.* The latter work has been recorded and staged in India. Mathias has also collaborated with Ruth Warrick, star of *Citizen Kane,* on an international production of *The Secret Bread,* from which a scene appears in Unit Ten of this book. This play was awarded the Huntington Hartford First Prize for Poetic Drama. Poet Muriel Rukeyser praised Mathias as "one of our major epic lyric poets." "The Divine Theme" which appears below is the introduction to a "Fugue for the Avatar, part VII" in *Vision from the Bridge of Fire: The Advent of Avatar Meher Baba* (on his centennial birthday celebration).

from *The Divine Theme*

Sun-cherries in India
The Himalayas stretch westward
The valleys grow lush with the peach blossom,
with the blossom of the pear;
In Kangra, valley of songs,
The apples signal His Beneficence.

But in Meherabad,
His Silence rests.
There the Arti is sung for Him,
Deep on the holy hilltop.
Their voices deeply resound
Within the tomb
And outside the tomb.
"In counter-point," sings His Painter.
*"They make a song within
And a song without."*
    It is said:
*"When an earthen pot is broken
The space within is one
    with the space without . . ."*

165

H.O.T. RESPONSES

In your cooperative group, discuss the following:

1. Locate the key images in the first stanza of "The Divine Theme." Why do you think the poet chooses these lush words?

2. In the second stanza, a spiritual song is chanted to stir the entombed body of the avatar Meher Baba. Compare the section that is printed in italics with the first part of the second stanza. How is this singing going to help the avatar?

3. After reading the final six lines in italics, can you predict what spiritual change will take place?

4. Can you compare this spiritual event to other religious events? Explain why they are similar.

CREATIVE PRODUCT

1. Work independently, and create your own poem or song based upon your personal spiritual beliefs. Share your product with your group when it is completed.

MAURICE KENNY

Legacy

FOCUS

Maurice Kenny is a Mohawk Native American born in northern New York State, between the St. Lawrence and Black Rivers. He is the publisher of Strawberry Press and is a lecturer on Studies in American Indian Literature. His work is translated in French and Russian. "Legacy" is a poem that captures the Native American's oneness with nature, in a cultural and religious sense. Read "Legacy" with the purpose of learning what Kenny's legacy is.

Legacy

Legacy

my face is grass
    color of April rain;
arms, legs are the limbs
    of birch, cedar;
my thoughts are winds
    which blow;
pictures in my mind
    are the climb up hill
    to dream in the sun;
    hawk feathers, and quills
    of porcupine running
    the edge of the stream
    which reflects stories
    of my many mornings
    and the dark faces of night
    mingled with victories
    of dawn and tomorrow;
corn of the fields and squash . . .
    the daughters of my mother
    who collect honey
    and all the fruits;

meadow and sky are the end of my day,
    the stretch of my night
    yet the birth of my dust;
my wind is the breath of a fawn
    the cry of the cub
    the trot of the wolf
    whose print covers
    the tracks of my feet;
my word, my word,
    loaned
legacy, the obligation I hand
    to the blood of my flesh
    the sinew of the loins
to hold to the sun
    and the moon
which direct the river
    that carries my song
    and the beat of the drum
to the fires of the village
    which endures.

H.O.T. RESPONSES

1. Discuss the many metaphors that relate to nature, to animals, and to the Native American or to the poet himself.

2. Walt Whitman, who lived during the American Civil War, was one of America's first great poets. He wrote *Leaves of Grass,* a book of poems that exalted man and nature (man as part of everything about him, including nature). Whitman was expressing a pantheistic view, which identifies God with the various forces and workings of nature. How does "Legacy" compare to this pantheistic view?

3. What is this Native American poet's . . . "word, loaned legacy, the obligation I hand to the blood of my flesh"?

4. From the poet's perspective, how important is his song or poem? How does it relate to the Native Americans' heritage and future?

CREATIVE PRODUCT

1. Write a poem that compares you to your heritage, culture, or race, using Kenny's pantheistic style.

2. Use many images, and don't be too concerned about sense; let your imagination lead you to the images you can create. Share your product and illustrate it.

Unit Seven

THEME:
RELATIONSHIPS: FAMILY AND
FRIENDS

INTRODUCTION

In this unit, the authors write about the importance of affectional ties and how these relationships affect our behavior and psyches. Sometimes we long for these relationships to be better than they actually are, and must somehow face up to the reality that family and friends do not always live up to our expectations. Such is the case in William Melvin Kelley's short story, "A Visit to Grandmother," and in Estrella D. Alfon's troubling short story, "Magnificence."

On the other hand, some remembrances can be reassuring and help us overcome difficulties in times of stress—or they can serve as a lesson, as in Brian Morton's *The Dylanist,* when Sally recalls how much her father valued being prepared.

As you read the literature in this unit, compare the kinds of relationships depicted here with your own experiences and memories—good and bad.

WILLIAM MELVIN KELLEY

A Visit to Grandmother

FOCUS

William Melvin Kelley often writes about "the plight of Negroes, as individual beings, in America." Born in New York City, he was educated at Harvard University where he received the Dana Reed Prize in 1960, and later was awarded fellowships to the New York Writers Conference, and the Bread Loaf Writers Conference. Kelley also won the prestigious Richard and Hinda Rosenthal Foundation Award of the National Institute of Arts and Letters for his novel, *A Different Drummer,* in 1962. His second novel, *A Drop of Patience,* was published in 1965. Many of his stories have appeared in *Negro Digest, Esquire,* and *Mademoiselle.* Although Kelley is a prose writer, his writing is quite poetic and he often uses the metaphor and simile in his descriptive passages as you will note in "A Visit to Grandmother." In this story, Chig learns on a visit to his grandmother in Nashville that his father did not have a very good relationship with his mother or brother, GL. Chig also gains a deeper insight with regard to his father.

A Visit to Grandmother

Chig knew something was wrong the instant his father kissed her. He had always known his father to be the warmest of men, a man so kind that when people ventured timidly into his office, it took only a few words from him to make them relax, and even laugh. Doctor Charles Dunford cared about people.

But when he had bent to kiss the old lady's black face, something new and almost ugly had come into his eyes: fear, uncertainty, sadness, and perhaps even hatred.

Ten days before in New York, Chig's father had decided suddenly he wanted to go to Nashville to attend his college class reunion, twenty years out. Both Chig's brother and sister, Peter and Connie, were packing for camp and besides were too young for such an affair. But Chig was seventeen, had nothing to do that summer, and his father asked if he would like to go along. His father had given him additional reasons: "All my running buddies got their diplomas and were snapped up by them crafty young gals, and had kids within a year— now all those kids, some of them gals, are your age."

The reunion had lasted a week. As they packed for home, his father, in a far too off-hand way, had suggested they visit Chig's grandmother. "We this close. We might as well drop in on her and my brothers."

So, instead of going north, they had gone farther south, had just entered her house. And Chig had a suspicion now that the reunion had been only an excuse to drive south, that his father had been heading to this house all the time.

His father had never talked much about his family, with the exception of his brother, GL, who seemed part con man, part practical joker and part Don Juan; he had spoken of GL with the kind of indulgence he would have shown a cute, but ill-behaved and potentially danger-ous, five-year old.

Chig's father had left home when he was fif-teen. When asked why, he would answer: "I wanted to go to school. They didn't have a Negro high school at home, so I went up to Knoxville and lived with a cousin and went to school."

They had been met at the door by Aunt Rose, GL's wife, and ushered into the living room. The old lady had looked up from her seat by the window. Aunt Rose stood between the visitors.

The old lady eyed his father. "Rose, who that? Rose?" She squinted. She looked like a doll, made of black straw, the wrinkles in her face running in one direction like the head of a broom. Her hair was white and coarse and grew out straight from her head. Her eyes were brown—the whites, too, seemed light brown— and were hidden behind thick glasses, which remained somehow on a tiny nose. "That Hiram?" That was another of his father's brothers. "No, it ain't Hiram; too big for Hiram." She turned then to Chig. "Now that man, he look like Eleanor, Charles's wife, but Charles wouldn't never send my grandson to see me. I never even hear from Charles." She stopped again.

"It Charles, Mama. That who it is." Aunt Rose, between them, led them closer. "It Charles come all the way from New York to see you, and brung little Charles with him."

The old lady stared up at them. "Charles? Rose, that really Charles?" She turned away, and reached for a handkerchief in the pocket of her clean, ironed, flowered housecoat, and wiped her eyes. "God have mercy. Charles." She spread her arms up to him, and he bent down and kissed her cheek. That was when Chig saw his face, grimacing. She hugged him; Chig watched the muscles in her arms as they tightened around his father's neck. She half rose out of her chair. "How are you, son?"

Chig could not hear his father's answer.

She let him go, and fell back into her chair, grabbing the arms. Her hands were as dark as the wood, and seemed to become part of it. "Now, who that standing there? Who that man?"

"That's one of your grandsons, Mama." His father's voice cracked. "Charles Dunford, junior. You saw him once, when he was a baby, in Chicago. He's grown now."

"I can see that, boy!" She looked at Chig squarely. "Come here, son, and kiss me once." He said. "What they call you? Charles too?"

"No, ma'am, they call me Chig."

She smiled. She had all her teeth, but they were too perfect to be her own. "That's good. Can't have two boys answering to Charles in the same house. Won't nobody at all come. So you that little boy. You don't remember me, do you. I used to take you to church in Chicago, and you'd get up and hop in time to the music. You studying to be a preacher?"

"No, ma'am. I don't think so. I might be a lawyer."

"You'll be an honest one, won't you?"

"I'll try."

"Trying ain't enough! You be honest, you hear? Promise me. You be honest like your daddy."

"All right. I promise."

"Good. Rose, where's GL at? Where's that thief? He gone again?"

"I don't know, Mama." Aunt Rose looked embarrassed. "He say he was going by his liquor store. He'll be back."

"Well, then where's Hiram? You call up those boys, and get them over here—now! You got enough to eat? Let me go see." She started to get up. Chig reached out his hand. She shook him off. "What they tell you about me, Chig? They tell you I'm all laid up? Don't believe it. They don't know nothing about old ladies. When I want help, I'll let you know. Only time I'll need help getting anywheres is when I dies and they lift me into the ground."

She was standing now, her back and shoulders straight. She came only to Chig's chest.

She squinted up at him. "You eat much? Your daddy ate like two men."

"Yes, ma'am."

"That's good. That means you ain't nervous. Your mama, she ain't nervous. I remember that. In Chicago, she'd sit down by a window all afternoon and never say nothing, just knit." She smiled. "Let me see what we got to eat."

"I'll do that, Mama." Aunt Rose spoke softly. "You haven't seen Charles in a long time. You sit and talk."

The old lady squinted at her. "You can do the cooking if you promise it ain't because you think I can't."

Aunt Rose chuckled. "I know you can do it, Mama."

"All right. I'll just sit and talk a spell." She sat again and arranged her skirt around her short legs.

Chig did most of the talking, told all about himself before she asked. His father only spoke when he was spoken to, and then, only one word at a time, as if by coming back home, he had become a small boy again, sitting in the parlor while his mother spoke with her guests.

When Uncle Hiram and Mae, his wife, came they sat down to eat. Chig did not have to ask about Uncle GL's absence; Aunt Rose volunteered an explanation: "Can't never tell where the man is at. One Thursday morning he left here and next thing we knew, he was calling from Chicago, saying he went up to see Joe Louis fight. He'll be here though; he ain't as young and foot-loose as he used to be." Chig's father had mentioned driving down that GL was about five years older than he was, nearly fifty.

Uncle Hiram was somewhat smaller than Chig's father; his short-cropped kinky hair was half gray, half black. One spot, just off his forehead, was totally white. Later Chig found out it had been that way since he was twenty. Mae (Chig could not bring himself to call her Aunt) was a good deal younger than Hiram, pretty enough so that Chig would have looked at her twice on the street. She was a honey-colored woman, with long eye lashes. She was wearing a white sheath.

© 1996 by The Center for Applied Research in Education

At dinner, Chig and his father sat on one side, opposite Uncle Hiram and Mae; his grandmother and Aunt Rose sat at the ends. The food was good; there was a lot and Chig ate a lot. All through the meal, they talked about the family as it had been thirty years before, and particularly about the young GL. Mae and Chig asked questions; the old lady answered; Aunt Rose directed the discussion, steering the old lady onto the best stories; Chig's father laughed from time to time; Uncle Hiram ate.

"Why don't you tell them about the horse, Mama?" Aunt Rose, over Chig's weak protest, was spooning mashed potatoes onto his plate. "There now, Chig."

"I'm trying to think." The old lady was holding her fork halfway to her mouth, looking at them over her glasses. "Oh, you talking about that crazy horse GL brung home that time."

"That's right, Mama." Aunt Rose nodded and slid another slice of white meat on Chig's plate.

Mae started to giggle, "Oh, I've heard this. This is funny, Chig."

The old lady put down her fork and began: Well, GL went out of the house one day with an old, no-good chair I wanted him to take over to the church for a bazaar, and he met up with this man who'd just brung in some horses from out West. Now, I reckon you can expect one swindler to be in every town, but you don't rightly think there'll be two, and God forbid they should ever meet—but they did, GL and his chair, this man and his horses. Well, I wished I'd-a been there; there must-a been some mighty high-powered talking going on. That man with his horses, he told GL them horses was half-Arab, half-Indian, and GL told that man the chair was an antique he'd stole from some rich white folks. So they swapped. Well, I was a-looking out the window and seen GL dragging this animal to the house. It looked pretty gentle and its eyes was most closed and its feet was shuffling.

"GL, where'd you get that thing?" I says.

"I swapped him for that old chair, Mama," he says. "And made myself a bargain. This is even better than Papa's horse."

Well, I'm a-looking at this horse and noticing how he be looking more and more wide awake every minute, sort of warming up like a teakettle until, I swears to you, that horse is blowing steam out its nose.

"Come on, Mama," GL says, "come on and I'll take you for a ride." Now George, my husband, God rest his tired soul, he'd brung home this white folks' buggy which had a busted wheel and fixed it and was to take it back that day and GL says, "Come on, Mama, we'll use this fine buggy and take us a ride."

"GL," I says, "no, we ain't. Them white folks'll burn us alive if we use their buggy. You just take that horse right on back." You see, I was sure that boy'd come by that animal ungainly.

"Mama, I can't take him back," GL says.

"Why not?" I says.

"Because I don't rightly know where that man is at," GL says.

"Oh," I says. "Well, then I reckon we stuck with it." And I turned around to go back into the house because it was getting late, near dinner time, and I was cooking for ten.

"Mama," GL says to my back. "Mama, ain't you coming for a ride with me?"

"Go on, boy. You ain't getting me inside kicking range of that animal." I was eyeing that beast and it was boiling hotter all the time. I reckon maybe that man had drugged it. "That horse is wild, GL," I says.

"No, he ain't. He ain't. That man say he is buggy and saddle broke and as sweet as the inside of a apple."

My oldest girl, Essie, had-a come out on the porch and she says: "Go on, Mama. I'll cook. You ain't been out of the house in weeks."

"Sure, come on, Mama," GL says. "There ain't nothing to be fidgety about. This horse is gentle as a rose petal." And just then that animal snorts so hard it sets up a little dust storm around its feet.

"Yes, Mama," Essie says, "you can see he gentle." Well, I looked at Essie and then at that horse because I didn't think we could be looking at the same animal. I should-a figured how Essie's eyes ain't never been so good.

175

"Come on, Mama," GL says.

"All right," I says. So I stood on the porch and watched GL hitching that horse up to the white folks' buggy. For a while there, the animal was pretty quiet, pawing a little, but not much. And I was feeling a little better about riding with GL behind that crazy-looking horse. I could see how GL was happy I was going with him. He was scurrying around that animal buckling buckles and strapping straps, all the time smiling, and that made me feel good.

Then he was finished, and I must say, that horse looked mighty fine hitched to that buggy and I knew anybody what climbed up there would look pretty good too. GL came around and stood at the bottom of the steps, and took off his hat and bowed and said: "Madam," and reached out his hand to me and I was feeling real elegant like a fine lady. He helped me up to the seat and then got up beside me and we moved out down our alley. And I remember how colored folks come out on their porches and shook their heads, saying: "Lord now, will you look at Eva Dunford, the fine lady! Don't she look good sitting up there!" And I pretended not to hear and sat up straight and proud.

We rode on through the center of town, up Market Street, and all the way out where Hiram is living now, which in them days was all woods, there not being even a farm in sight and that's when that horse must-a first realized he weren't at all broke or tame or maybe thought he was back out West again, and started to gallop.

"GL," I says, "now you ain't joking with your mama, is you? Because if you is, I'll strap you purple if I live through this."

Well, GL was pulling on the reins with all his meager strength, and yelling, "Whoa, you. Say now, whoa!" He turned to me just long enough to say, "I ain't fooling with you, Mama. Honest!"

I reckon that animal weren't too satisfied with the road, because it made a sharp right turn just then, down into a gully and struck out across a hilly meadow. "Mama," GL yells. "Mama, do something!"

I didn't know what to do, but I figured I had to do something so I stood up, hopped down onto the horse's back and pulled it to a stop.

Don't ask me how I did that; I reckon it was that I was a mother and my baby asked me to do something, is all.

"Well, we walked that animal all the way home; sometimes I had to club it over the nose with my fist to make it come, but we made it, GL and me. You remember how tired we was, Charles?"

" I wasn't here at the time." Chig turned to his father and found his face completely blank, without even a trace of a smile or a laugh.

"Well, of course you was, son. That happened in . . . in . . . it was a hot summer that year and—"

"I left here in June of that year. You wrote me about it."

The old lady stared past Chig at him. They all turned to him; Uncle Hiram looked up from his plate.

"Then you don't remember how we all laughed?"

"No, I don't, Mama. And I probably wouldn't have laughed. I don't think it was funny." They were staring into each other's eyes.

"Why not, Charles?"

"Because in the first place, the horse was gained by fraud. And in the second place, both of you might have been seriously injured or even killed." He broke off their stare and spoke to himself more than to any of them: "And if I'd done it, you would've beaten me good for it."

"Pardon?" The old lady had not heard him; only Chig had heard.

Chig's father sat up straight as if preparing to debate. "I said that if I had done it, if I had done just exactly what GL did, you would have beaten me good for it, Mama." He was looking at her again.

"Why you say that, son?" She was leaning toward him.

"Don't you know? Tell the truth. It can't hurt me now." His voice cracked, but only once. "If GL and I did something wrong, you'd beat me first and then be too . . . tired to beat him. At dinner, he'd always get seconds and I wouldn't. You'd do things with him, like ride in that buggy, but if I wanted you to do something with me, you were always too busy." He paused and considered whether to say what he finally did say: "I cried when I left here. Nobody loved me, Mama. I cried all the way up to Knoxville. That was the last time I ever cried in my life."

"Oh, Charles." She started to get up, to come around the table to him.

He stopped her. "It's too late."

"But you don't understand."

"What don't I understand? I understood then; I understand now."

Tears now traveled down the lines in her face, but when she spoke, her voice was clear. "I thought you knew. I had ten children. I had to give all of them what they needed most." She nodded. "I paid more mind to GL. I had to. GL could-a ended up swinging if I hadn't. But you was smarter. You was more growed up than GL when you was five and he was ten, and I tried to show you that by letting you do what you wanted to do."

"That's not true, Mama. You know it. GL was light-skinned and had good hair and looked almost white and you loved him for that."

"Charles, no. No, son. I didn't love any one of you more than any other.

"That can't be true." His father was standing now, his fists clenched tight. "Admit it, Mama . . . please!" Chig looked at him, shocked; the man was actually crying.

"It may not-a been right what I done, but I ain't no liar." Chig knew she did not really understand what had happened, what he wanted of her. "I'm not lying to you, Charles."

Chig's father had gone pale. He spoke very softly. "You're about thirty years too late, Mama." He bolted from the table. Silverware and dishes rang and jumped.

Chig heard him hurrying up to their room.

They sat in silence for awhile and then heard a key in the front door. A man with a new, lacquered straw hat came in. He was wearing brown and white two-tone shoes with very pointed toes and a white summer suit. "Say now! Man! I heard my brother was in town. Where he at? Where that rascal?"

He stood in the doorway, smiling broadly, an engaging, open, friendly smile, the innocent smile of a five-year-old.

H.O.T. RESPONSES

1. Discuss, in your group, why you think Charles took Chig to see his grandmother, knowing all along that this would be a difficult visit?

2. Have you ever experienced a similarly painful visit with family members or friends? Was your negative experience anticipated like Charles' must have been? Explain.

177

3. What did Chig's father mean when he said, "You're about thirty years too late, Mama."? To what is he referring?

4. Did you believe Chig's grandmother when she gives the following excuse to his father? Explain.

   I paid more mind to GL, I had to. GL could-a ended up swinging if I hadn't. But you was smarter. You was more growed up than GL when you was five and he was ten, and I tried to show you that by letting you do what you wanted to do.

5. Charles is the honest son. He has strong convictions and is very serious compared with GL. When and how is this dramatized in the story?

6. How is the story about GL meeting up with a swindler like himself similar to some other stories you have read? Explain.

7. What is your opinion about how the story ends? Why does the author use the word "smile" three times in the final sentence?

CREATIVE PRODUCT

1. Grandmother seemed most amused about GL meeting up with another swindler and says: "Well, I wished I'd-a been there; there must-a been some mighty high-powered talking going on." Can you imagine what that "high-powered talking" might have been like? Now, recreate this "high-powered talking" as dialogue by retelling the tale in your own words.

2. Write a folk tale in which one swindler meets another swindler.

VIRGINIA DRIVING HAWK SNEVE

The Medicine Bag

FOCUS

Virginia Driving Hawk Sneve grew up on the Sioux Rosebud Reservation in South Dakota. Currently, she writes in the summer and is a counselor at Rapid City Central High School in South Dakota during the school year.

Sneve is most concerned about the misconceptions of Native Americans, and therefore writes to provide a perspective that is more realistic. Her first book, *Jimmy Yellow Hawk,* was awarded the Interracial Council for Minority Books for Children Award. She has written several books for younger children, while "The Medicine Bag" is a story for older children; it is based upon a real incident.

As you read this story, try to understand the embarrassment of someone who is trying to assimilate into the American culture, but who has to face the truth of his ancestral heritage. Can you understand why Martin was so worried about what the neighborhood would think about his Sioux grandfather?

THE MEDICINE BAG

My kid sister Cheryl and I always bragged about our Sioux grandpa, Joe Iron Shell. Our friends, who had always lived in the city and knew about Indians only from movies and TV, were impressed by our stories. Maybe we exaggerated and made Grandpa and the reservation sound glamorous, but when we'd return home to Iowa after our yearly summer visit to Grandpa, we always had some exciting tale to tell.

We always had some authentic Sioux article to show our listeners. One year Cheryl had new moccasins that Grandpa had made. On another visit he gave me a small, round, flat rawhide drum that was decorated with a painting of a warrior riding a horse. He taught me a real Sioux chant to sing while I beat the drum with a leather-covered stick that had a feather on the end. Man, that really made an impression.

We never showed our friends Grandpa's picture. Not that we were ashamed of him, but because we knew that the glamorous tales we told didn't go with the real thing. Our friends would have laughed at the picture because Grandpa wasn't tall and stately like TV Indians. His hair wasn't in braids but hung in stringy gray strands on his neck, and he was old. He was our great-grandfather, and he didn't live in a teepee but all by himself in a part log, part tar-paper shack on the Rosebud Reservation in South Dakota. So when Grandpa came to visit us, I was so ashamed and embarrassed I could've died.

There are a lot of yippy poodles and other fancy little dogs in our neighborhood, but they usually barked singly at the mailman from the safety of their own yards. Now it sounded as if a whole pack of mutts were barking together in one place.

I got up and walked to the curb to see what the commotion was. About a block away I saw a crowd of little kids yelling, with the dogs yipping and growling around someone who was walking down the middle of the street.

I watched the group as it slowly came closer and saw that in the center of the strange procession was a man wearing a tall black hat. He'd pause now and then to peer at something in his hand and then at the houses on either side of the street. I felt cold and hot at the same time as I recognized the man. "Oh, no!" I whispered. "It's Grandpa!"

I stood on the curb, unable to move, even though I wanted to run and hide. Then I got mad when I saw how the yippy dogs were growling and nipping at the old man's baggy pant legs and how wearily he poked them away with his cane. "Stupid mutts," I said as I ran to rescue Grandpa.

When I kicked and hollered at the dogs to get away, they put their tails between their legs and scattered. The kids ran to the curb where they watched me and the old man.

"Grandpa," I said and felt pretty dumb when my voice cracked. I reached for his beat-up old tin suitcase, which was tied shut with a rope. But he set it down right in the street and shook my hand.

"*Hau, Takoza,* Grandchild," he greeted me formally in Sioux.

All I could do was stand there with the whole neighborhood watching and shake the hand of the leather-brown old man. I saw how his gray hair straggled from under his big black hat, which had a drooping feather in its crown. His rumpled black suit hung like a sack over his stooped frame. As he shook my hand, his coat fell open to expose a bright red satin shirt with a beaded bolo tie under the collar. His get-up wasn't out of place on the reservation, but it sure was here, and I wanted to sink right through the pavement.

"Hi," I muttered with my head down. I tried to pull my hand away when I felt his bony hand trembling and looked up to see fatigue in his face. I felt like crying. I couldn't think of anything to say, so I picked up Grandpa's suitcase, took his arm, and guided him up the driveway to our house.

Mom was standing on the steps. I don't know how long she'd been watching, but her hand was over her mouth, and she looked as if she couldn't believe what she saw. Then she ran to us.

"Grandpa," she gasped. "How in the world did you get here?"

She checked her move to embrace Grandpa, and I remembered that such a display of affection is unseemly to the Sioux and would embarrass him.

"*Hau,* Marie," he said as he shook Mom's hand. She smiled and took his other arm.

As we supported him up the steps, the door banged open and Cheryl came bursting out of the house. She was all smiles and was so obviously glad to see Grandpa that I was ashamed of how I felt.

"Grandpa!" she yelled happily. "You came to see us!"

Grandpa smiled, and Mom and I let go of him as he stretched out his arms to my ten-year-old sister, who was still young enough to be hugged.

"*Wicincala,* little girl," he greeted her and then collapsed.

He had fainted. Mom and I carried him into her sewing room, where we had a spare bed.

After we had Grandpa on the bed, Mom stood there helplessly patting his shoulder.

"Shouldn't we call the doctor, Mom?" I suggested, since she didn't seem to know what to do.

"Yes," she agreed with a sigh. "You make Grandpa comfortable, Martin."

I reluctantly moved to the bed. I knew Grandpa wouldn't want to have Mom undress him, but I didn't want to, either. He was so skinny and frail that his coat slipped off easily. When I loosened his tie and opened his shirt collar, I felt a small leather pouch that hung from a thong around his neck. I left it alone

and moved to remove his boots. The scuffed old cowboy boots were tight, and he moaned as I put pressure on his legs to jerk them off.

I put the boots on the floor and saw why they fit so tight. Each one was stuffed with money. I looked at the bills that lined the boots and started to ask about them, but Grandpa's eyes were closed again.

Mom came back with a basin of water. "The doctor thinks Grandpa is suffering from heat exhaustion," she explained as she bathed Grandpa's face. Mom gave a big sigh, "*Oh, hinh,* Martin. How do you suppose he got here?"

We found out after the doctor's visit. Grandpa was angrily sitting up in bed while Mom tried to feed him some soup.

"Tonight you let Marie feed you, Grandpa," spoke my dad, who had gotten home from work just as the doctor was leaving. "You're not really sick," he said as he gently pushed Grandpa back against the pillows. "The doctor said you just got too tired and hot after your long trip."

Grandpa relaxed, and between sips of soup, he told us of his journey. Soon after our visit to him, Grandpa decided that he would like to see where his only living descendants lived and what our home was like. Besides, he admitted sheepishly, he was lonesome after we left.

I knew that everybody felt as guilty as I did—especially Mom. Mom was all Grandpa had left. So even after she married my dad, who's a white man and teaches in the college in our city, and after Cheryl and I were born, Mom made sure that every summer we spent a week with Grandpa.

I never thought that Grandpa would be lonely after our visits, and none of us noticed how old and weak he had become. But Grandpa knew, and so he came to us. He had ridden on buses for two and a half days. When he arrived in the city, tired and stiff from sitting so long, he set out, walking, to find us.

He had stopped to rest on the steps of some building downtown, and a policeman found him. The cop, according to Grandpa, was a good man who took him to the bus stop and waited until the bus came and told the driver to let Grandpa out at Bell View Drive. After Grandpa got off the bus, he started walking again. But he couldn't see the house numbers on the other side when he walked on the sidewalk, so he walked in the middle of the street. That's when all the little kids and dogs followed him.

I knew everybody felt as bad as I did. Yet I was so proud of this eighty-six-year-old man who had never been away from the reservation, having the courage to travel so far alone.

"You found the money in my boots?" he asked Mom.

"Martin did," she answered, and roused herself to scold. "Grandpa, you shouldn't have carried so much money. What if someone had stolen it from you?"

Grandpa laughed. "I would've known if anyone had tried to take the boots off my feet. The money is what I've saved for a long time— a hundred dollars—for my funeral. But you take it now to buy groceries so that I won't be a burden to you while I am here."

"That won't be necessary, Grandpa," Dad said. "We are honored to have you with us, and you will never be a burden. I am only sorry that we never thought to bring you home with us this summer and spare you the discomfort of a long trip."

Grandpa was pleased. "Thank you," he answered. "But do not feel bad that you didn't bring me with you, for I would not have come then. It was not time." He said this in such a way that no one could argue with him. To Grandpa and the Sioux, he once told me, a thing would be done when it was the right time to do it, and that's the way it was.

"Also," Grandpa went on, looking at me, "I have come because it is soon time for Martin to have the medicine bag."

We all knew what that meant. Grandpa thought he was going to die, and he had to follow the tradition of his family to pass the medicine bag, along with its history, to the oldest male child.

"Even though the boy," he said, still looking at me, "bears a white man's name, the medicine bag will be his."

I didn't know what to say. I had the same hot and cold feeling that I had when I first saw Grandpa in the street. The medicine bag was the dirty leather pouch I had found around his neck. "I could never wear such a thing," I almost said aloud. I thought of having my friends see it in gym class or at the swimming pool and could imagine the smart things they would say. But I just swallowed hard and took a step toward the bed. I knew I would have to take it.

But Grandpa was tired. "Not now, Martin," he said, waving his hand in dismissal. "It is not time. Now I will sleep."

So that's how Grandpa came to be with us for two months. My friends kept asking to come see the old man, but I put them off. I told myself that I didn't want them laughing at Grandpa. But even as I made excuses, I knew it wasn't Grandpa that I was afraid they'd laugh at.

Nothing bothered Cheryl about bringing her friends to see Grandpa. Every day after school started, there'd be a crew of giggling little girls or round-eyed little boys crowded around the old man on the patio, where he'd gotten in the habit of sitting every afternoon.

Grandpa would smile in his gentle way and patiently answer their questions, or he'd tell them stories of brave warriors, ghosts, and animals; and the kids listened in awed silence. Those little guys thought Grandpa was great.

Finally, one day after school, my friends came home with me because nothing I said stopped them. "We're going to see the great Indian of Bell View Drive," said Hank, who was supposed to be my best friend. "My brother has seen him three times, so he oughta be well enough to see us."

When we got to my house, Grandpa was sitting on the patio. He had on his red shirt, but today he also wore a fringed leather vest that was decorated with beads. Instead of his usual cowboy boots, he had solidly beaded moccasins on his feet that stuck out of his black trousers. Of course, he had his old black hat on—he was seldom without it. But it had been brushed, and the feather in the beaded head-band was proudly erect, its tip a brighter white. His hair lay in silver strands over the red shirt collar.

I stared just as my friends did, and I heard one of them murmur, "Wow!"

Grandpa looked up, and when his eyes met mine, they twinkled as if he were laughing inside. He nodded to me, and my face got all hot. I could tell that he had known all along I was afraid he'd embarrass me in front of my friends.

"*Hau, hoksilas,* boys," he greeted and held out his hand.

My buddies passed in a single file and shook his hand as I introduced them. They were so polite I almost laughed. "How, there, Grandpa," and even a "How-do-you-do, sir."

"You look fine, Grandpa," I said as the guys sat on the lawn chairs or on the patio floor.

"*Hanh,* yes," he agreed. "When I woke up this morning, it seemed the right time to dress in the good clothes. I knew that my grandson would be bringing his friends."

"You guys want some lemonade or some-thing?" I offered. No one answered. They were listening to Grandpa as he started telling how he'd killed the deer from which his vest was made.

Grandpa did most of the talking while my friends were there. I was so proud of him and amazed at how respectfully quiet my buddies were. Mom had to chase them home at supper time. As they left, they shook Grandpa's hand again and said to me,

"Martin, he's really great!"

"Yeah, man! Don't blame you for keeping him to yourself."

"Can we come back?"

But after they left, Mom said, "No more vis-itors for a while, Martin. Grandpa won't admit it, but his strength hasn't returned. He likes having company, but it tires him."

That evening Grandpa called me to his room before he went to sleep. "Tomorrow," he said, "when you come home, it will be time to give you the medicine bag."

I felt a hard squeeze from where my heart is supposed to be and was scared, but I answered, "OK, Grandpa."

All night I had weird dreams about thunder and lightning on a high hill. From a distance I heard the slow beat of a drum. When I woke up in the morning, I felt as if I hadn't slept at all. At school it seemed as if the day would never end, and when it finally did, I ran home.

Grandpa was in his room, sitting on the bed. The shades were down, and the place was dim and cool. I sat on the floor in front of Grandpa, but he didn't even look at me. After what seemed a long time, he spoke.

"I sent your mother and sister away. What you will hear today is only for a man's ears. What you will receive is only for a man's hands." He fell silent, and I felt shivers down my back.

"My father in his early manhood," Grandpa began, "made a vision quest to find a spirit guide for his life. You cannot understand how it was in that time when the great Teton Sioux were first made to stay on the reservation. There was a strong need for guidance from *Wakantanka,* the Great Spirit. But too many of the young men were filled with despair and hatred. They thought it was hopeless to search for a vision when the glorious life was gone and only the hated confines of a reservation lay ahead. But my father held to the old ways.

"He carefully prepared for his quest with a purifying sweat bath, and then he went alone to a high butte top to fast and pray. After three days he received his sacred dream—in which he found, after long searching, the white man's iron. He did not understand his vision of find-ing something belonging to the white people, for in that time they were the enemy. When he came down from the butte to cleanse himself at the stream below, he found the remains of a campfire and the broken shell of an iron kettle. This was a sign that reinforced his dream. He took a piece of the iron for his medicine bag, which he had made of elk skin years before, to prepare for his quest.

183

"He returned to his village, where he told his dream to the wise old men of the tribe. They gave him the name Iron Shell, but neither did they understand the meaning of the dream. The first Iron Shell kept the piece of iron with him at all times and believed it gave him protection from the evils of those unhappy days.

"Then a terrible thing happened to Iron Shell. He and several other young men were taken from their homes by the soldiers and sent far away to a white man's boarding school. He was angry and lonesome for his parents and the young girl he had wed before he was taken away. At first Iron Shell resisted the teacher's attempts to change him, and he did not try to learn. One day it was his turn to work in the school's blacksmith shop. As he walked into the place, he knew that his medicine had brought him there to learn and work with the white man's iron.

"Iron Shell became a blacksmith and worked at the trade when he returned to the reservation. All of his life he treasured the medicine bag. When he was old and I was a man, he gave it to me, for no one made the vision quest any more."

Grandpa quit talking, and I stared in disbelief as he covered his face with his hands. His shoulders were shaking with quiet sobs, and I looked away until he began to speak again.

"I kept the bag until my son, your mother's father, was a man and had to leave us to fight in the war across the ocean. I gave him the bag, for I believed it would protect him in battle, but he did not take it with him. He was afraid that he would lose it. He died in a faraway place."

Again Grandpa was still, and I felt his grief around me.

"My son," he went on after clearing his throat, "had only a daughter, and it is not proper for her to know of these things."

He unbuttoned his shirt, pulled out the leather pouch, and lifted it over his head. He held it in his hand, turning it over and over as if memorizing how it looked.

"In the bag," he said as he opened it and removed two objects, "is the broken shell of the iron kettle, a pebble from the butte, and a piece of the sacred sage." He held the pouch upside down and dust drifted down.

"After the bag is yours, you must put a piece of prairie sage within and never open it again until you pass it on to your son." He replaced the pebble and the piece of iron and tied the bag.

I stood up, somehow knowing I should. Grandpa slowly rose from the bed and stood upright in front of me holding the bag before my face. I closed my eyes and waited for him to slip it over my head. But he spoke.

"No, you need not wear it." He placed the soft leather bag in my right hand and closed my other hand over it. "It would not be right to wear it in this time and place where no one will understand. Put it safely away until you are again on the reservation. Wear it then, when you replace the sacred sage."

Grandpa turned and sat again on the bed. Wearily he leaned his head against the pillow. "Go," he said. "I will sleep now."

"Thank you, Grandpa," I said softly, and left with the bag in my hands.

That night Mom and Dad took Grandpa to the hospital. Two weeks later I stood alone on the lonely prairie of the reservation and put the sacred sage in my medicine bag. ❧

H.O.T. RESPONSES

1. Discuss with your group the significance of the narrator's comment:

    We never showed our friends Grandpa's picture. Not that we were ashamed of him, but we knew that the glamorous tales we told didn't go with the real thing.

2. Discuss why Martin might be ashamed of his grandfather's "get-up" and why he "wanted to sink right through the pavement." Is this kind of behavior understandable or is it inexcusable?

3. Explain why Cheryl's response to seeing her grandfather is so much more genuine than Martin's. What does Martin learn about himself through his younger sister's behavior?

4. How does Joe Iron Shell's daughter try to compensate for her "modern" lifestyle? Is she successful?

5. Tradition or ritual is a common link to all cultures. Grandpa knows he is going to die soon, and so, as a Sioux, must "follow the tradition of his family to pass the medicine bag, along with its history, to the oldest male child." What other Native American rituals or traditions have you learned? Discuss this information with your group.

6. In your group, share similar and contrasting family traditions. How are they similar or different?

7. This ritual or rite of passage includes the oldest male child. What ritual are you aware of that includes only a female?

8. Discuss the drama and power of the relationships created in this story:

> Old and Young
> Native American and Interracial
> Historical and Modern
> Male and Female

9. What passage shows the grandfather's sensitivity and awareness of the modern culture?

CREATIVE PRODUCT

1. Create your own medicine bag or family bag, and choose three important objects to place in it: (1) One object should be real and represent your own culture and relationship with your family. (2) One object should be created by you. (3) One object should be gathered from nature.

2. Share your medicine bag objects with your group, and relate their personal significance to you, to your family, and to your culture.

3. Write a poem or a story about your medicine bag or your "family" bag.

FOCUS

Brian Morton's first novel, *The Dylanist,* met with critical acclaim from most critics. Morton has also published several essays and articles in journals, magazines, and newspapers. He is an editor and writer for the journal, *Dissent.*

As you read this excerpt from Brian Morton's novel, *The Dylanist,* note that it is written from the point of view of a female—the main character, Sally. It is rare that an author writes from the point of view of the opposite sex, and the critics were quick to point out that Morton had done so superbly.

In this brief chapter, Sally remembers her father, Burke, a well-known union leader, who has dedicated his life to improving the working conditions and salaries of his union workers, and who has taught her an important value, which she will carry with her throughout life. In the excerpt that follows, Sally learns another lesson in the form of a parable about the famous New York Yankee, Joe DiMaggio.

from The Dylanist

Burke spoke in parables. He never told you large general truths about how to live. He told you about DiMaggio.

He liked to talk about the day Ted Williams hit a huge fly ball to the monuments in center field. Running flat-out with his back to the infield, DiMaggio made an over-the-shoulder catch. The next batter hit a dinky little pop-up just behind second base; Burke, following the flight of the ball, expected to see it drop in—but DiMaggio, playing the hitter perfectly, was already there. He didn't even have to move.

Burke never drew any morals, but Sally thought of this as his lesson in the value of being prepared.

The tale closest to Burke's heart, and therefore to Sally's, was about the way DiMaggio retired. One of the many ways he set an example was in how he gave up the game. Unlike the greats who hang on after their talents are spent, muddying the memory of their greatness, DiMaggio retired at the peak of his form. He was hitting as well as ever; he seemed to be as fast as ever; and it seemed he'd be able to keep it up for years. But DiMaggio knew that he'd lost a step; he knew his swing was a fraction of a second slow. It wasn't reflected in the box score yet, but in a year or two, it would be. So DiMaggio allowed those who loved him to remember him as he was in his prime: he had one more championship season, and then he retired.

One effect of these stories was to turn Sally into a baseball fan. Baseball was a language she needed to know, because it was a language in which her father revealed himself.

"I hope I go out like that myself, when it's time to go," Burke once said. "Joltin' Joe."

H.O.T. RESPONSES

1. Families and cultures pass down tradition in a variety of ways as you learned by reading "The Medicine Bag." In this story, Burke speaks in parables, or stories that—in themselves—teach general truths about how to live. From these stories, we learn what our culture and family values are.

   What does the parable about Joe DiMaggio teach Sally to value? Do you agree with this point of view? Discuss this with your group, and share other values that you have learned from stories you have heard from your own relatives.

2. Can you give other examples of individuals you know or have read about who ended their careers or fame in their prime? Tell their stories.

3. In contrast, are there examples of individuals who continued after their prime and brought embarrassment to themselves and their loved ones? Cite examples and explain.

CREATIVE PRODUCT

1. Write a short story in which your narrator is the opposite gender from you.

2. Write a second story in which the narrator is a different race from you.

3. Write a story in which someone from your own cultural background relates a parable or a story that teaches you a lesson or value.

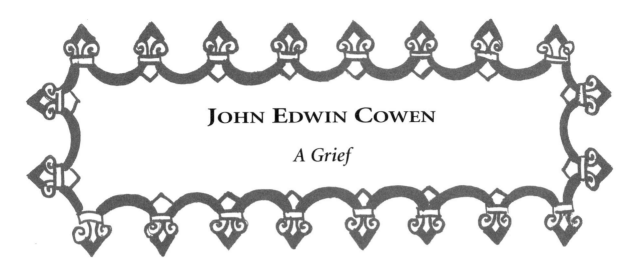

FOCUS

"A Grief" is an elegy or a poem written to someone who has died. Usually, an elegy is written in memory of a loved one, or in some cases, elegies have been written to memorialize another poet, a president, or a monarch.

In this instance, John Edwin Cowen is writing about a dedicated teacher and friend, Hilde Marx, who died in the prime of her life. As you read this poem, note how the repetition of certain words, such as *grief, rose, toll, death* are used to create a haunting or lamenting song.

A Grief

(a grief)(and a grief)
and a grind after all
and to those with too much
rose, the presages of
death impose

(a grief)(and a grief)
and a grave bell to toll
for love prospers not
though it gather a perfect
rose, and a tall dark
parable of gold

(a grief)(and a grief)
and I must lace up my
life, and lift up my mind
:Sing please to my death
and toll   only once)   my time.

© 1996 by The Center for Applied Research in Education

191

H.O.T. RESPONSES

1. Have someone from your small group read "A Grief" with feeling. Then discuss how the repetition of certain words creates a sad tone or mood.

2. Why do you think the poet has chosen to enclose the first line of each stanza in parentheses?

3. How can a person have "too much rose" (lines 3–4)?

4. What is meant by the lines, "a tall dark/parable of gold"?

5. Summarize the final stanza in your own words. Each line is a metaphor; therefore, your summary should include each of the last four lines after (a grief) (and a grief).

CREATIVE PRODUCT

1. Write an elegy for someone you have loved or for some famous person whom you have admired.

ESTRELLA D. ALFON

Magnificence

FOCUS

Estrella D. Alfon attracted public attention when her "O Perfect Day," which had first appeared in the *Philippine Magazine,* was published in *Story,* an American magazine devoted entirely to the short story.

Known for her forthrightness of manner and her sense of humor, Ms. Alfon worked as associate editor of the *Manila Time Magazine,* as editor of *Yours,* and as a director of the Philippine Association of Women Writers.

National artist of literature, José Garcia Villa, who is quite chary of his praise, hails Estrella D. Alfon as one of the best short story writers in the history of the medium. It is sad to note that this personable writer, known affectionately as "Mama," recently died; however, her work lives on and is as contemporary as ever. Her story, "Magnificence," makes a dramatic statement about a problem that plagues us more so today, in spite of the fact that it was published as early as 1960 in *Magnificence and Other Stories*—long before the term "child abuse" was brought to our social consciousness.

MAGNIFICENCE

There was nothing to fear, for the man was always so gentle, so kind. At night when the little girl and her brother were bathed in the light of the big shaded bulb that hung over the big study table in the downstairs hall, the man would knock gently on the door, and come in. He would stand for a while just beyond the pool of light, his feet in the circle of illumination, the rest of him in shadow. The little girl and her brother would look up at him where they sat at the big table, their eyes bright in the bright light, and watch him come fully into the light. A dark little man with protuberant lips, his eyes glinting in the light, but his voice soft, his manner slow. He would smell very faintly of sweat and pomade, but the children didn't mind although they did notice, for they waited for him every evening as they sat at their lessons like this. He'd throw his visored cap on the table, and it would fall down with a soft plop, then he'd nod his head to say one was right, or shake it to say one was wrong.

It was not always that he came. They could remember perhaps two weeks when he remarked to their mother that he had never seen two children looking so smart. The praise had made their mother look over them as they stood around listening to the goings-on at the meeting of the neighborhood association, of which their mother was president. Two children, one a girl of seven, and a boy of eight. They were both very tall for their age, and their legs were the long gangly legs of fine spirited colts. Their mother saw them with eyes that held pride, and then to partly gloss over the maternal gloating she exhibited, she said to the man, in answer to his praise. But their homework! they're so lazy with them. And the man said, I have nothing to do in the evenings, let me help them. Mother nodded her head and

said, if you want to bother yourself. And the thing rested there, and the man came in the evenings therefore, and he helped solve fractions for the boy, and write correct phrases in language for the little girl.

In those days, the rage was for pencils. School children always have rages going at one time or another. Sometimes it is for paper butterflies that are held on sticks, and whirr in the wind. The Japanese bazaars promoted a rage for those. Sometimes it is for little lead toys found in the folded waffles that Japanese confection-makers had such light hands with. At this particular time, it was for pencils. Pencils big but light in circumference not smaller than a man's thumb. They were unwieldy in a child's hands, but in all schools then, where Japanese bazaars clustered, there were all colors of these pencils selling for very low, but unattainable to a child budgeted at a "ba-on" of a centavo a day. They were all of five centavos each, and one pencil was not at all what one had ambitions for. In rages, one kept a collection. Four or five pencils, of different colors, to tie with strings near the eraser end, to dangle from one's book-basket, to arouse the envy of the other children who probably possessed less.

Add to the man's gentleness his kindness in knowing a child's desires, his promise that he would give each of them not one pencil, but two. And for the little girl, who he said was very bright and deserved more, he would get the biggest pencil he could find.

And every evening after that the two children would wait for him, watch him come feet first into the pool of light, watch him bathed in the brightness of the incandescent bulb, and wait eagerly for him to give them the pencils he had promised them.

© 1996 by The Center for Applied Research in Education

One evening he did bring them. The evenings of waiting had made them look forward to this final giving, and when they got the pencils they whooped with joy. The little boy had two pencils, one green, one blue. And the little girl had three pencils, two of the same circumference as the little boy's but colored red and yellow. And the third pencil, a jumbo size pencil really, was white, and had been sharpened, and the little girl jumped up and down, and shouted with glee. Until their mother called from down the stairs. What are you shouting about? And they told her, shouting gladly, Vicente, for that was his name. Vicente had brought the pencils he had promised them.

Thank him, their mother called. The little boy smiled and said, Thank you. And the little girl smiled, and said, Thank you, too. But the man said, are you not going to kiss me for those pencils? They both came forward, the little girl and the little boy, and they both made to kiss him, but Vicente slapped the boy smartly on his lean hips, and said, Boys do not kiss boys. And the little boy laughed and scampered away, and then ran back and kissed him anyway.

The little girl went up to the man shyly, put her arms about his neck as he crouched to receive her embrace and kissed him on the cheeks.

The man's arms tightened suddenly about the little girl, until the little girl squirmed out of his arms, and laughed a little breathlessly, disturbed but innocent, looking at the man with a smiling little question of puzzlement.

The next evening, he came around again. All through that day, they had been very proud in school, showing off their brand new pencils. All the little girls and boys had been envying them. And their mother had finally to tell them to stop talking about pencils. Pencils, for now that they had, the boy two, and the girl three, they were asking their mother to buy more, so that they could each have five, and three at least in the jumbo size that the little girl's third pencil was. Their mother said, Oh stop it, what will you do with so many pencils, you can only write with one at a time.

And the little girl muttered under her breath, I'll ask Vicente for some more.

Their mother replied, He's only a bus conductor, don't ask him for too many things. It's a pity and this observation their mother said to their father, who was eating his evening meal between paragraphs of the book on masonry rites that he was reading. It is a pity, said the mother. People like those, they make friends with people like us, and they feel it is nice to give us gifts, or the children toys and things. You'd think they wouldn't be able to afford it.

The father grunted, and said, The man probably needed a new job, and was softening his way through to him by going at the children like that. And the mother said, No, I don't think so, he's a rather queer young man, I think he doesn't have many friends, but I have watched him with the children, and he seems to dote on them.

The father grunted again, and did not pay any further attention.

Vicente was earlier than usual that evening. The children immediately put their lessons down, telling him of the envy of their schoolmates, and would he buy them more please?

Vicente said to the little boy, Go and ask if you can let me have a glass of water. And the little boy ran away to comply, saying behind him. But buy us some more pencils, huh, buy us more pencils, and then went up the stairs to their mother.

Vicente held the little girl by the arm, and said gently, "Of course I will buy you more pencils, as many as you want."

And the little girl giggled and said, "Oh, then I will tell my friends, and they will envy me, for they don't have as many or as pretty."

Vicente took the girl up lightly in his arms, holding her under the armpits, and held her to sit down on his lap and he said, still gently, "What are your lessons tomorrow?" And the little girl turned to the paper on the table where she had been writing with the jumbo pencils, and she told him that was her lesson but it was easy.

Then go ahead and write, and I will watch you.

Don't hold me on your lap, said the little girl, I am very heavy, you will get very tired.

The man shook his head and said nothing, but held her on his lap just the same.

The little girl kept squirming, for somehow she felt uncomfortable to be held thus, her mother and father always treated her like a big girl, she was always told never to act like a baby. She looked around at Vicente, interrupting her careful writing to twist around.

His face was all in sweat, and his eyes looked very strange, and indicated to her that she must turn around, attend to the homework she was writing.

But the little girl felt very queer, she didn't know why, all of a sudden she was immensely frightened, and she jumped up away from Vicente's lap.

She stood looking at him, feeling that queer frightened feeling, not knowing what to do. By and By, in a very short while her mother came down the stairs, holding in her hand a glass of zarzaparilla. The little boy followed her. The mother said, I brought you some zarzaparilla, Vicente.

But Vicente had jumped up too as soon as the little girl had jumped from his lap. He snatched at the papers that lay on the table and held them when he heard the mother's coming.

The mother looked at him, stopped in her tracks, and advanced into the light. She had been in the shadow. Her voice had been like a bell of safety to the little girl. But now she advanced into the glare of the light that held like a tableau the figures of Vicente holding the little girl's papers to him, and the little girl looking up at him frightenedly, in her eyes dark pools of wonder and fear and question.

The little girl looked at her mother, and saw the beloved face transfigured by some sort of glow. The mother kept coming into the light, and when Vicente made as if to move away into the shadow, she said, very low, but very heavily, Do not move.

She put the glass of soft drink down on the table, where in the light one could watch the little bubbles go up and down in the dark liquid. The mother said to the little boy, Oscar, finish your lessons. And then turning to the little girl, she said, come here. The little girl went to her, and the mother knelt down, for she was a tall woman and she said, turn around. Obediently the little girl turned around, and her mother passed her hands over the little girl's back.

Go upstairs, she said.

The mother's voice was of such a heavy quality and of such awful timbre that the little girl could only nod her head, and without looking at Vicente again, she raced up the stairs. The little boy bent over his lessons.

The mother went to the cowering man, and marched him with a glance out of the circle of light that held the little boy. Once in the shadow, she extended her hand, and without any opposition took away the papers that Vicente was holding to himself. She stood there saying nothing as the man fumbled with his hands and with his fingers, and she waited, until he had finished. She was going to open her mouth but she glanced at the boy and closed it, and with a look and an inclination of the head, she bade Vicente go up the stairs.

The man said nothing, for she said nothing either. Up the stairs went the man, and the mother followed him behind. When they had reached the upper landing, the woman called down to her son, Son, come up and go to your room.

The little boy did as he was told, asking no questions for indeed he was feeling sleepy already.

As soon as the boy was gone, the mother turned on Vicente.

Finally, the woman raised her hand, and slapped him full hard in the face. He retreated down one tread of the stairs with the force of the blow, but the mother followed him. With her other hand she slapped him on the other side of the face again. And so down the stairs they went, the man backwards, his face continually open to the force of the woman's slapping. Alternately she lifted right hand and left hand and made him retreat before her until they reached the bottom landing.

He made no resistance, offered no defense. Before the silence and the grimness of her attack he cowered, retreating, until out of his mouth issued something like a whimper.

The mother thus shut his mouth, and with those hard forceful slaps she escorted him right to the door. As soon as the cool air of the free night touched him, he recovered enough to turn away and run, into the shadows that ate him up. The woman looked after him, and closed the door. She turned off the blazing light over the study table, and went slowly up the stairs.

The little girl watched her mother come up the stairs. She had been witness, watching through the shutters of a window that overlooked the stairs, to the picture of magnificence her mother made as she slapped the man down the stairs and out into the dark night.

When her mother reached her, the woman held her hand out to the child. Always also, with the terrible indelibility that one associates with terror, the girl was to remember the touch of that hand on her shoulder, heavy, kneading at her flesh, the woman herself stricken almost dumb, but her eyes eloquent with that angered fire. She knelt. She felt the little girl's dress and took it off with haste that almost made her sob. Hush! the mother said. Take a bath quickly.

Her mother presided over the bath that the little girl took, scrubbed her, and soaped her, and then wiped her gently all over and changed her into new clothes that smelt with the clean fresh smell of clothes that had hung in the light of the sun. The clothes that she had taken off the little girl, she bundled into a tight wrenched bunch, which she threw into the kitchen range.

Take also the pencils, said the mother to the watching newly bathed, newly changed child. Take them and throw them into the fire. But when the girl turned to comply, the mother said, No, tomorrow will do. And taking the little girl by the hand, she led her to her little girl's bed, made her lie down and tucked the covers gently about her as the girl dropped off into quick slumber.

197

H.O.T. RESPONSES

In your cooperative group:

1. Explain why the setting of this story is so ominous, or threatening by referring to the following:

   a. The first sentence of the story.

   b. The second and third sentences.

   c. The description of Vicente.

   d. Vicente's early treatment of the little boy in contrast to that of his little sister.

   e. The little girl's "puzzlement" as Vicente's arms tightened about her.

   f. The mother's intuition about Vicente: ". . . He's a rather queer young man, I think he doesn't have many friends, but I have watched him with children and he seems to *dote* on them."

2. Why do you think the mother does not act on her intuition? And why is her husband so indifferent to her stated observation?

3. In the future, how do you think the mother will teach her children to react to such advances?

4. Why do you think it is so important to teach young people to JUST SAY NO! as a way of educating children to protect themselves against child abuse?

5. How can this story be used to help your younger brothers and sisters to be more cautious in order to prevent such incidents from happening to them?

6. How do you think the mother handled this violation of her daughter's human dignity? Were you surprised that she did not call upon her husband for help?

7. Why do you suppose she had her daughter wait to throw the pencils away? Was this a good thing to do, psychologically?

8. Why is "Magnificence" a perfect title for this story?

CREATIVE PRODUCT

1. Create a "What If ? Scenario," similar in style to that which appears in Unit Five; however, use child abuse or sexual abuse as your subject.

2. Share your scenario with your cooperative group. Also share your work with your classroom teacher and your health teacher to see if they might want to use it to advise children on how to respond to similar situations.

Author's Comment on Child Abuse and Sexual Abuse

Counselors advise children and adults to rely on their instincts and suspicions when they find themselves in situations that feel awkward. Educators *insist:* JUST SAY, NO! and remove yourself from a potentially bad situation at once. It is better to be safe than sorry! Therefore, do not worry about being sure of your feelings or about embarrassing the individual who causes you to feel uncomfortable or suspicious. Once you are safe, it is important to express your doubts or suspicions to a trusted adult. Be confident that telling is all right!

In the story, "Magnificence," the mother had failed to act upon her instincts or intuition based on her own observation that Vicente *doted* on children. This story, however, was written thirty-five years ago, long before this problem received any widespread attention. Nevertheless, it is still reported that problems such as the one illustrated by this story (and far worse) happen when individuals fail to act on their suspicions or "gut-level" feelings. This story and commentary should convince you that to do otherwise may be *very* foolish.

CIRILO F. BAUTISTA

She of the Quick Hands: My Daughter

FOCUS

Cirilo F. Bautista is a poet, critic, essayist, and contributing editor to *Panorama,* a literary magazine published in Manila, Philippines. Bautista is the author of several volumes of poetry; he is a prolific writer, whose prose and poetry are published extensively in the Philippines as well as in international literary journals and magazines. He is the recipient of the prestigious Palanca Poetry Award and his poems have been anthologized in *The Doveglion Book of Philippine Poetry* (1975) and in *The New Doveglion Book of Philippine Poets,* expanded edition (1994), edited by José Garcia Villa.

Villa regards Bautista's contributions to this national anthology as some of the "best poems in English written by a Filipino." "She of the Quick Hands: My Daughter" is a poem written by a sensitive, observant father who is awed by his two-year-old daughter's magical innocence and curiosity, as well as his own innocence as a new, and somewhat imperfect, parent. This poem is exquisitely well crafted in that it is carefully patterned in three-lined stanzas, in rhyme scheme, and in rhythm. Yet, when the poem is read, these patterns are subtle—visually as well as aurally; that is, the poem has a modern, colloquial feel while the traditional form of its rhythm and its rhyme is quiet and unobtrusively satisfying.

As you read the poem, first for sheer enjoyment, and then for meaning, take notice of its formal elegance.

She of the Quick Hands: My Daughter

She of the quick hands: my daughter
From what fibre has she sprung
What bones   where is she bound for

As she leaps and catches the tongue
Of sun only two years old
Yet questioning right or wrong

The color of grass   why trees are cold
And I only her father cannot
Explain the universe in her hold

Am just a part of it   begot
And not begetting it
In my parenthood have forgot

The innocence   the dancing it
Arranges in the human bone
As she does now meaning it

Less to her than to the stone
Whirling in an image of letter
In a light pure to her alone

In a light purer with laughter
Striking me with a new wisdom
She of the quick feet: my daughter

H.O.T. RESPONSES

1. With a partner from your cooperative group, discuss the awe the poet is feeling.

2. Can you grasp the meaning of the metaphor in the second stanza? Take turns summarizing its meaning.

3. Try to explain the father's feeling of inadequacy, which is expressed in stanzas 3, 4, and 5.

4. What kind of innocence is the poet describing?

5. Explain the following two lines:

   As she does now meaning it
   Less to her than to the stone

6. What is the "new wisdom" acquired by the poet? Why do you think this happens?

7. Can you explain the first and last lines of this poem?

CREATIVE PRODUCT

1. To see how well you understand the form of this poem, use it as a model to create your own poem. Your poem should reflect the theme of this unit, "Relationships: Family and Friends."

2. Follow Bautista's rhyme scheme and stanzaic patterns. Notice how Bautista's rhymes are *slant rhymes:* daughter/for, tongue/wrong. Also notice how the second line rhymes with the first and third line of each succeeding stanza, for example, sprung/tongue/wrong.

   Note on Slant Rhymes: Remember that *slant rhymes* are not *exact rhymes* as *sun* and fun *are,* although they are close enough in sound and harmonics to qualify as a rhyme. Some modern poets prefer the slight tonal difference between *tongue* and *wrong,* for example, because they find such rhymes more subtle and, therefore, more intriguing.

203

GLORIA POTTER

slowly like a shade

FOCUS

In Unit One, you read a poem by Gloria Potter which ended with the lines:

Masks can
ask much

Gloria Potter is also an excellent craftsperson as a poet and uses words with great skill and imagination. Her poem, "slowly like a shade," can be considered a concrete poem because it actually creates the image of a shade by the lowering of one line at a time. Through the use of repetition, and layering of one line upon another, a visual image of a shade being lowered is accomplished visually as well as linguistically.

As you read this poem, try to get a feel for the mood of the poem. Also, try to think about what kind of relationship she is describing. Is it a good family relationship, or a not-so-good relationship? Now you can begin lowering the shade yourself as you begin reading this intriguing poem.

slowly like a shade

slowly, like a shade

understand why-so,so
slowly, like a shade

the son,the daughter
understand why-so,so
slowly, like a shade

winding now it seems
the son,the daughter
understand why-so,so
slowly, like a shade

nor shameful is that
winding now it seems
the son,the daughter
understand why-so,so
slowly, like a shade

long, white in waves
nor shameful is that
winding now it seems
the son,the daughter
understand why-so,so
slowly, like a shade

allow a letting down
long, white in waves
nor shameful is that
winding now it seems
the son,the daughter
understand why-so,so
slowly, like a shade

H.O.T. RESPONSES

1. In your cooperative group, explain how *technique* is used to enhance the meaning in this poem.

2. Do you think the last stanza could have been presented just as effectively if it were printed as the entire poem? Explain your point of view.

3. Do you think that the parent of "the son, the daughter" alluded to in the poem, has had a good relationship with her children? Explain your view by pointing to key words or phrases in this poem.

4. Do you think the line that appears above the poem is necessary? Explain the reason(s) for your answer to this question.

CREATIVE PRODUCT

1. Create your own concrete poem; that is, have your imagination and language lead you to create a concrete image for your poem. Cowen's poem, "Dakotas," takes the shape of a knife; Potter's poem represents a shade. Poems have been written in different shapes, including a diamond, a beard, a chalice, an anvil, and many others.

2. Write a story that shows the relationship between a parent and a child. Create a plot that dramatizes the closeness or conflict between parent and child.

© 1996 by The Center for Applied Research in Education

Unit Eight

THEME:
FOLK TALES FROM
DIFFERENT CULTURES

INTRODUCTION

Through storytelling we learn more about ourselves and others. We learn about human failings, about our shortcomings, our strengths, and our mistreatment of others. *Folk tales* are brief stories that get passed down generation after generation by word of mouth; sometimes they get written down and are later published. Similarly, *myths* about how the world or people were created were told by ancient cultures. They told their myths to explain their universe long before scientific explanations were available.

The tales that follow deal with shortcomings in human behavior. Often animals or nature are portrayed as heroes or heroines in which humans are shown how they should behave. For instance, the prince in the Romanian tale, "The Rose Prince," grows to be a young man, only to realize that war is futile. He decides to return to nature so that his people will live in peace.

"The Emperor's New Clothes" is a Danish tale that shows how vanity can lead one to foolish behavior, and that even an Emperor can become a fool. *Greed* is another human shortcoming, so is longing for eternal youth, and both of these human desires are judged in the Puerto Rican tale, "Lazy Peter and His Three Cornered Hat," and in the Japanese tale, "The Fountain of Youth."

One African American myth will tell how their ancestors believed the Sun and Moon were created. Other tales tell how animals can, at times, outwit humans. Another warns us that modern technology can become dehumanizing if we are not cautious.

As you read these tales, see what lessons you can learn and apply to your own character development.

RICARDO E. ALEGRIA

Lazy Peter and His Three-Cornered Hat

Translated by Elizabeth Culbert

FOCUS

"Lazy Peter and His Three-Cornered Hat" is a Puerto Rican folk tale written by Ricardo E. Alegria and translated by Elizabeth Culbert. As you read this tale, think about how Lazy Peter tries to outsmart and take advantage of the farmer. Then try to recall how GL, the swindler, in "A Visit to Grandmother" is similar to Lazy Peter. Think about how Lazy Peter and GL have similar attitudes toward life.

Later, you will read a tale, "The Emperor's New Clothes," in which two swindlers take advantage of the Emperor. You will want to consider all of these charlatans and compare them to their modern counterparts.

LAZY PETER AND HIS THREE-CORNERED HAT

Translated by Elizabeth Culbert

This is the story of Lazy Peter, a shameless rascal of a fellow who went from village to village making mischief. One day Lazy Peter learned that a fair was being held in a certain village. He knew that a large crowd of country people would be there selling horses, cows, and other farm animals and that a large amount of money would change hands. Peter, as usual, needed money, but it was not his custom to work for it. So he set out for the village, wearing a red three-cornered hat.

The first thing he did was to stop at a stand and leave a big bag of money with the owner, asking him to keep it safely until he returned for it. Peter told the man that when he returned for the bag of money, one corner of his hat would be turned down, and that was how the owner of the stand would know him. The man promised to do this, and Peter thanked him. Then he went to the drugstore in the village and gave the druggist another bag of money, asking him to keep it until he returned with one corner of his hat turned up. The druggist agreed, and Peter left. He went to the church and asked the priest to keep another bag of money and to return it to him only when he came back with one corner of his hat twisted to the side. The priest said fine, he would do this.

Having disposed of three bags of money, Peter went to the edge of the village where the farmers were buying and selling horses and cattle. He stood and watched for a while until he decided that one of the farmers must be very rich indeed, for he had sold all of his horses and cows. Moreover, the man seemed to be a miser who was never satisfied but wanted always more and more money. This was Peter's man! He stopped beside him. It was raining, and instead of keeping his hat on to protect his head, he took it off and wrapped it carefully in his cape, as though it were very valuable. It puzzled the farmer to see Peter stand there with the rain falling on his head and his hat wrapped in his cape.

After a while he asked, "Why do you take better care of your hat than of your head?"

Peter saw that the farmer had swallowed the bait, and smiling to himself, he said that the hat was the most valuable thing in all the world and that was why he took care to protect it from the rain. The farmer's curiosity increased at this reply, and he asked Peter what was so valuable about a red three-cornered hat. Peter told him that the hat worked for him; thanks to it, he never had to work for a living, because whenever he put the hat on with one of the corners turned over, people just handed him any money he asked for.

The farmer was amazed and very interested in what Peter said. As money-getting was his greatest ambition, he told Peter that he couldn't believe a word of it until he saw the hat work with his own eyes. Peter assured him that he could do this, for he, Peter, was hungry, and the hat was about to start working, since he had no money with which to buy food.

With this, Peter took out his three-cornered hat, turned one corner down, put it on his head, and told the farmer to come along and watch the hat work. Peter took the farmer to the stand. The minute the owner looked up, he handed over the bag of money Peter had left with him. The farmer stood with his mouth open in astonishment. He didn't know what to make of it. But of one thing he was sure—he had to have that hat!

Peter smiled and asked if he was satisfied, and the farmer said yes, he was. Then he asked Peter if he would sell the hat. This was just what Lazy Peter wanted, but he said no, he was not interested in selling the hat, because with it, he never had to work and he always had money. The farmer said he thought that was unsound reasoning because thieves could easily steal a hat, and wouldn't it be safer to invest in a farm with cattle? So they talked, and Peter pretended to be impressed with the farmer's arguments. Finally he said yes, he saw the point, and if the farmer would make him a good offer he would sell the hat. The farmer, who had made up his mind to have the hat at any price, offered a thousand pesos. Peter laughed aloud and said he could make as much as that by just putting his hat on two or three times.

As they continued haggling over the price, the farmer grew more and more determined to have that hat, until finally he offered all he had realized from the sale of his horses and cows—ten thousand pesos in gold. Peter still pretended not to be interested, but he chuckled to himself, thinking of the trick he was about to play on the farmer. All right, he said, it was a deal. Then the farmer grew cautious and told Peter that before he handed over the ten thousand pesos, he would like to see the hat work again. Peter said that was fair enough. He put on the hat with one of the corners turned up and went with the farmer to the drugstore. The moment the druggist saw the turned-up corner, he handed over the money Peter had left with him. At this the farmer was convinced and very eager to set the hat to work for himself. He took out a bag containing ten thousand pesos in gold and was about to hand it to Peter when he had a change of heart and thought better of it. He asked Peter please to excuse him, but he had to see the hat work just once more before he could part with his gold. Peter said that that was fair enough, but now he would have to ask the farmer to give him the fine horse he was riding as well as the ten thousand pesos in gold. The farmer's interest in the hat revived, and he said it was a bargain!

Lazy Peter put on his hat again, doubled over one of the corners, and told the farmer that since he still seemed to have doubts, this time he could watch the hat work in the church. The farmer was delighted with this, his doubts were stilled, and he fairly beamed thinking of all the money he was going to make once that hat was his.

They entered the church. The priest was hearing confession, but when he saw Peter with his hat, he said, "Wait here, my son," and he went to the sacristy and returned with the bag of money Peter had left with him. Peter thanked the priest, then knelt and asked for a blessing before he left. The farmer had seen everything and was fully con-

vinced of the hat's magic powers. As soon as they left the church, he gave Peter the ten thousand pesos in gold and told him to take the horse also. Peter tied the bag of pesos to the saddle, gave the hat to the farmer, begging him to take good care of it, spurred his horse, and galloped out of town.

As soon as he was alone, the farmer burst out laughing at the thought of the trick he had played on Lazy Peter. A hat such as this was priceless! He couldn't wait to try it. He put it on with one corner turned up and entered the butcher shop.

The butcher looked at the hat, which was very handsome indeed, but said nothing. The farmer turned around, then walked up and down until the butcher asked him what he wanted. The farmer said he was waiting for the bag of money. The butcher laughed aloud and asked if he were crazy. The farmer thought that there must be something wrong with the way he had folded the hat. He took it off and doubled another corner down. But this had no effect on the butcher. So he decided to try it out some other place. He went to the mayor of the town.

The mayor, to be sure, looked at the hat but did nothing. The farmer grew desperate and decided to go to the druggist who had given Peter a bag of money. He entered and stood with the hat on. The druggist looked at him but did nothing.

The farmer became very nervous. He began to suspect that there was something very wrong. He shouted at the druggist, "Stop looking at me and hand over the bag of money!"

The druggist said he owed him nothing, and what bag of money was he talking about, anyway? As the farmer continued to shout about a bag of money and a magic hat, the druggist called the police. When they arrived, he told them that the farmer had gone out of his mind and kept demanding a bag of money. The police questioned the farmer, and he told them about the magic hat he had bought from Lazy Peter. When he heard the story, the druggist explained that Peter had left a bag of money, asking that it be returned when he appeared with a corner of his hat turned up. The owner of the stand and the priest told the same story. And I am telling you the farmer was so angry that he tore the hat to shreds and walked home. ❧

H.O.T. RESPONSES

After you have read this tale, work with one partner from your cooperative group to solve the following:

1. What is meant by the following saying? "If only he could have put his cleverness to good use, he could have amounted to something!" (Think of this saying in the context of the tale "Lazy Peter and His Three-Cornered Hat.")

2. How are Lazy Peter and GL similar?

3. Why do you think the author allows the swindler to succeed in tricking the farmer?

4. To whom is the moral of this story aimed? Do you think it is successful?

5. If you had written this tale, would you have had the ending turn out differently? If so, how?

CREATIVE PRODUCT

1. You and your partner should collaborate in rewriting this tale so that the "trick" backfires on the trickster as it did on GL.

2. Create your own tale, using the "swindler" or "trickster" theme, but have the swindler lose in the end.

HANS CHRISTIAN ANDERSEN

The Emperor's New Clothes

FOCUS

Hans Christian Andersen was born in Denmark in 1805 and although his dream was to become an actor, he never realized this goal, but began writing tales for children. Before his death in 1875, he wrote 168 tales including "The Emperor's New Clothes," and "The Ugly Duckling," which are widely read around the world even today. As you read this tale, consider how foolish even an emperor can be.

The Emperor's New Clothes

Many years ago there was an Emperor who was so excessively fond of new clothes that he spent all his money in dress. He did not trouble himself in the least about his soldiers; nor did he care to go either to the theater or the chase, except for the opportunities they afforded him for displaying his new clothes. He had a different suit for each hour of the day; and as of any other king or emperor one is accustomed to say, "He is sitting in council," it was always said of him, "The Emperor is sitting in his wardrobe."

Time passed away merrily in the large town which was his capital; strangers arrived every day at the court. One day two rogues, calling themselves weavers, made their appearance. They gave out that they knew how to weave stuffs of the most beautiful colors and elaborate patterns, the clothes manufactured from which should have the wonderful property of remaining invisible to everyone who was unfit for the office he held, or who was extraordinarily simple in character.

"These must indeed be splendid clothes!" thought the Emperor. "Had I such a suit, I might at once find out what men in my realm are unfit for their office, and also be able to distinguish the wise from the foolish! This stuff must be woven for me immediately." And he caused large sums of money to be given to both the weavers, in order that they might begin their work directly.

So the two pretended weavers set up two looms and affected to work very busily, though in reality they did nothing at all. They asked for the most delicate silk and the purest gold thread, put both into their own knapsacks, and then continued their pretended work at the empty looms until late at night.

"I should like to know how the weavers are getting on with my cloth," said the Emperor to himself, after some little time had elapsed. He was, however, rather embarrassed when he remembered that a simpleton, or one unfit for his office, would be unable to see the manufacture. To be sure, he thought, he had nothing to risk in his own person, but yet he would prefer sending somebody else to bring him intelligence about the weavers and their work before he troubled himself in the affair. All the people throughout the city had heard of the wonderful property the cloth was to possess; and all were anxious to learn how wise, or how ignorant, their neighbors might prove to be.

"I will send my faithful old Minister to the weavers," said the Emperor at last, after some deliberation. "He will be best able to see how the cloth looks; he is a man of sense, and no one can be more suitable for his office than he is."

So the honest old Minister went into the hall, where the knaves were working with all their might at their empty looms. "What can be the meaning of this?" thought the old man, opening his eyes very wide; "I cannot discover the least bit of thread on the looms!" However, he did not express his thoughts aloud.

The impostors requested him very courteously to be so good as to come nearer their looms, and then asked him whether the design pleased him and whether the colors were not very beautiful, at the same time pointing to the empty frames. The poor old Minister looked and looked; he could not discover anything on the looms for a very good reason: there was nothing there. "What!" thought he again. "Is it possible that I am a simpleton? I have never thought so myself, and at any rate if I am so, no one must know it. Can it be that I am unfit for my office? No, that must not be said either. I will never confess that I could not see the stuff."

"Well, sir Minister!" said one of the knaves, still pretending to work. "You do not say whether the stuff pleases you."

"Oh, it is admirable!" replied the old Minister, looking at the loom through his spectacles. "This pattern, and the colors—yes, I will tell the Emperor without delay how very beautiful I think them."

"We shall be much obliged to you," said the impostors, and then they named the different colors and described the patterns of the pretended stuff. The old Minister listened attentively to their words in order that he might repeat them to the Emperor; and then the knaves asked for more silk and gold, saying that it was necessary to complete what they had begun. However, they put all that was given them into their knapsacks and continued to work with as much apparent diligence as before at their empty looms.

The Emperor now sent another officer of his court to see how the men were getting on and to ascertain whether the cloth would soon be ready. It was just the same with this gentleman as with the Minister: he surveyed the looms on all sides but could see nothing at all but the empty frames.

"Does not the stuff appear as beautiful to you as it did to my lord the Minister?" asked the impostors of the Emperor's second ambassador, at the same time making the same gestures as before and talking of the design and colors which were not there.

"I certainly am not stupid!" thought the messenger. "It must be that I am not fit for my good, profitable office! That is very odd; however, no one shall know anything about it." And accordingly he praised the stuff he could not see and declared that he was delighted with both colors and patterns. "Indeed, please Your Imperial Majesty," said he to his sovereign when he returned, "the cloth which the weavers are preparing is extraordinarily magnificent."

The whole city was talking of the splendid cloth which the Emperor had ordered to be woven at his own expense.

And now the Emperor himself wished to see the costly manufacture while it was still on the loom. Accompanied by a select number of officers of the court, among whom were the two honest men who had already admired the cloth, he went to the crafty impostors, who, as soon as they were aware of the Emperor's approach, went on working more diligently than ever, although they still did not pass a single thread through the looms.

"Is not the work absolutely magnificent?" said the two officers of the crown already mentioned. "If Your Majesty will only be pleased to look at it! What a splendid design! What glorious colors!" and at the same time they pointed to the empty frames, for they imagined that everyone but themselves could see this exquisite piece of workmanship.

"How is this?" said the Emperor to himself. "I can see nothing! This is indeed a terrible affair! Am I a simpleton? Or am I unfit to be an emperor? That would be the worst thing that could happen. Oh, the cloth is charming!" said he aloud. "It has my entire approbation." And he smiled most graciously and looked at the empty looms, for on no account would he say that he could not see what two of the officers of his court had praised so much. All his retinue now strained their eyes, hoping to discover something on the looms, but they could see no more than the others; nevertheless they all exclaimed, "Oh! How beautiful!" and advised His Majesty to have some new clothes made from this splendid material for the approaching procession. "Magnificent! Charming! Excellent!" resounded on all sides, and everyone was uncommonly gay. The Emperor shared in the general satisfaction and presented the impostors with the riband of an order of knighthood to be worn in their buttonholes, and the title of "Gentlemen Weavers."

The rogues sat up the whole of the night before the day on which the procession was to take place, and had sixteen lights burning so that everyone might see how anxious they were to finish the Emperor's new suit. They pretended to roll the cloth off the looms, cut the air with their scissors, and sewed with needles without any thread in them. "See!" cried they at last. "The Emperor's new clothes are ready!"

And now the Emperor, with all the grandees of his court, came to the weavers; and the

© 1996 by The Center for Applied Research in Education

216

rogues raised their arms as if in the act of holding something up, saying, "Here are your Majesty's trousers! Here is the scarf! Here is the mantle! The whole suit is as light as a cobweb; one might fancy one has nothing at all on when dressed in it; that, however, is the great virtue of this delicate cloth."

"Yes, indeed!" said all the courtiers, although not one of them could see anything of this exquisite manufacture.

"If Your Imperial Majesty will be graciously pleased to take off your clothes, we will fit on the new suit in front of the looking glass."

The Emperor was accordingly undressed, and the rogues pretended to array him in his new suit, the Emperor turning around from side to side before the looking glass.

"How splendid His Majesty looks in his new clothes, and how well they fit!" everyone cried out. "What a design! What colors! These are indeed royal robes!"

"The canopy which is to be borne over Your Majesty in the procession is waiting," announced the Chief Master of the Ceremonies.

"I am quite ready," answered the Emperor. "Do my new clothes fit well?" asked he, turning himself round again before the looking glass in order that he might appear to be examining his handsome suit.

The lords of the bedchamber, who were to carry His Majesty's train, felt about on the ground as if they were lifting up the ends of the mantle, and pretended to be carrying something; for they would by no means betray anything like simplicity or unfitness for their office.

So now the Emperor walked under his high canopy in the midst of the procession, through the streets of his capital; and all the people standing by, and those at the windows, cried out, "Oh, how beautiful are our Emperor's new clothes! What a magnificent train there is to the mantle! And how gracefully the scarf hangs!" In short, no one would allow that he could not see these much-admired clothes, because in doing so, he would have declared himself either a simpleton or unfit for his office. Certainly, none of the Emperor's various suits had ever excited so much admiration as this.

"But the Emperor has nothing at all on!" said a little child. "Listen to the voice of innocence!" exclaimed his father, and what the child had said was whispered from one to another.

"But he has nothing at all on!" at last cried out all the people. The Emperor was vexed, for he knew that the people were right; but he thought, "The procession must go on now!" And the lords of the bedchamber took greater pains than ever to appear holding up a train, although in reality there was no train to hold. 🍃

H.O.T. RESPONSES

1. Why do you think the two impostors would dare to carry out their scheme on the Emperor?

2. Explain why people can feel so insecure that they won't trust their own eyes.

3. Why does it take a child's revelation, before others dare reveal their own thoughts?

4. Why do you think the procession continues, even though the Emperor learns the truth about his new clothes?

5. What do you think about the ending of this tale?

6. Put into your own words what the lesson of this tale teaches all of us.

CREATIVE PRODUCT

1. Write your own tale, using "vanity" as the theme. Be sure that a lesson can be learned from your tale.

JOSÉ GARCIA VILLA

The Emperor's New Sonnet

FOCUS

The Filipino-American poet, José Garcia Villa has written a humorous parody of the well-known folk tale, "The Emperor's New Clothes," by Hans Christian Andersen. Consider the humor of Villa's sonnet after you have read Andersen's famous tale.

The Emperor's New Sonnet

219

H.O.T. RESPONSES

1. Why is Villa's poem a humorous parody of Hans Christian Andersen's tale?

2. What other parodies have you read or seen in art?

3. Why is Villa's "The Emperor's New Sonnet" considered a concrete poem?

CREATIVE PRODUCT

1. Write a tale that is a parody of another tale or story you have read. Write it so that the reader recognizes that you are writing a parody of a very well-known work.

2. Write a poem that mocks or pokes fun at something everyone takes seriously.

3. Write a tale about a frustrated poet who says he has invented a new brand of invisible ink.

SHARON CREEDEN

The Rose Prince

FOCUS

"The Rose Prince" is a Romanian tale retold by Sharon Creeden, whose fascination with storytelling drew her from a legal career to spinning tales. Before she became a storyteller several years ago, Sharon Creeden graduated from the University of Puget Sound Law School, and was a King County Juvenile Court Prosecutor. In 1986, Ms. Creeden was a performer at the National Storytelling Festival, which an estimated 4,000 people attended.

As you read this Romanian tale, think about the relationship of humans to nature. Also think about how the metaphor plays an important role in making this fascinating story come to life.

THE ROSE PRINCE

Once upon a time, a rose bush grew at the edge of a forest. The bush had beautiful roses; each blossom was more splendid than the last. One day, the bush produced a bud lovelier than all the others. When the bud opened, there was a human child inside. The rose had given birth to a son.

The Queen of the country was walking near the rim of the forest when she heard a baby's cry. She followed the sound to the rose bush and found the child lying on the petals. The Queen wrapped the baby in her veil and carried him to the palace.

Several weeks later King Laurin returned from battle. He found the Queen in her rose bower. She was swinging a wicker cradle hung from satin ribbons. The King saw the infant inside the cradle and smiled. King Laurin and Queen Rhoda accepted the child as their own.

They were childless and the Queen was long past childbearing age. Once the palace had been filled with the laughter of seven sons. But one by one the laughing voices were stilled as each prince was slain in the ceaseless war that raged across the country. The reason for the war was forgotten because it was so ancient. But now King Laurin fought to avenge the deaths of his seven sons.

The Rose Prince grew in strength and grace. The King taught him to ride horseback and to swordfight. The Queen taught him to play his lute and to write poetry.

As the Prince reached manhood, he was to be knighted. On the eve of the ceremony, he sat alone in the chapel and watched over his armor. The Queen came and sat with him. She told him of his birth and the rose bush who was his mother.

During the pink dawn, the Prince knelt before the King and pledged to right the ancient wrongs. He kissed the Queen farewell and rode to battle by the King's side. By the time the sun was overhead, the Prince was on a battlefield surrounded by the sound of screams and the smell of blood. He saw the King cut from his horse and run through with a lance. He heard the dying King call to him to avenge his death. He felt the anger burn in his brain. He reared his horse and pursued the King's slayer towards the forest. The Prince knocked the man from his horse and cut the lance from his hand.

As he lifted his sword to strike again, he saw the wild roses under the pines. There was blood on the roses. In an instant, he felt the hatred that clouded his brain. The Prince told the soldier, "Flee—while I am still in my right mind." The soldier ran; the Prince was alone in the serenity of the forest. He vowed to end the carnage.

The Rose Prince returned to the battlefield. He gathered the fallen banners of all the countries and held them high over his head.

"Stop the battle," his voice rang out. One by one, the soldiers stopped fighting. The battle ceased. The Prince spoke softly of surrender and reconciliation. The soldiers began to cast off their armor and weapons. One by one, each turned and went home.

The Prince walked to the forest. He called out, "I am of you. Where is the rose bush that bore the splendid blossoms?"

A nightingale replied, "She is dead. She was a noble tree and had a prince for a flower."

"I am that prince. The juice of the rose still runs in my veins. I wish to return to a life of fragrance and beauty. I wish to leave this human life."

The nightingale said, "Dear Prince, I will stay with you and sing your soul back to a rose."

The Prince knelt on the spot where he was born. At nightfall, the nightingale began to sing. The melody cast out all memory of the world of men. The Prince sank into the moss and loam; his limbs took root in the earth. By dawn, a tall and thornless rose tree had bloomed. And for as long as the rose tree lived, there was peace in the land. ❧

© 1996 by The Center for Applied Research in Education

H.O.T. RESPONSES

1. With one of the students from your cooperative group, discuss how the rose bush is used as a literary device to teach humans a lesson.

2. If the Prince were born of human parents, what dimension of this tale would be lost?

3. Explain how this story creates mixed emotions of joy and sadness.

4. As in poetry, the nightingale is personified, and its song enables the Prince to return to his Rose mother. Explain the importance of the nightingale as a symbol.

CREATIVE PRODUCT

1. Many poets have written about the nightingale. As a library assignment, read John Keats' "Ode to a Nightingale" and compare this romantic's poem to "The Rose Prince." Write a brief paper showing how both nightingales cast spells returning Prince and Poet to their origins.

2. Create a tale in which nature, in the form of an animal, flower, tree, or insect, transforms the human into a better person.

LAFCADIO HEARN

The Fountain of Youth

FOCUS

"The Fountain of Youth" is a traditional Japanese folk story or fairy tale, retold by Lafcadio Hearn. The desire to search for a fountain of youth, or to create a potion to prolong youth, has been a fascination of people from all cultures. Stories about this fascination have been passed down for hundreds of years.

Folklore has it that the Spanish explorer Juan Ponce de Léon once claimed to have discovered the "Fountain of Youth" when he landed at St. Augustine, Florida. Unfortunately, he was wounded in a surprise attack by Seminole braves, and died shortly thereafter, in 1521, at the age of sixty-one.

As you read this tale, think about the moral it teaches, and why wishing for eternal youth is a questionable value.

THE FOUNTAIN OF YOUTH

*L*ong, long ago there lived somewhere among the mountains a woodcutter and his wife. They were very old, and had no children. Every day the husband went alone to the forest to cut wood, while the wife sat weaving at home.

One day the old man went farther into the forest than was his custom, to seek a certain kind of wood; and he suddenly found himself at the edge of a little spring he had never seen before. The water was strangely clear and cold, and he was thirsty; for the day was hot, and he had been working hard. So he doffed his great straw hat, and knelt down, and took a long drink. That water seemed to refresh him in a most extraordinary way.

Then he caught sight of his own face in the spring, and started back. It was certainly his own face, but not at all as he was accustomed to see it in the old mirror at home. It was the face of a very young man! He could not believe his eyes.

He put up both hands to his head, which had been quite bald only a moment before. It was covered with thick black hair. And his face had become smooth as a boy's; every wrinkle was gone.

At the same moment he discovered himself full of new strength. He started in astonishment at the limbs that had been so long withered by age; they were now shapely and hard with dense young muscle.

Unknowingly he had drunk at the Fountain of Youth; and that draught had transformed him.

First, he leaped high and shouted for joy; then he ran home faster than he had ever run before in his life. When he entered his house his wife was frightened,—because she took him for a stranger; and when he told her the wonder, she could not at once believe him.

But after a long time he was able to convince her that the young man she now saw before her was really her husband; and he told her where the spring was, and asked her to go there with him. Then she said:

"You have become so handsome and so young that you cannot continue to love an old woman;—so I must drink some of that water immediately. But it will never do for both of us to be away from the house at the same time. Do wait here while I go."

And she ran to the woods all by herself.

She found the spring and knelt down, and began to drink. Oh! how cool and sweet that water was! She drank and drank and drank, and stopped for breath only to begin again.

Her husband waited for her impatiently; he expected to see her come back changed into a pretty slender girl. But she did not come back at all. He got anxious, shut up the house, and went to look for her. When he reached the spring, he could not see her. He was just on the point of returning when he heard a little wail in the high grass near the spring. He searched there and discovered his wife's clothes and a baby,—a very small baby, perhaps six months old!

For the old woman had drunk too deeply of the magical water; she had drunk herself far back beyond the time of youth into the period of speechless infancy.

He took up the child in his arms. It looked at him in a sad, wondering way. He carried it home,—murmuring to it,—thinking strange melancholy thoughts.

H.O.T. RESPONSES

1. Are the husband and wife truly guilty of seeking eternal youth? Explain your point of view.

2. Why does the husband become a handsome young man, while his wife is reduced to a wailing infant?

3. Explain the mysteriousness of the last sentence in this tale.

4. If you were retelling this story, would you have told it the same way? If so, why? If not, why not?

5. Did you anticipate this strange ending? It is, indeed, an imaginative way to conclude a story. What story have you read that can compare with this surprise ending? (Share your remembered story and retell it to a partner from your group.)

6. Research the Ponce de Léon legend of the Fountain of Youth and report what you learn.

CREATIVE PRODUCT

1. Create your own Fountain of Youth story. Try to create a dramatic, surprise ending.

THREE RETOLD FOLK TALES (61–63)

Robin Kim, "The Tiger and the Dried Persimmon"
(A Korean Tale)

Ancy Samuel, "The Tailor"
(An Indian Story)

Richard Gonzales, "Why the Sun and the Moon Live in the Sky"
(An African Tale)

INTRODUCTION

The following three folk tales are retold by student authors and contributors to *Imagine,* a publication of the Teaneck, New Jersey, Thomas Jefferson Middle School Writers Club, established by their teacher and advisor, Eva Benevento. The folk tales appeared in the issue entitled *Imagine: A Gift to All People; Cultural Diversity,* April, 1994, which was devoted to a celebration of culture—yours and mine. Each story is so well written by these young middle school authors that their tales appear here with those of established and notable writers.

Robin Kim's "The Tiger and the Persimmon" (A Korean Tale) is very humorous. It is woven together by a series of "mistaken identities," a theme used by authors since the beginning of civilization; even today, movies and Broadway comedies are developed by utilizing the mistaken identity concept. As you read the tale, take note that each of these mistakes is woven into a successful and entertaining tale.

Ancy Samuel's "The Tailor" (An Indian Story), shows how an angry elephant gets even with an abusive tailor. Folk tales often depict animals as being superior to human beings, or having better values. Read this story and anticipate what the elephant has in store for the tailor, Pari.

Richard Gonzales' tale, "Why the Sun and the Moon Live in the Sky" (An African Tale) is a creation myth, a common story told by ancient peoples of all cultures to explain the mysteries of their universe.

ROBIN KIM—THE TIGER AND THE DRIED PERSIMMON

(A Korean Folk Tale)

Once there was a huge tiger who lived in a mountain cave. He always walked around boasting about his strength. Every time he said, "I dare anyone to match my strength," all of the animals ran away screaming.

When winter came, the snow piled up higher and higher. It piled up so high that the tiger couldn't dig out of his cave. One day he got so hungry, he slowly and painfully got out of his cave.

The snow made all of the mountains white, and food was hard to find. The tiger began wandering around in the snow. He reached a farm, walked up to the barn, and looked inside. He found a nice fat cow sleeping in the hay. The tiger stared at the cow with a very hungry look.

Then he heard a small child crying. The sound came from the house. The tiger was curious about the sound and decided to sneak up to the room where he saw the child and his mother. The mother was trying to stop her child from crying by trying to scare him into silence. She said, "There's a tiger outside and he is going to eat you."

The tiger heard this and thought the mother had seen him. He said to himself, "I had better be careful." The child cried even louder and the tiger didn't like the idea of the child not being afraid of him.

The mother then tried something different. She said, "Look, a dried persimmon." When she said that, the child stopped crying.

The tiger saw that the child stopped crying and thought that the persimmon must be a beast stronger and scarier than he was. He even thought that if he sat there for a long time, the persimmon would eat him, so he went back to the barn.

As soon as he was inside, he saw a black thing creeping to the barn door. The tiger was convinced that it was a persimmon, so he just sat there shaking, afraid to move. The black shape patted the tiger and said, "This one is really nice and fat." The black thing was really a thief who had come to steal the cow. The thief thought the furry tiger was the cow because it was dark and he couldn't see very well. The tiger thought for sure it was the end of his life, so he closed his eyes in terror, ready to be eaten. When the thief led the tiger out of the barn, he saw that it was a tiger and he was just as scared as the tiger.

Realizing that, the tiger thought, "Now's my chance!" He started to run, but the thief jumped on his back thinking that the tiger was about to eat him. The tiger ran faster heading for the mountains, but that only made the thief hold on tighter. The thief spotted a branch, reached out and grabbed it as the tiger kept running toward the cave.

When the tiger reached the cave, he realized that the thief was gone. After he caught his breath, he said, "That was close! Today I was almost eaten by a persimmon!"

H.O.T. RESPONSES

1. Work with a partner from your cooperative group and make a list of each case of mistaken identity that occurs in this tale.

2. Why is the word "persimmon" so important to this tale? Did you know the meaning of "persimmon" when you first read it? (Be sure to learn the meaning of this word if you do not know it at this point.)

3. Is there any lesson that can be learned from this tale? Explain your answer.

4. Have you ever overreacted to a situation because of a case of mistaken identity in which you were involved? Share with your partner how and why you overreacted to this situation.

CREATIVE PRODUCT

1. Create a tale of your own, using mistaken identity to build your plot or action.

2. Ask your parents or relatives to tell you a tale that they remember from their youth, and record it in your journal.

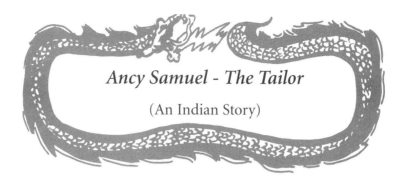

Ancy Samuel - The Tailor

(An Indian Story)

Once there was a tailor whose name was Thunikaren Paripil. (Let's call him Pari.) Pari's shop opened at 6:30 in the morning and closed at 8:30 at night.

There was a master and his elephant who went to the river every day so that the master could give the elephant a bath. It just so happened that Pari's shop stood right in the middle of the road traveled by the elephant and his master.

Every day at about 7:30, as the tailor was well into his sewing, the master and the elephant would pass. The elephant would reach out his trunk and the tailor would give him a banana.

One day, when the elephant came and reached out his trunk, the tailor looked for a banana, but there wasn't one in sight! What was he going to do?

He thought of playing a little joke. He thought, "Why don't I poke him with a needle instead!"

As the elephant passed, the tailor poked him with the needle. The elephant was very angry, but did not do any harm to Pari. However, he had something in store for Pari. (Did you think that he would let Pari off?)

While the elephant was taking a bath, he was doing more than just standing there like a dumb elephant. He was sucking up as much water as he could into his trunk. After his bath, he and his master were on the road and had to pass the tailor's shop. As they passed the shop, the elephant sprayed all of the water into the tailor's shop. The shop was totally ruined. When the elephant started to roar, the tailor took off full speed. The tailor stumbled over some rocks but didn't even care about any cuts or scratches. He just was glad to get away without being drowned.

H.O.T. RESPONSES

1. Do you think the elephant in this tale had reason to be angry? Or did you think that it was all right for Pari, the tailor, to play a joke on the elephant as he did?

2. Why is the author's use of the phrase, "standing there like a dumb elephant" a good choice for the ensuing action?

3. Do you think the elephant's retaliation was too severe? Explain your answer.

4. Have you ever observed an animal's reaction to bad treatment in ways that might lend realism to this tale?

CREATIVE PRODUCT

1. Create your own tale in which an animal triumphs over a human and, in turn, teaches a lesson.

2. Ask some adults if they recall tales about animals. Record any tales you are told and retell one of them to your cooperative group.

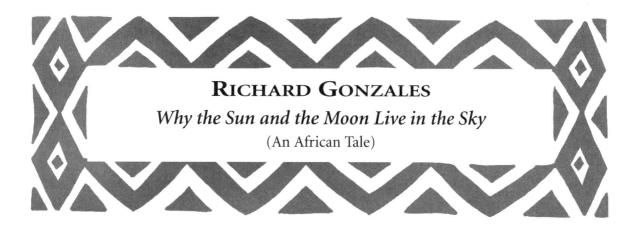

RICHARD GONZALES

Why the Sun and the Moon Live in the Sky

(An African Tale)

Many, many times the Sun and the Moon wanted their dear friend Water to come and visit them in their home. Water kept saying that his family was so big that they would not fit without somebody getting wet. Neither the Sun nor the Moon wanted to get wet.

So, they built a new home, a very big home, a very pretty home, and then invited Water to come and visit. Again, Water was not sure, but he agreed to come anyway.

When the day came, the Sun and the Moon were so excited. Water kept coming and coming until the Sun and the Moon had to go outside. Fish, plants, whales, and dolphins came, and little by little, Sun and Moon moved up in the air. Before Sun and Moon realized it, they were in the sky. And that, my friends, is how the Sun and Moon came to live in the sky.

H.O.T. RESPONSES

1. Explain how the author uses the poetic form of "personification" to write his tale.

2. Why do you think water was a good choice for explaining why Sun and Moon live in the Sky?

3. What other examples could be used to further explain why Sun and Moon live in the Sky?

CREATIVE PRODUCT

1. Imagine that you are living long, long before Galileo was born. Write a tale explaining daylight and darkness, or winter and spring.

2. Also, write a myth explaining the existence of birds, animals, and fish.

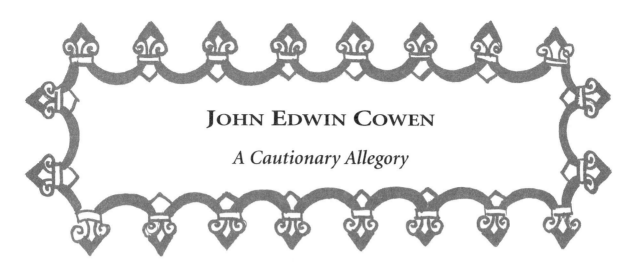

FOCUS

An alarming prediction was made by G. Fortier in 1983; he stated, "Words will be replaced by electronic signals automatically encoded and decoded in the brain; Wagschal has predicted the demise of the written word as our primary means of communicating by the year 2001." Fortier further predicts, based upon his research in the areas of artificial intelligence and neuroscience, "Through the use of appropriate amplifiers and receivers, a direct brain to brain communication in 'brain language' will become possible."

The haunting possibility of these futuristic views of reading instruction has led to the writing of the allegory that follows. The allegory is not meant to detract from the wonderful and myriad possibilities that computers can have for the teaching of reading. Its purpose, however, is to serve as a simple reminder that we are indeed *human*, and that we must—above all else—maintain this humanity throughout our continuous pursuit of knowledge.

A CAUTIONARY ALLEGORY

*O*nce upon a time, in the year 2048, there lived a boy n amed Macintosh, so named after a relic computer once owned by his grandfather.

Macintosh was to celebrate his tenth birthday. Yet, on this day, Macintosh was very sad. He had been admonished by his father for speaking. For speaking was contrary to the custom of the children of the time. "Silence was the golden rule," he had been taught from the time he attended school at age three. From that day forward, Macintosh learned how to read and conceptualize without ever saying, hearing, or seeing a word. For at this early age, Macintosh's brain was attached to an electronic apparatus known as an impress teaching device, which taught him everything he had to know about reading and understanding.

Perhaps he thought he was strange because he was forever practicing speech. But for some unknown reason, he was moved by the sound of words. He received great pleasure when words tripped off his tongue, fell from his lips, and resounded ever so sweetly in his ears. Yet, whenever Macintosh spoke, the other children would grimace, frantically cover their ears, and run away, as though these strange and foreign sounds disrupted their entire beings.

This was not all that troubled Macintosh. He had recently uncovered a leather-bound book amongst his grandfather's belongings, stored in a huge metal trunk. Macintosh soon discovered that leafing through this leather-bound treasure brought him great pleasure. He also learned that this primitive learning device was once used by children long before the electronic impress method was invented, and that the beautiful language he admired was written by an ancient poet named Walt Whitman. "Why," he would ask himself, "do adults prefer silence to speech, impress teaching to reading or human discussion, and why do they outlaw beautiful books like Whitman's?"

These thoughts would make him grow sadder and sadder. He could tell no one, just now, what great joy his new discovery gave him. But, he imagined how one day he, alone, would spread the word and teach others how much the book could benefit them, and how deprived their civilization was without books.

"One day," he imagined, "I shall stand on a mountaintop and wave my book for all the world to see. I shall shout Walt Whitman's words for everyone to hear. And, the world will become humanly free to savor the beauteous sound of *the word*—through the BOOK."

H.O.T. RESPONSES

1. See if you and your cooperative group can define *Allegory,* which is a kind of folk tale, but with a specific purpose or message.

2. Compare the allegory to the futuristic predictions discussed in the "Focus" section. What predictions are depicted in the allegory?

3. Can you explain how Macintosh could be so unique that he would practice speech when no one else was able to do so?

4. Do you think it is at all possible that Macintosh could read and love the poetry of an ancient poet like Walt Whitman and be moved as greatly as he was?

5. Read Walt Whitman's poem, "When Lilacs Last in the Dooryard Bloom'd." This poem was written as an elegy to Abraham Lincoln after his assassination by John Wilkes Booth. This poem appeared in his work, *Leaves of Grass*.

6. Do you think the author of this allegory has indeed cautioned us about the potential problems of technology?

CREATIVE PRODUCT

1. Write a modern allegory of your own. You may caution against politics, social problems, or other modern issues.

2. Write a sequel to "A Cautionary Allegory," using Cowen's as a model.

Unit Nine

THEME:
TALKING TO THE ANIMALS

INTRODUCTION

Humans, regardless of race or ethnic origin, have always had an affinity and special feeling for animals. The biblical account of Noah and the ark accentuates this important bond. The fact that Noah would select a pair of each of God's creatures to survive the infamous flood is evidence of the human-animal connection.

Literature from all cultures, throughout the ages, provides examples of this natural relationship. Ferocious animals, or even the strange domestic creatures described in Manohar Shetty's poem—the lowly cockroach or the loathsome bat—deserve mention; so does the lady alligator in Vanderborg's zany poem. Villa would rather invite a tiger for a weekend over some timid, uninteresting animal or human. At the same time, Villa is quick to mention the beauty and grace of two lovely giraffes.

Countee Cullen's "Christopher Cat" describes the first of nine lives of his friend and coauthor, and Cirilo F. Bautista describes the life and experiences of the sea gull.

Of course, not all is perfect, for just as in real life, the bizarre and the unexpected may happen, as in the case of "The Boy Who Drew Cats." Also, Flory Perini's sensitive poem describes how animals may sometimes be used or abused by humans.

As you read through this unit, think of your own observations of the animal world. Consider your own experiences, good and bad, and think about what kind of world this would be if we did not have animals with whom we could talk, to whom we could relate, or whom we could observe.

MANOHAR SHETTY

Domestic Creatures

FOCUS

Manohar Shetty was born in Bombay, India, in 1953, and educated at the University of Bombay. He now lives in Panjim, India, where he is a journalist and editor of *GOA Today.* His short stories have appeared in *Debonair* and *Indian Horizons,* and he has published two collections of poetry, *A Guarded Space* and *Borrowed Time.*

His poem "Domestic Creatures" and several others recently appeared in *The Oxford India Anthology of Twelve Modern Indian Poets,* edited by Arvind Krishna Mehrota, himself a well-known poet, translator, and critic-historian. In this anthology of modern Indian poetry in English are considered to be twelve of the most outstanding poets writing today.

As you read about Shetty's five unusual domestic creatures, consider his fine use of description as well as his use of metaphor and simile to bring into focus their actual likeness.

Domestic Creatures

LIZARD

Tense, wizened,
Wrinkled neck twisting,
She clears
The air of small
Aberrations
With a snapping tongue,
A long tongue.

Domestic Creatures
(cont'd)

PIGEON

Swaddled cosily, he
Settles by the window,
Burping softly;
Eyelids half-closed,
Head sinking
In a fluffy
Embroidered pillow.

SPIDER

The swollen-headed spider
Spins yarns from her corner.
Tenuous threads of her tales
Glitter like rays
From the fingertips of a saint.

She weaves on, plays along,
Hangs from a hoary strand,
Rolls, unrolls: a yoyo,
A jiggling asterisk: a footnote:
Little characters transfixed
In the clutches of her folds.

COCKROACH

Open the lid, he tumbles out
Like a family secret;
Scuttles back into darkness;
Reappears, feelers like
Miniature periscopes,
Questioning the air;
Leaves tell-tale traces:
Wings flaky as withered
Onion skin, fresh
Specks scurrying
In old crevices.

Domestic Creatures
(cont'd)

BATS

After dark, no longer hung umbrellas,
Black bull's-eyes, or wrapped
Shut as catatonics, they swept
Through moon-glided windows,
Gliding across the walls
Like giant bow-ties; over heads
Sleeping in neat rows,
Dreaming of creaking capes,
Catacombs, crimson teeth
Dipping into sweet veins.

Awakened by the whooshing shadows,
Blood rising at their inverted lives,
With towels and blazers we slapped
Them to the cold floor: they flapped,
Toes twitching, the rowing tracery
Of wings grounded, huddled,
Pouting foxfaces startled
By the stark lights. Later, we heard
Of their soundless cries.

H.O.T. RESPONSES

1. First read about each of the five domestic creatures, then each member of your cooperative group should select one and be prepared to discuss the poem in depth. For instance, in "Lizard" what is significant about clearing the air *"of small aberrations?"* You need to know that an *aberration* is an oddity or a curiosity.

2. Why is the poet's choice of these domestic creatures an oddity in and of itself?

3. What is the word, "burping" really describing in "Pigeon"?

4. In "Spider," why do you think Manohar Shetty uses the metaphor, "From the fingertips of a saint"?

5. Also in "Spider," explain the choice of the metaphors throughout the second stanza.

6. In "Cockroach," why do you think the poet chooses to have the cockroach "tumble out like a family secret?"

7. Do you think the cockroach's wings are as the poet describes them? (The poet Mae Swenson once described a cockroach as being "blonde.") Which image is closer to your observation? Use your own descriptive word(s).

8. Shetty uses several metaphors and similes to describe bats. Which one do you prefer? Explain why.

9. Explain your reactions to the poet's dramatic ending in "Bats."

CREATIVE PRODUCT

1. Think about other possible "strange" creatures that can inhabit a house, and write your own poems describing them.

2. Describe insects using metaphors and similes.

3. Choose one of the creatures Manohar Shetty has written about, and create your own poetic description. Compare the two.

CHRISTOPHER CAT IN COLLABORATION WITH COUNTEE CULLEN
from *My Lives and How I Lost Them (Life No. 1)*

FOCUS

An author may choose to collaborate and share the writing of a book with another author. It is rare, however, when a cat and a human share in such a partnership. Actually these two authors collaborated once before when they wrote the *Lost Zoo,* a novel about the animals (including one of Christopher Cat's ancestors) who were lucky enough to travel with Noah on his ark, and about those who were not as lucky.

One might say that Christopher Cat and Countee Cullen are natural collaborators, since they are good friends who have lived together for a long time. They have both agreed to share the first chapter of their book with us, which Christopher Cat refers to as "Life No. 1." You are probably aware that cats are granted nine lives to live, so if you find Christopher Cat's first life interesting to read about, you will probably want to read about his remaining eight lives.

Countee Cullen, the human author of this book, is also the poet who wrote "Tableau" and "Yet Do I Marvel," two poems that appear earlier—in Unit Four and Unit Six of this text. This great African American author taught English and creative writing at Frederick Douglass Junior High in New York City, and the Countee Cullen Regional Library, a branch of the New York Public Library, was named in his honor. (To date, no library has been dedicated to Christopher Cat.)

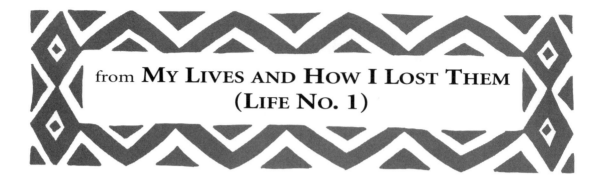

from MY LIVES AND HOW I LOST THEM (LIFE NO. 1)

In every household where there is more than one child, there is bound to be one so gifted in some way, in obedience, perhaps, or in affection for its parents, that it becomes, even against their wills, its parents' favorite. In every litter of kittens there will always be one so graceful, so cateristically obedient, so filled with all the kittenish virtues, that the mother cat and the father cat, even against *their* wills, must acknowledge it their favorite kitten. So, when the animals were made, and the great Creator of them all beheld them, it may not have been His instant intention to think of any of them as His favorite creature, but to love them all equally. The long line stretched before him. There were mighty lions, with silken manes and swift claws. There were clever, mischievous monkeys. There were striped snakes with varied patterns on their shiny backs. There were tigers with skins of gold and black velvet. There were thousands of bright-colored birds. There were millions of insects. Every animal under the sun was there. Each had its place in the great Creator's affections, and to each He granted the gift of life, but of *one* life only. Not even to man, to whom He gave all power over us, did He give more than *one* life. But looking at the first cat which frisked and capered in thanks before Him, the great Creator, against His will almost, knew that here was His favorite animal, and added eightfold to the first cats' lives, and to the lives of all cats to come.

Thus, now in the third year of my *ninth* and *last* life, I think it no show of conceit or vanity to set down those happenings of my previous eight lives which were full of such adventure and excitement as I shall never know again. For now, aware that I have but one more life to live, I look twice before I pounce once, and the safest place I know is my own home and fireside.

Children are born in houses and hospitals. Birds are born in nests; various other animals in dens and stalls. Some are born in holes in the ground, others in the water. Each kind of animal seems to have its appointed place of birth. Perhaps it is because we have so many lives to live that we cats do not mind much *where* we are born. Box or basket, closet or cellar, field, bureau drawer, neglected satchel or useless attic trunk, it does not matter to us, as long as we are born. And no stranger place could have been found than the cast-off, but still smooth and silklined opera hat in which my brothers and sisters and I uttered our first meows.

There were six of us, three girls and three boys who were given the names of Carole, Claudia, Christobelle, Carlos, Claude—and myself, Christopher, named after my father. As you will observe, we were named in pairs: Carole and Carlos, Claudia and Claude, Christobelle and Christopher. All through our lives, though we were all fond of one another, each of us was a wee bit fonder of the one whose name was like his own. That one we considered our twin. Consequently, Christobelle was my twin and my favorite sister.

I was the first one to receive a name, and though I am now eight lives old, going on nine, I still remember the occasion as clearly as though it were yesterday.

My first recollection of the beginning of my lives is of a great darkness in which I needn't be afraid because close to me was a warm, sweet-smelling, singing someone against whom my brothers and sisters and I cuddled in happiness while she caressed us with her tongue. That was my mother. My next most vivid remembrance is of a deep, booming voice that came straight out of the dark, and of which, deep as it was, I knew I had no reason to be afraid.

"Well, Clarissa?" said the voice. That was the first time I knew that my mother's name was Clarissa.

"Well, Christopher?" said my mother; and that was the first time I knew that my father's name was Christopher.

"How are you, Clarissa?" asked my father.

"Look at them, Christopher, six lovely kittens!" said my mother. "Do you like them, Christopher?"

"I will look at them in time, Clarissa," said my father in a very sedate manner, "but first I want to know how *you* are!"

"Oh, Christopher!" said my mother, and you have never in your life, nor have I in all nine of mine, heard two words so filled with pleasure. "I am very well, and very happy."

"Then," said my father, "I will look at the kittens."

I could feel his long silken whiskers, of which I later learned that he was tremendously proud (and with good reason) brush over me, as he poked his head into the opera hat and sniffed at us.

"Clarissa," he said finally, "these are the finest kittens in the world. Now, don't move an inch until I return; there is something I want to do. Mind now, don't go away!"

"Well, really," laughed my mother, "with these six little ones to rear, I don't imagine that I *could* go very far."

"That was just a manner of speaking, Clarissa," cried my father laughingly, and I heard him bounding away from us.

"Now I wonder what Christopher has on his mind," murmured my mother.

She was not left long in doubt. In a short while, my father was back. I could feel his whiskers brushing me again; and I suppose my brothers and sisters must have felt them too if, sleeping as they usually were in those early days, they could feel anything at all. Suddenly I felt something soft and smooth slip around my neck. I didn't know what it was, and it frightened me a little at first. I held my breath and lay very still.

"Clarissa," I heard my father say, "I have already told you that these are the finest kittens in the world. I am certain you are the finest mother. Therefore, I have brought you my finest possessions—my blue ribbons, one for each kitten, and my most prized Royal Blue for you."

"Oh, Christopher, you shouldn't, you really shouldn't," my mother protested. "Poor plain me, wearing your Royal Blue! Why I have never even been entered in a contest in all my lives, and here you want me to wear your Royal Blue! Really, Christopher, really, really, really!" I thought she was going to cry.

At that time, although even my feeble and kittenish mind could sense that my father had done something which pleased my mother mightily, I had no real idea of what had happened. It was only later when we were much older, that our mother told us what it all meant. My father, as we found out, was a very distinguished cat. Half cream colored, and half bold, bright orange, with large golden-yellow eyes, he was indeed as handsome a cat as you would find in a journey around the world. Moreover, he had a pedigree, being a direct descendant of that Christopher Cat who sailed in Noah's Ark. His whiskers were magnificent, and his tail so large and bushy that I am sure many a fine lady would have been proud to have it waving from her best Sunday bonnet. With my father, beauty was certainly its own reward, for he had won numerous medals (gold ones of course!) and bright blue ribbons, all simply because he was so handsome. My mother, on the other hand, could by no stretch of the imagination, be called beautiful, not even by us (and we were her children, and naturally thought her the most marvelous being in the world). Good she was, kind, unselfish, gentle, courteous to everyone, not given to gossip about her neighbors, graceful and playful, but, no, not beautiful. And not a medal had she ever won. She was just a plain striped tabby whose simplicity had won my elegant father's affections. Whenever my father had been taken away to be entered in a contest, my mother had been as excited as he, and though his owners might brush and comb him to their taste later on, my mother always brushed and combed him first for luck. "Bring back a ribbon, Christopher," she always cried after him. And he never disappointed her.

For a long, long time my mother had ached to have one of those ribbons around her own plain neck, just once to feel this sign of perfection. But in his thoughtlessness my father, although he brought her each ribbon to inspect, had never suggested that she try one on. And she, in her timidity, had never dared make the suggestion herself. You can imagine, then, how happy she was when my father decorated her and us six kittens at the time of our birth.

I have not forgotten that I set out to tell you how I happened to be the first of us kittens to receive a name. But each event in its own time and importance is what I always say.

It seems that there was no thought of naming any of us for quite a while. We were such helpless creatures at first that all we could do was eat and sleep, sleep and eat. We could meow lustily enough, but we couldn't stand on our little legs and, worst of all, we couldn't see a wink! As I grew older I learned of a law which the human being calls the law of fair exchange. It seems that for every happiness there must be a little sorrow. I have often thought that this law begins to work with us cats as soon as we are born. For, although there stretches out before us the promise of nine lives, something not granted any other form of living creature, there is also the undeniable fact that for nine days, and sometimes even longer, we are deprived of the pleasure of seeing. We live at first in a world of darkness.

I hesitate to give the impression that I was a kitten prodigy, but looking back over events as they actually happened, I can come to no other conclusion than that from the very beginning I was unusual. I am no more to blame for my superior qualities than my father for his handsomeness, or my mother for her gentleness and plainness. At any rate, it was to my unusual

and quick development that I owe the loss of my first life.

Long before my brothers and sisters had begun to think of anything but food and sleep, my agile mind had begun to wonder if there were not more to the world than the circular walls of an old opera hat. My legs began to kick about in spite of myself; I began to crawl back and forth across my brothers and sisters, up and down my mother's body which, in my blindness, seemed as huge as a mountain. My early crawling seemed to surprise my mother and to please her at the same time. She would sing to me as I crawled over her, and when she thought I had crawled enough, she would reach back, take me in her teeth and gently set me down beside my sleeping brothers and sisters.

"This little fellow is overanxious," I heard her say once to my father.

"How surprised they will be to find out what the world is like," my father replied.

Then, just as I thought, there *was* more to the world than this old opera hat! What was I waiting for? What were we all waiting for? But I dared not do anything about it as long as my mother was guarding me. I bided my time. And then one day, my chance came!

My mother had fallen asleep (my brothers and sisters were already asleep as usual) and there was no one awake in the opera hat but me. Very gently I began to crawl along my mother's back; up and up I climbed, higher and higher, until finally I stood on my mother's head. I reached up cautiously, but there seemed to be nothing there above me, nothing but space. I kept reaching higher and higher, until finally I pulled myself up on the rim of the hat. My eyes not yet having opened, I could see nothing, but I had a strange, new feeling. The air here was different. I seemed to be surrounded by more space than was good for me. I wanted to get back to my mother, but I didn't know how. And I was afraid to cry out. Suddenly I felt dizzy. My brain swam. The whole world swam. Then off I fell, down, down, straight down the whole length of that opera hat on to what I afterward learned was the floor. The breath went from my body as the air goes sighing from a balloon into which you thrust a pin.

© 1996 by The Center for Applied Research in Education

How long I lay there lifeless on that hard floor I cannot say, but through the darkness that surrounded me, I finally heard my mother weeping and my father trying to comfort her.

"Oh, Christopher, why did I ever go to sleep?" my mother was saying. "It's all my fault. The poor little fellow, the only one that looks exactly like you (that was the first time I knew that!) I'm sure he's done for!"

"Nonsense, Clarissa," replied my father. "He's not done for at all. He has probably just lost one of his lives, a little early if you ask me, but I'm sure it's no more serious than that. Here, move away a bit with your sniffling, and let me get to him."

My father began to roll me over and over, to work my paws up and down, and to lick my face with his tongue. Then he began to blow his breath through my nostrils. All the while my mother was crying as if she were the dead one, while my brothers and sisters, awake now and missing our mother from the opera hat, were all meowing at the tops of their very well-devel-

oped lungs. The noise was enough to bring back to life anybody who had an extra life to spare, and I soon began to breathe again and to stir.

My mother pounced on me, hugged and kissed me, and scolded me by turns. She jumped with me back in the opera hat. "I have half a mind to cuff you soundly," she threatened as she hugged me tight. I didn't know what cuffing meant at that time, but I was to learn in time how distasteful it is.

Just when I could feel those familiar long whiskers brushing my face, and I knew that my father was looking in at us. "I wouldn't cuff him, Clarissa," he said. "The boy has spunk. He pleases me. In fact I think we ought to call him Christopher. In fact we *will* call him Christopher."

And that's how I lost my first life and was named after my father.

And even as my father named me, my eyes opened, and I could see how wonderful and wide, beyond my dizziest expectations, the world was!

H.O.T. RESPONSES

1. Categorize the term "cateristically obedient" as it appears in paragraph 1.

2. Do you agree with Christopher Cat's explanation as to why cats were given nine lives, eightfold more than humans? Explain your answer.

3. What passages point to the fact that one of the authors of this story is a poet, that is, the use of tactile (touch) and visual imagery?

4. What is the meaning of "the law of fair exchange?"

5. How did being a "prodigy" cost Christopher Cat his first life? Can you compare this unusual development to the life of a young human?

6. Describe into what kind of family Christopher Cat was born. If you were a cat, would this be the kind of family you would want to have?

7. If you had a chance to choose what kind of animal you could be, what animal would you choose to be? Explain why. Share your choice with members from your collaborative group.

8. Although this story was written for younger students, why do you think it can be read by anyone, regardless of age?

CREATIVE PRODUCT

1. Describe a pet of yours. If you have not had a pet, describe one that you would like to have.

2. Write your own version of how Christopher Cat loses his second, seventh, or eighth life.

LAFCADIO HEARN

The Boy Who Drew Cats

FOCUS

In Unit Eight, you read another Japanese fairy tale, retold by Lafcadio Hearn, "The Fountain of Youth," a haunting tale with a surprise ending.

The tale you are about to read, "The Boy Who Drew Cats" is a very strange and surprising tale as well; however, these are not the sweet, cuddly cats to which you may be accustomed, like Christopher Cat. These cats are created from the wildest of artistic imaginations.

THE BOY WHO DREW CATS

$\mathcal{A}$ long, long time ago, in a small country-village in Japan, there lived a poor farmer and his wife, who were very good people. They had a number of children, and found it very hard to feed them all.

The elder son was strong enough when only fourteen years old to help his father; and the little girls learned to help their mother almost as soon as they could walk.

But the youngest child, a little boy, did not seem to be fit for hard work. He was very clever,—cleverer than all his brothers and sisters; but he was quite weak and small, and people said he could never grow very big. So his parents thought it would be better for him to become a priest than to become a farmer. They took him with them to the village-temple one day, and asked the good old priest who lived there, if he would have their little boy for his acolyte, and teach him all that a priest ought to know.

The old man spoke kindly to the lad, and asked him some hard questions. So clever were the answers that the priest agreed to take the little fellow into the temple as an acolyte, and to educate him for the priesthood.

The boy learned quickly what the old priest taught him, and was very obedient in most things. But he had one fault. He liked to draw cats during study-hours, and to draw cats even where cats ought not to have been drawn at all.

Whenever he found himself alone, he drew cats. He drew them on the margins of the priest's books, and on the screens of the temple, and on the walls, and on the pillars. Several times the priest told him this was not right; but he did not stop drawing cats. He drew them because he could not really help it. He had what is called "the genius of an *artist,*" and just for that reason he was not quite fit to be an acolyte;—a good acolyte should study books.

One day after he had drawn some very clever pictures of cats upon a paper screen, the old priest said to him severely: "My boy, you must go away from this temple at once. You will never make a good priest, but perhaps you will become a great artist. Now let me give you a last piece of advice, and be sure you never forget it. *Avoid large places at night;—keep to small!*"

The boy did not know what the priest meant by saying, *"Avoid large places;—keep to small."* He thought and thought, while he was tying up his little bundle of clothes to go away; but he could not understand those words, and he was afraid to speak to the priest any more, except to say good-by.

He left the temple very sorrowfully, and began to wonder what he should do. If he went straight home he felt sure his father would punish him for having been disobedient to the priest: so he was afraid to go home.

All at once he remembered that at the next village, twelve miles away, there was a very big temple. He had heard there were several priests at the temple; and he made up his mind to go to them and ask them to take him for their acolyte.

Now that big temple was closed up but the boy did not know this fact. The reason it had been closed up was that a goblin had frightened the priests away, and had taken possession of the place. Some brave warriors had afterward gone to the temple at night to kill the goblin; but they had never been seen alive again.

255

Nobody had ever told these things to the boy —so he walked all the way to the village hoping to be kindly treated by the priests.

When he got to the village it was already dark, and all the people were in bed; but he saw the big temple on a hill at the other end of the principal street, and he saw there was a light in the temple. People who tell the story say the goblin used to make the light, in order to tempt lonely travelers to ask for shelter.

The boy went at once to the temple, and knocked. There was no sound inside. He knocked and knocked again; but still nobody came. At last he pushed gently at the door, and was quite glad to find that it had not been fastened. So he went in, and saw a lamp burning,—but no priest.

He thought some priest would be sure to come very soon, and he sat down and waited. Then he noticed that everything in the temple was gray with dust, and thickly spun over with cobwebs. So he thought to himself that the priests would certainly like to have an acolyte, to keep the place clean. He wondered why they had allowed everything to get so dusty. What most pleased him, however, were some big white screens, good to paint cats upon.

Though he was tired, he looked at once for a writing-box, and found one, and ground some ink, and began to paint cats.

He painted a great many cats upon the screens; and then he began to feel very, very sleepy. He was just on the point of lying down to sleep beside one of the screens, when he suddenly remembered the words, *"Avoid large places;—keep to small!"*

The temple was very large; he was all alone; and as he thought of these words,—though he could not quite understand them—he began to feel for the first time a little afraid; and he resolved to look for a *small place* in which to sleep. He found a little cabinet, with a sliding door, and went into it, and shut himself up. Then he lay down and fell fast asleep.

Very late in the night he was awakened by a most terrible noise,—a noise of fighting and screaming. It was so dreadful that he was afraid even to look through a chink of the little cabinet: he lay very still, holding his breath for fright.

The light that had been in the temple went out; but the awful sounds continued, and became more awful, and all the temple shook.

After a long time silence came; but the boy was still afraid to move. He did not move until the light of the morning sun shone into the cabinet through the chinks of the little door.

Then he got out of his hiding-place very cautiously, and looked about. The first thing he saw was that all the floor of the temple was covered with blood. And then he saw, lying dead in the middle of it, an enormous, monstrous rat,—a goblin-rat,—bigger than a cow!

But who or what could have killed it? There was no man or other creature to be seen. Suddenly the boy observed that the mouths of all the cats he had drawn the night before, were red and wet with blood. Then he knew that the goblin had been killed by the cats which he had drawn. And then also, for the first time, he understood why the wise old priest had said to him,

"Avoid large places at night;—keep to small."

Afterwards that boy became a very famous artist. Some of the cats which he drew are still shown to travelers in Japan.

H.O.T. RESPONSES

1. Lucy Calkins, a Professor at Teachers College, Columbia University, and a well-known teacher of writing, once said that the best writers are "obsessed" about writing; that is, they write and write every chance they get. Describe how the acolyte is "obsessed" as well, and the reason why the priest told him: "You will never make a good priest, but perhaps you will become a great artist."

2. How does the boy's obsession for art save his life, while at the same time, nearly cause his death? Explain your point of view.

3. Why do you think the priest warned the boy to "avoid large places at night; keep to small!" Is there a logical explanation for the priest's foresight? Explain your answer.

4. How do you account for the fact that the goblin rat, bigger than a cow, happened to be in the "large place" the same night the boy arrived at the temple?

5. Why do you think the boy decided to become an acolyte (assistant) instead of pursuing a career as an artist?

6. What kind of cats do you suppose this young artist liked to draw?

CREATIVE PRODUCT

1. Draw a cat as you imagine the young artist drew his.

2. Make a mask in the shape and image of a cat.

3. Write your own tale about a young person who is "obsessed" about doing something that creates a dramatic situation.

JOSÉ GARCIA VILLA

Inviting a Tiger for a Weekend

FOCUS

The Filipino American poet, José Garcia Villa has written two beautiful poems about animals in contrasting styles. "Inviting a Tiger for a Weekend" is a unique and daring gesture. "The Parlement of Giraffes" is a sweet poem showing the loveliness of spirit and physical grace that giraffes possess.

In "Inviting a Tiger for a Weekend," Villa summons two legendary individuals, St. Augustine, who was the protector of birds; and poet William Blake, who also wrote a poem about a tiger. Blake's famous poem begins: "Tiger, tiger, burning bright / in the forests of the night, / what immortal hand or eye / could frame thy fearful symmetry?"

As you read the following poem, see how these allusions to Augustine and Blake relate to its meaning.

Inviting a Tiger for a Weekend

Inviting a tiger for a weekend.
The gesture is not heroics but discipline.
The memoirs will be splendid.

Proceed to dazzlement, Augustine.
Banish little birds, graduate to tiger.
Proceed to dazzlement, Augustine.

Any tiger of whatever colour
The same as jewels any stone
Flames always essential morn.

The guest is luminous, peer of Blake.
The host is gallant, eye of Death.
If you will do this you will break.

The little religions for my sake.
Invite a tiger for a weekend,
Proceed to dazzlement, Augustine.

259

H.O.T. RESPONSES

In your cooperative group, discuss the following:

1. Why do you think the poet believes that his desire to invite a tiger for a week-end requires *discipline*?

2. In your own words, explain the meaning of the second stanza. Refer to Augustine.

3. "Luminous" is a derivative of the word *illuminate,* meaning very bright. Why does Villa say his guest is "luminous"? Why is his guest a peer (friend) of Blake? (Refer to the "Focus" section and the lines quoted from William Blake's poem before answering this question.)

4. Discuss the meaning of the next two mysterious lines:

   If you will do this you will break
   The little religions for my sake.

CREATIVE PRODUCT

1. Think about the most exciting guest (an animal) you would like to invite for a weekend. Write a story or a poem to describe this encounter.

2. What if you were an animal? What famous person would you like to visit? Describe the conversation you would have with this famous person.

JOSÉ GARCIA VILLA

The Parlement of Giraffes

FOCUS

This poem by the Filipino American poet, Villa, is also the very essence of the theme of this unit—"Talking to the Animals." *Parlement* is the French word for speaking. Notice that this poem begins, "I was speaking of oranges to a lady," so that it develops a relationship between humans and animals.

"The Parlement of Giraffes" is a beautiful love poem, in which two giraffes come to pay homage to two young lovers. It is from this tender and innocent, silent communication between animal and human that love becomes ever so heightened and meaningful.

The language of this poem is as graceful as are the two giraffes. "The Parlement of Giraffes," however, is about a level of communication that is natural and is what the great American naturalist, Ralph Waldo Emerson refers to as the highest form of spiritual understanding—that which springs from our senses and from our minds as we encounter nature and animals.

As you read this poem, listen to the rhythm and the sound of the words, which create a pleasant mood similar to the tone and musical quality of a parable from the Bible. You may even hear the giraffes speaking if you listen hard enough.

The Parlement of Giraffes

I was speaking of oranges to a lady
of great goodness when O the lovely

giraffes came. Soon it was all their
splendor about us and my throat

ached with the voice of great larks.
O the giraffes were so beautiful as

if they meant to stagger us by such
overwhelming vision: Let us give

each a rose said my beautiful lady
of great goodness and we sent the

larks away to find roses. It was
while the larks were away that

the whitest giraffe among them
and the goldest one among them

O these two loveliest ones sought
and found us: bent before us two

kneeling with their divine heads
bowed. And it was then we knew

why all this loveliness was sent
us: the white prince and the golden

princess kneeling: to adore us
brightly: we the Perfect Lovers.

H.O.T. RESPONSES

Choose a partner from your cooperative group and discuss the following:

1. How does the word, "oranges" create a mood at the outset of this charming poem?

2. Explain the metaphor:

   . . . my throat ached with the
   voice of great larks.

3. How is the rose used as a symbol in this poem?

4. Why are the giraffes described as *whitest* and *goldest?*

5. Why does the poet write that once the two giraffes bowed before the two lovers, they knew why the giraffes were sent to them?

6. Explain the purpose of this poem and how it relates to the theme in this unit.

CREATIVE PRODUCT

1. Write a tale about giraffes that creates a mood similar to that achieved in Villa's poem.

2. Create a poem that uses the tone of the parable or the folk tale similar to the tone and musical quality of "Parlement of Giraffes."

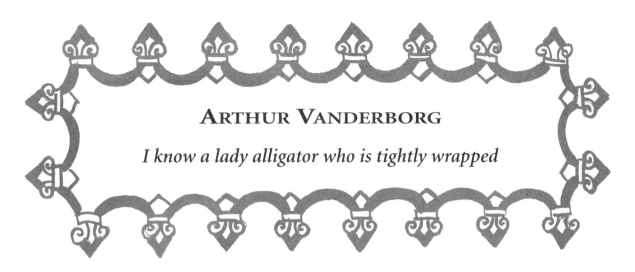

ARTHUR VANDERBORG

I know a lady alligator who is tightly wrapped

FOCUS

Arthur Vanderborg is a poet and a short story writer and is the author of a book of poems entitled *Who Is Mr. Vanderborg?* published by King and Cowen (1979). Vanderborg's poetry is a zany, well-crafted, unique style, though his use of language and punctuation is reminiscent of E.E. Cummings and José Garcia Villa. Vanderborg studied under Villa in his advanced poetry workshop at the New School for Social Research for several years, and is the recipient of the Doveglion Poetry Award. Mr. Vanderborg is of Northern European descent and lives in New York City.

I know a lady alligator who is tightly wrapped

I know a lady alligator who is tightly wrapped
(But not upstairs her mind is skin tight and her
Body bumped (never fight a lady alligator she
Entwines you like a snake but stronger for her
Bumps hold too. she likes to claim the skin
Especially (her own is coarse No never fight

I tried it once she wrapped up tightly even
To my mind she rampaged me and slept between my
Screaming too this lady alligator then connected
Me to her she kept on closing in until i too had
Bumps and i was tightly wrapped. she certainly
Would not let go (i did escape but never fought

I simply tickled all her bumps then Ran never
Fight a lady alligator (though i'll try again

H.O.T. RESPONSES

1. Alligator wrestling is a sport practiced by some adventurous and high risk-taking animal trainers. Do you think the author of this poem falls into this category? Explain.

2. Why do you suppose the poet describes the alligator as being "tightly wrapped/(But not upstairs her mind is skin tight . . .")?

3. The poet seems to have a "love-hate" relationship with this lady alligator. Can you venture to say why?

4. After a while, the poet begins to take on characteristics of the alligator. Why does this occur? Have you ever observed humans who seem to take on the appearance or personality of their pets? Explain your observations.

5. Did you enjoy the humor of the escape strategy used by the poet?

6. Once he gets away, why does the poet write: "(though i'll try again"?

7. The poet uses the open parenthesis on five different occasions. How does this unique use of punctuation affect the language and rhythm in the poem?

8. Compare Arthur Vanderborg's poem to an E.E. Cummings poem.

© 1996 by The Center for Applied Research in Education

CREATIVE PRODUCT

1. Think about an animal that would be as humorous to write about as Vanderborg's lady alligator, then create a humorous poem or story of your own.

2. Try writing a poem, using parentheses and other unusual punctuation to create a variation in its rhythmic movement.

3. Recall a humorous animal poem or story and write a modified version of it to share with your cooperative group.

CIRILO F. BAUTISTA

The Sea Gull

FOCUS

In a previous unit, you read Cirilo F. Bautista's poem about his daughter. "The Sea Gull" is also a very sensitive poem that depicts the sea gull as a determined, tireless bird who clings to life, living off human droppings, or cast-off objects, or "broken loves."

    As you read this poem, consider how, in some respect, the sea gull is not too unlike some humans you know.

The Sea Gull

It has no choice but to live. It is a brave
Thing to go flapping
And flipping in a wave
Of air, in a swing
Of water that is the hair of wind, the face
Of ships and diamonds riding to important
Places. Burnt and burnt
By the sunny maze
Of clouds and fogs, it tails the cargo of queens
And ambassadors,
Spies and stevedores,
      And never gets tired it seems;
      It never gets tired, really,
For the preservation
Of its ancestry
Which clings to its tail like a persistent nightmare
Depends on how quick it is to sweep down, how soon,
And no not sooner,
          To claim the human droppings of
        Fishbones, coffeecups, tattered gloves,
      And broken loves
    From the blind clutch of the sea, on one hand,
   And, on the other, the cruel mocking of the land.

H.O.T. RESPONSES

1. Why does the sea gull have no choice but to live?

2. Why do you suppose Bautista repeats the following word: "Burnt and burnt . . ."?

3. Make a list of all of the different end-rhymes found in this well-crafted poem.

4. Why is the mood of this poem so somber?

5. Can you explain the meaning of the metaphor, in the final stanza, that refers to "broken loves"?

6. Does the shape of this poem create a concrete image for you? If so, explain what it is.

CREATIVE PRODUCT

1. Sea gulls often remind us of boat trips or vacations at the seashore. Begin a story or a poem in which sea gulls are the first images that you recall.

2. The short book, *Jonathan Livingston Seagull,* by Richard Bach, is a wonderful descriptive book about the life of a sea gull. It is short enough to read in one sitting. Read it and write a poem about a sea gull.

FOCUS

Flory J. Perini was born of Italian American immigrants and several of his poems reflect his parents' experiences growing up in a small village in Italy. Mr. Perini is an outstanding educator who began his career at Teaneck High School as an English teacher, and later became a Supervisor of English, Language Arts, and Humanities. He is also an adjunct professor at Fairleigh Dickinson University, and a member of the Writing Committee for the New Jersey State Department of Education. He has published a number of articles on multicultural literature in journals, and has been a valued member of the Multicultural Management Team for the Teaneck School District. In large measure, the following quote from *The Record,* (a Bergen County, New Jersey, newspaper) can be attributed to this educator, author, poet, lecturer: "Teaneck is taking multiculturalism seriously . . . Will other districts have the courage to follow?" (1992)

Perini's narrative poem, "Napoleon House in New Orleans," was inspired by a visit to Napoleon House, and to a nearby former slave exchange in New Orleans. As you reflect upon this poem, see if you can relate the interconnectedness of this former slave exchange to the African American driver and to the horse.

Napoleon House in New Orleans

In the crannied courtyard of the Napoleon House,
Of ancient brick, wood, and stone, with flowers and vines
Seeping out of timeless cracks to catch the sunlight,
Tourists absorbed themselves in a confluence of
Tastes and classical music
Of an age past.

"This place was built for Napoleon who never quite got here,"
The waiter told them.

In the distance, a vanquished horse,
Trotting and clinking on the cobblestones,
Tugged a carriage to the corner, and stopped.
In the blazing afternoon sun, a black driver,
Explaining New Orleans history to tourists,
Wiped his sweat and pointed to a building
Opposite the Napoleon House.
"This is the famous Slave Exchange," he proclaimed.
"Where slaves were bought and sold at market."
The salaried historian delivered his scheduled message,
And undetected to those in his carriage,
Looked away from the building as if his words,
Dutifully delivered, were more than a distant piece of history,
Made clean and impassive by time.

With the changing of the light,
The driver collected himself and
Sharply cracked his whip at the horse.
At once, the late, beautiful beast, worn and bony,
Decorated with a gawdy straw hat,
Raised his bowed head, denied his
Strength, beauty and freedom and continued
The endless journey through confused time,
Past the Slave Exchange of former days,
A hapless, bound slave.

© 1996 by The Center for Applied Research in Education

H.O.T. RESPONSES

Each member of your cooperative group should assume the responsibility for reading a portion of this poignant, narrative poem aloud.
Then discuss the following related questions:

1. Time is emphasized throughout this poem, as is the historical context in which the poem is placed. Explain how these historical events have shaped the world.

2. Relate the poet's impressions of the past to the present time.

3. Explain the poet's use of the term, "salaried historian."

4. Why does Perini refer to the horse as: "the late, beautiful beast . . ."?

5. Explain the meaning of the last stanza in the context of history.

6. What does this horse symbolize for the poet?

7. What paradoxes or strange parallels are made in this poem, for example, (a) the role of the black driver; (b) history "... made clean and impassive by time"; (c) the former Slave Exchange; (d) the tourists; (e) Napoleon House; (f) the horse?

8. What is significant about the line: "With the changing of the light ..."?

CREATIVE PRODUCT

1. Think about a historical place you may have visited. Reflect upon some of the thoughts you had at the time. What judgments did you make that are worth sharing about your experience? Write about your reactions or personal insights.

2. Select a famous person in history and write a poem or a story that gives a different slant or perspective on this individual.

Unit Ten

THEME:
THE PLAY'S THE THING

INTRODUCTION

In this unit, the play is featured as another literary form or genre. In the previous nine units, the genres introduced included: poetry, short stories, essays, folk tales, and articles. The play, also referred to as *drama* or *theater,* uses many of the elements found in these other genres, such as metaphor, simile, and meter (poetic rhythm) from poetry—as well as dialogue, plot, and climax from the short story and novel.

The play, however, is not written to be savored on the page as is the poem or the short story. The main function of the play is its performance, in which words and actions are dramatized by actors and actresses on the stage. Therefore, very little description of characters, of scenery, or of plot is written by the playwright. Stage directions and other cues are stated briefly for functional use. The success of the play comes as a result of the characters' dialogue and their actions, which are interpreted and dramatized by actors to an audience of spectators.

When the playwright, the director, and the actors are in sync, the play evokes direct and physical responses from the spectators, who may laugh or cry, or become anxious or fearful.

William Shakespeare knew how the dramatic effects of a play create such emotions; therefore, in *Hamlet,* he employs the use of a play within a play, *The Mousetrap,* to evoke guilt and anxiety in Prince Hamlet's Uncle Claudius who Hamlet suspects is his father's assassin. In this scene, Hamlet reveals that he intends to trap his uncle, and proclaims, "The play's the thing!"

Similarly, playwright Michael Mathias' play within a play, based on *The Hunt of the Unicorn,* is used by the character, William de Champeaux, to expose the love affair between Heloise and Abelard.

The play has been used as a major literary genre throughout the ages and is embraced by most cultures, as is illustrated by the playwrights included in this unit: William Shakespeare (English–Northern European); Michael Mathias (Welsh American); Lottie E. Porch (African American); Rabindranath Tagore (Asian Indian) and Motokiyo Zeami (Asian Japanese).

To be appreciated fully, these plays should be acted out in the classroom.

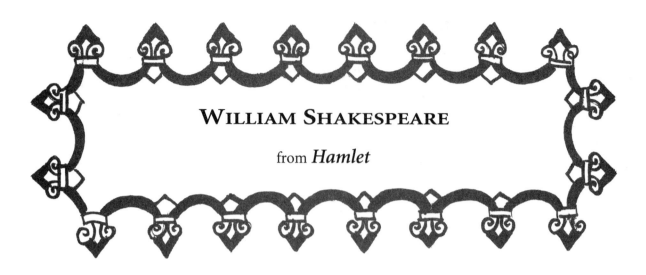

FOCUS

The name "William Shakespeare" is synonymous with great drama and with exact use of language. Shakespeare was also a great poet and his exquisite use of the metaphor is as evident in his plays as it is in his sonnets. Shakespeare, who was born in 1564 and died in 1616, wrote at the time when Queen Elizabeth I reigned in England. Elizabeth was a cultured, well-read ruler and patron of the arts, financially supporting the theater, art, music, and dance—thereby giving birth to a golden age of literature and the arts, referred to in history as the *Elizabethan Age.*

William Shakespeare wrote tragedies and comedies, and actors performed his plays at the Globe Theater to packed audiences composed of commoners and royalty.

Hamlet is one of Shakespeare's greatest tragedies. Hamlet, Prince of Denmark, comes home to learn that his father, the King, has died suddenly and mysteriously, and that his mother has just as suddenly married his uncle Claudius. It becomes evident to Hamlet that his father was most likely murdered by his uncle. To be sure, Hamlet asks a group of players to re-enact a similar murder scene in the presence of his uncle and his mother. The following mime play which appears in Act III, Scene II, is a prologue or preview of The Mousetrap, which is a re-enactment of a murder similar to that of Hamlet's father. The actors pantomime the action of this prologue, and do not speak; hence, the term "dumb-show." The dumb-show shows how Hamlet's father, the King, is murdered:

Hautboys play. The dumb-show enters.

Enter a King and a Queen very lov-
ingly; the Queen embracing him, and
he her. She kneels, and makes show of
protestation unto him. He takes her up,
and declines his head upon her neck:
he lays him down upon a bank of
flowers: she, seeing him asleep, leaves
him. Anon comes in another man, takes
off his crown, kisses it, pours poison in
the sleeper's ears, and leaves him. The
Queen returns; finds the King dead, and
makes passionate action. The Poisoner
with some three or four comes in again,
seems to condole with her. The dead
body is carried away. The Poisoner woos
the Queen with gifts: she seems harsh
awhile, but in the end accepts his love.

The following scene is a famous soliloquy, or solo speech, given by Hamlet. In this speech, he explains how troubled and melancholy he is, because he has been unable to avenge his father's death, and has strong enough suspicions to know that his father's murderer is his uncle Claudius. This soliloquy appears at the end of Act II, Scene II.

In Act III, Scene II, *The Mousetrap* is staged so that Hamlet can observe his uncle, now, King Claudius, and his mother, the Queen.

As you will have learned by reading the soliloquy, Hamlet lays a trap that will prove that Claudius is the murderer, and says: ". . . the play's the thing/wherein I'll catch the conscience of the King."

from *Hamlet*

end of Act II, Scene II

Hamlet. Ay, so, God be wi' ye;
    Now I am alone.
O what a rogue and peasant slave am I!
Is it not monstrous that this player here
But in a fiction, in a dream of passion,
Could force his soul so to his own conceit
That from her working all his visage
  wanned,
Tears in his eyes, distraction in his aspect,
A broken voice, and his whole functions
  suiting

279

from *Hamlet*

end of Act II, Scene II (cont'd)

> With forms to his conceit? and all for
>   nothing,
> For Hecuba.
> What's Hecuba to him, or he to Hecuba,
> That he should weep for her? What would
>   he do
> Had he the motive and the cue for passion
> That I have? He would drown the stage
>   with tears
> And cleave the general ear with horrid
>   speech,
> Make mad the guilty and appal the free,
> Confound the ignorant, and amaze indeed
> The very faculties of eyes and ears;
> Yet I,
> A dull and muddy-mettled rascal, peak
> Like John-a-dreams, unpregnant of my
>   cause,
> And can say nothing; no, not for a king,
> Upon whose property and most dear life
> A damned defeat was made. Am I a
>   coward?
> Who calls me villain? breaks my pate across,
> Plucks off my beard and blows it in my
>   face,
> Tweaks me by the nose, gives me the lie I'
>   the throat
> As deep as to the lungs? who does me this,
>   ha?
> Swounds, I should take it: for it cannot be
> But I am pigeon-livered, and lack gall
> To make oppression bitter, or ere this
> I should ha' fatted all the region kites
> With this slave's offal. Bloody, bawdy vil-
>   lain!
> Remorseless, treacherous, lecherous, kind-
>   less villain!

from *Hamlet*

end of Act II, Scene II (cont'd)

O vengeance!
Why, what an ass am I! This is most brave,
That I, the son of a dear father murdered,
Prompted to my revenge by heaven and
    hell,
Must like a whore, unpack my heart with
    words,
And fall a-cursing, like a very drab
A stallion!
Fie upon't, foh! About, my brains; hum, I
    have heard
That guilty creatures sitting at a play
Have by the very cunning of the scene
Been struck so to the soul, that presently
They have proclaimed their malefactions;
For murder, though it have no tongue, will
    speak
With most miraculous organ. I'll have these
    players
Play something like the murder of my
    father
Before mine uncle; I'll observe his looks,
I'll tent him to the quick; if a' do blench
I know my course. The spirit that I have
    seen
May be a devil, and the devil hath power
To assume a pleasing shape; yea, and per-
    haps
Out of my weakness and my melancholy,
As he is very potent with such spirits,
Abuses me to damn me; I'll have grounds
More relative than this; the play's the thing
Wherein I'll catch the conscience of the
    king.

Exit.

from *Hamlet*

end of Act III, Scene II

Hamlet. Madam, how like you this play?

Queen. The lady doth protest too much,
    methinks.

Hamlet. O, but she'll keep her word.

King. Have you heard the argument? Is there
    no offence in't?

Hamlet. No, no, they do but jest, poison in
    jest; no offence i' the world.

King. What do you call the play?

Hamlet. The Mousetrap. Marry how? Trop-
    ically. This play is the image of a murder
    done in Vienna; Gonzago is the duke's
    name, his wife Baptista; you shall see anon
    tis a knavish piece of work, but what o'
    that? your majesty and we that have free
    souls, it touches us not; let the galled jade
    wince, our withers are unwrung.

Enter Lucianus.

This is one Lucianus, nephew to the king.

Ophelia. You are as good as a chorus, my
    lord.

Hamlet. I could interpret between you and
    your love, if I could see the puppets dally-
    ing.

Ophelia. You are keen, my lord, you are keen.

Hamlet. It would cost you a groaning to take
    off mine edge.

Ophelia. Still better and worse.

Hamlet. So you must take your husbands.
    Begin murderer, leave thy damnable faces,
    and begin. Come: "the croaking raven doth
    bellow for revenge."

Lucianus. Thoughts black, hands apt, drugs
    fit, and time agreeing,

  Confederate season, else no creature
    seeing,

Thou mixture rank, of midnight weeds
    collected,

from *Hamlet*

end of Act III, Scene II

With Hecate's ban thrice blasted, thrice
   infected,
Thy natural magic and dire property
On wholesome life usurps immediately.

Pours the poison in his ears.

Hamlet. A' poisons him i' the garden for his
   estate. His name's Gonzago; the story is
   extant, and written in very choice Italian;
   you shall see anon how the murderer gets
   the love of Gonzago's wife.
Ophelia. The king rises.
Hamlet. What, frightened with false fire?
Queen. How fares my lord?
Polonius. Give o'er the play.
King. Give me some light; away!
Polonius. Lights, lights, lights!

H.O.T. RESPONSES

Before trying to respond to the following questions, read and reread the two scenes silently and independently. Then take roles in your cooperative group and read the scenes out loud. Work together in your cooperative group to answer the following:

1. Why does Prince Hamlet give the title, *The Mousetrap,* to the play acted before his uncle? Could this trap be used effectively today? Give examples.

2. Why does Hamlet's girlfriend, Ophelia, tell him that he is ". . . as good as a chorus . . ."?

3. To whom is Hamlet referring in the line: "Come, the croaking raven doth bellow for revenge . . ."?

4. In his soliloquy (Act II, Scene II), Hamlet says:

   For murder, though it have no
   tongue, will speak with most
   miraculous organ.

   Explain the meaning of this metaphor.

5. At which moment in the play does Claudius reveal his guilt? Why does he respond so, at this point in the play-within-a-play?

6. Why do you think it was so difficult for Hamlet to avenge the death of his father? Do you think it was because he was a coward? Explain.

© 1996 by The Center for Applied Research in Education

CREATIVE PRODUCT

1. Study the "dumb-show" that appears in the "Focus" section. Perform this mime with your cooperative group as it must have been done in Shakespeare's time.

2. As a class project, view a videocassette of *Hamlet,* and discuss its fascinating plot and characters as well as its tragic elements.

3. *Renaissance Man,* starring Danny DeVito, is a funny film in which a former advertising executive loses his job and winds up teaching *Hamlet* to a low-level group of soldiers in a training camp. The film shows how great a work *Hamlet* truly is, and how meaningful and how relevant this play is today.

4. The entire class should see this videocassette—to review the humorous, yet poignant, film in terms of its treatment of *Hamlet.* Write a review of *Renaissance Man* so that other students may learn more about Shakespeare's *Hamlet.*

MICHAEL MATHIAS

from *The Secret Bread*

© 1996 by The Center for Applied Research in Education

FOCUS

Michael Mathias is a lyrical Welsh American whose poem, "The Divine Theme," appeared earlier in Unit Six, Activity Nine. His play, *The Secret Bread,* is based on the love story of Peter Abelard and the beautiful Heloise, niece of a canon in the cathedral of Paris. He became her tutor—an intimate of her uncle's home—and he won her love. A son was born of their love, and then came years of heart-break.

Peter Abelard (1079–1142) was one of the most brilliant theologians in France at a time when the great tides of spiritual awakening were flowing. A man of intense faith, he was a strikingly contradictory figure. The classroom was the breath of life to him and he attracted throngs of admiring students wherever he taught.

The purpose of the feast scene is to heighten the dramatic intensity by exposing the love affair between Heloise and Abelard to Fulbert and his guests. To drive Fulbert, Heloise's uncle, into a jealous rage, William de Champeaux has written a play-within-a-play based on *The Hunt of the Unicorn,* a medieval legend about the piercing and capturing of the unicorn, symbolizing the wounding and crucifixion of Christ.

William de Champeaux, Abelard's former teacher and jealous professional rival, planted the seeds of Fulbert's madness in a previous scene when he conspired with Abiathar, Heloise's nurse, to reveal to Fulbert that she followed Heloise to the Cathedral of Notre Dame where she witnessed her lovemaking to Abelard. William's mousetrap is to weave Abelard's love poems to Heloise into *The Hunt of the Unicorn* and to focus Fulbert's attention on the guilty reactions of Abelard as he provokes Abelard with satiric and biting asides. William intimates in his asides that the maiden who tempts the unicorn to her lap is Heloise. And when Abelard's love poem is read at the climax of the play-within-the-play, Abelard has disappeared with Heloise, driving Fulbert into madness: "Give over this play. For Death has suddenly entered here!" Thus through the dramatic function of the play-within-the-play, William has motivated Fulbert to have Abelard arrested for heresy.

As you read this wonderful scene from *The Secret Bread,* compare it to Act III, Scene II, in Shakespeare's *Hamlet.* Michael Mathias' romanticism and spiritualism transcend modernism; at times, you will believe you have been transported into another time and place.

from *The Secret Bread (a play)*

ACT II

SCENE 2
Triste:

(*Triste appears before the curtain.*)
(*To the audience.*) All you fattened people, with
stomachs full of food, come to Fulbert's feast, and
lose your stuffedness in dancing!
For I have heard tell that a man once lost five
pounds that way—but, alas, after all of that
dancing, he ate enough food to gain back the pounds
he lost, and an additional five pounds besides!
So you see, you have everything to gain and nothing
to lose, for such is Fulbert's feast. Oh, what a
feast!

But, let me ask you as I am standing here. Let me
ask you which food you treasure more—the food of
the stomach or the food of the mind?
Let us reason this out together. The food of the
stomach passes in and passes out. But the food of
the mind passes in, and never passes out again.
Unless you have a hole in your head, but then you
have no need for that food in the first place.
Ah, wonderful storing place, the brain, and how many
hundreds of feasts it can devour!
Therefore, when you come to Lord Fulbert's house,
partake not only the food of the body, but the
food of the mind. For the food of the body you can
only hold so much of. But the food of the mind
frees us from space, and always leaves us hungry.
Now then, this leads us to a very serious question.
Are the things which take up space more real than
the things which occupy no space at all? Or is it
vice-versa? Or is everything real?

Oh, my head aches! Here's a warning to all. If I
put enough thinking into my head,—'Tis easy
to conclude, that to make room for the surplus, I
would have to go out of my mind! Therefore, take
heed against too much thinking, lest your thoughts
take up room where your soul should be.
Very well, you have had both my invitation and my
warning! Take either or both, as it pleases you.

from *The Secret Bread (a play)*

ACT II

SCENE 2 (cont'd)

(*The music of the Festive Pipes is heard, and
down the aisles stream the players.*)

Oh, our words are all too sad, too flat, too stale
tonight! There's more music made with lips than
tambourines and cymbals! Kiss! Kiss! And sing
the stars to flight!

(*The men kiss the women. The music begins again.*)

All you who would be stung by cupid's arrow,
enter now our Court of Love!

(*The curtain opens.*)

William:	(Aside.) He'll not leave tonight!
Count:	Oh, what a glorious trap! I've never seen more gorgeous color, nor heartier laughter to catch a rabbit!
William:	I've inserted some of Abelard's poems in the play. Watch how he'll blush!
Young Man:	This apple is like love, which blindfolded we pursue. Every now and then, we feel its presence on our cheek, but always it evades our bite!
Young Girl:	I would much rather that it did, for if we held it in our hands, it would be eaten in an instant.
Fulbert:	Come! Sing with us of love, and sudden you will know why and what life is.
Triste:	Love is a church!
Abelard:	(Dressed as a knight with a lance.) Love is lost Eden that was first made; God relented and let some men wander back.
William:	There comes his pretty voice from behind that white mask. Oh, what dissembling masks we wear!

289

from *The Secret Bread (a play)*

ACT II

SCENE 2 (cont'd)

Count:	Is that Peter Abelard? I cannot tell one face from another amidst this blaze of color.
First Juggler:	Love makes jugglers of us all; we balance our hearts on our fingertips. Careful, careful! One slip and we break our hearts.
Second Juggler:	Or another's heart!
Third Juggler:	Or we toss them back and forth betwixt ourselves until, thrown too high, we cannot catch them in time!
Tight-rope Walker:	(Balancing on rope.) Look, all of you, how love lifts us as high as the sky, making us think we walk on clouds—yet it is only a thin wire under our feet. Take warning, all you pretty ladies and handsome gentlemen—one careless step, and you miss your footing! (*He pretends to fall off the wire; but hangs on by one foot. Women scream.*)
	Take heed, ladies! We must be skilled in love! Or fall!
Triste:	Can you learn what Life's about. Live a bit and Find it out!
Fulbert:	(*Leading Abiathar to a young man.*) Fling all your thought into the golden air! Come, clasp a maiden's hand and dance along.
Abiathar:	Kissing cannot be wicked in the Paris sun. (*She kisses the young man.*)
Heloise:	Now must I be what I most hate to be. But, courage, heart; what seems eternity will be a moment—a little while, and then farewell to masquerade!
Abelard:	Ah, Heloise, my white butterfly, That lent me wings that I might fly Where God is, in the highest region of the sky. Not sky above, but sky within.
William:	Did you see how she did blush as he passed by? Ah, if we had only ears could reach across the room to hear their whispers!

from *The Secret Bread (a play)*

© 1996 by The Center for Applied Research in Education

ACT II

SCENE 2 (cont'd)

Count:	Ah, Heloise, how you do light this room with color!
Heloise:	The flower is in your own eye, dear Count, and I am but a mere reflection of what is fair in you.
Count:	Mirror, you do reflect me well. I see myself as I have never been before.
Heloise:	Why, you have never looked with Beauty's eyes.
William:	Bring forth the players. 'Tis time for more serious entertainment.
Fulbert:	Oh, a play, a play! How delightful. What is its name?
William:	'Tis the "Hunt of the Unicorn"—a play I wrote myself with a touch or two added that you will like especially, dear Knight!
Count:	Oh, the unicorn, the unicorn is a most enchanting beast! Have you ever seen one William?
William:	'Tis a mythological beast, but tonight for your enjoyment, we'll bring him alive again, if you will all but lend your imaginations to the scene.
Narrator:	Imagine the end of a damp, dark day, The sky is filled with death. And odors of decay, Infest us from the forest bogs with every breath. Where is the sun? Has it hidden its light To give the unicorn a chance to run? Before we've got him in our sight? In the shadows of the trees, In the thickest wilderness, Stands a young man in royal dress Like a flag of France waving in the breeze. Beside him two companions stand, Dressed in garments of matching color, With questioning face and outstretched hand— Grim as soldiers going into war. Why are your faces so dark And filled with doubt?

291

from *The Secret Bread (a play)*

ACT II

SCENE 2 (cont'd)

© 1996 by The Center for Applied Research in Education

Hunter: All ye who stand with waiting spear,
Come follow us, the unicorn is near.

Narrator: Come, bring the hounds with fiercest fang.
They'll outrun the swiftest stang.
Even the unicorn whose cloven hoof
Can leap over tallest trees, highest roof!

Through the thick forest they go—
The greyhounds dashing before them—
Their eyes with fierce fires aglow,
Their mouths all the while foaming.

Such was the ravenous crowd at Golgotha
Which devoured the innocent lamb.
The man who had only to say "I am"
And through surrender find himself a king.

Though pinioned to a cross, he found a way to soar.
So will the unicorn be loose and free,
Though bound into captivity.

1st Comp. Look, there in the clearing
The unicorn is kneeling!

Chorus: The unicorn is kneeling!
The unicorn is kneeling!
The unicorn kneels in quiet prayer,
God's love with all mankind to share,
As one who prayed upon Gethsemane's rock
To overcome Death, the stumbling block.

Narrator: Fear thou, the lance of purity
Which opens wide our foul sin.
Come, hunters, advance with open eye.

The young men spring up from the trees
Their teeth and spears about to seize,

But the beast breaks loose like a startled breeze,
Kicks high his heels, lets fly his knees
As if to leap above the moon
And with his nostrils blast a terrible typhoon.
One dog he pierces through the heart
which utters such a fearful howl
That all in terror at once depart,
Even the greyhounds, without a howl,
Silently and swiftly flee.

292

from *The Secret Bread (a play)*

ACT II

SCENE 2 (cont'd)

Send out the maiden to the beast.
Only a virgin can capture the unicorn.
He comes to her lap as if to feast
And is as tender as a lamb just shorn.
Look, how softly the maid doth tread:
Such a whisper maketh her feet, as if upon a silken carpet,

Not a sign of fear, nor trace of dread.
She shines a lovely smile like to dispel all threat.

(*The Maiden sings to the Unicorn.*)

Chorus: The unicorn stands still in space.
A look of peace upon his face.
He cocks his head off to one side.
And lifts his feet as if to glide.

Narrator: With her song she puts him in a trance.
For see how gently he doth dance.

Unicorn: From the first you have been the gate
Through which I found God once again.
Once in those doors, I lost all hate.
I am no longer I
When He and thee are in my heart.
Within me is all of sky,
Which you have shown me from the start.

William: What think you of this verse, Sir Knight

Abelard: I think it is a trifle adolescent.

William: (*To Fulbert.*) 'Tis one of Abelard's verses. Did
you hear how his voice cracked beneath the mask?

Fulbert: Yet, 'tis nothing near to lewdness.

1st Comp. Drop by drop he sheds a tear.

2nd Comp. Step by step she draws him near.

Count: Thus are all men betrayed by women.

Narrator: She stroketh her soft white breast
And offers it to him for rest!
Now his hand he lieth in her lap,
And thus is caught within fair Beauty's trap!

from *The Secret Bread (a play)*

ACT II

SCENE 2 (cont'd)

Count:	Poor, poor unicorn! He's a most poetic beast, but like all beasts eventually made slave to passion.
Narrator:	See, see, how sweetly sleeps the unicorn Whilst in the sky shines red the moon. There where the unicorn hath made his bed, Softly, softly the hunters tread. One careless footstep, one startling sound Might wake the beast and turn him round From gentle sleep to fiercest rage. And all the while the maiden smiles. For women often with their cunning wiles, With tenderest stroke make lions weep!
Chorus:	Look how with a Judas kiss upon his cheek The maid transforms him to a lamb so meek . . . .
Narrator:	With silver spears the hunters stand which gleam like teeth extended from the hand.
Chorus:	Now must we do the deed— Now pierce his thigh. Our sins will purify With every drop he bleeds.
Narrator:	Thus with this spear they crucify And take the unicorn with startled cry!
Unicorn:	Forgive them, Father, this thing they do; The love You've granted me, give them too!
Narrator:	Thus did the Lord the world so glorify That every man will live, yet though he die, And no one knows the reason why One man could nature's laws defy! A time is coming, when pain will cease, When night will be no longer, When Love shall reign with Peace.
William:	Thus is every man by love betrayed!
Abelard:	And every man by love is saved!
Triste:	'Tis no doubt that Love is worth a poet's praise. So, come, players, philosophers, and poets all— let's hear your songs and see whether any will add wings to Cupid!

from *The Secret Bread (a play)*

ACT II

SCENE 2 (cont'd)

William:	I will offer a prize of twelve gold pieces for the winning poem.
Abelard:	(To Heloise.) Dear Butterfly, you begin!
Heloise:	I know not where to start.
	"I wear a mask. You wear a mask To make a trivial play."
Abelard:	"And with a mask To meet a mask Where is the Truth today?"
Heloise:	"Is Truth too whole a play?"
Abelard:	"Can both be true? Can this be you, And this you, too?"
Heloise:	"Or is one mask To make the task Of coward-hero easier For me, if not for you?"
Abelard:	"Yet Truth is more Than play."
Heloise:	(Whispering.) Meet me in my garden tonight!
William:	Mark that whisper, Count? There's lechery about!
Count:	(Aloud.) An excellent dialogue on the deceit of love!
William:	Dear Butterfly, your face is flushed!
Heloise:	Oh, I am ill, I fear!
William:	But stay a while; these songs will give you cheer!
Fulbert:	Let us pray so—the atmosphere needs lifting. That was a far too sombre play, William! And for such a happy eve!
William:	Truth is bitter.

from *The Secret Bread (a play)*

ACT II

SCENE 2 (cont'd)

    (The Jongleurs and Maidens each in turn recite a poem or song on love.)

1.	"Crystal love or red, It is drink of dread."
2.	"One sip sweet! Two then sweeter!"
3.	"Beyond four You need no more."
Fulbert:	Well said. Love's a powerful potion.
4.	"Most lovers question; The lady says "Yes"— You take possession without caress."
	"Tomorrow you will come, you say, But when was tomorrow enough for today?"
Fulbert:	There's a thirsty love!
5.	"How much is truth— How much is lying? How ever know? Fatal the trying."
William:	Ah, painful riddle is love!
6.	"My love loves another. So what can I do? Love the other one, too?"
Triste:	Love another one, too!
7.	"How much is truth, How much is lying? How ever know? Fatal the trying."
Count:	Love is not honest! Is it Heloise?
Heloise:	Love is honest in an honest heart.
William:	Well said!
8.	"If love were not so wicked, How lovely it would be For me to give a little kiss To you—occasionally.

© 1996 by The Center for Applied Research in Education

from *The Secret Bread (a play)*

ACT II

SCENE 2 (cont'd)

But, ah! To kiss is wicked—
A sin, the sages say:
And so I will not fancy it
Except when you're away.
(A thing I wish to know:
Are sages happy so?)"

9.   "I would be a dreaming river flowing
             Always far from the sea,
For sea is rest, and I—
             I would be going.

I would be a breathless comet cleaving
             Infinity,
Never returning—leaving—
             Eternally.

I would be a prayer—human yearning
             To be
God: I would be Love, eternally
             Burning."

Fulbert: There is an excellent poem!

Count: Come, little one, receive your prize.

9.   But, sir, I am not the author of this poem.

Fulbert: Who is?

William: Tell them who it is.

9.   Abelard!

Count: Abelard?

Fulbert: Come, come, then Abelard. Receive the prize.

William: Why, Abelard is gone—and so is Heloise!

Fulbert: Gone? Stop! Give o'er this music! Death has entered here!

(The music stops. Players and Jongleurs scatter.)

(Fulbert begins to exit.)

(CURTAIN)

297

H.O.T. RESPONSES

1. Write a brief summary of how the play-within-a-play is used successfully in *The Secret Bread* and compare it to *The Mousetrap* in *Hamlet*.

2. Although *The Secret Bread* was staged as late as 1993, what observations have you made about the language used by Michael Mathias?

3. See if you and your cooperative group can answer Triste's question to the audience:

    Are the things which take up space
    more real than the things which
    occupy no space at all? Or is it
    vice-versa? Or is everything real?

    Discuss this unusual question and explain its meaning.

4. Compare William's following line to some of the poems you read in Unit One: Masks Around the World:

    There comes his pretty
    voice behind that white mask.
    Oh, what dissembling masks we wear!

5. If the unicorn is as the count says, ". . . a most poetic beast," is there any other beast you might declare "poetic"?

6. Abelard and Heloise recite their own collaborative poem. It is about a mask. Summarize the meaning of this poem. How does it compare to Claribel Alegria's poem that appears in Unit One?

7. Think of two other individuals in history who fell in love, or who were never able to fulfill their dream. Name these two individuals and tell their story to members in your cooperative group.

CREATIVE PRODUCT

1. Use the two characters selected for your response in activity 7 above, and write a scene for a play that tells their story. (Your characters may come from history, from a tale, from a parable, from a religious story, or other source.)

RABINDRANATH TAGORE

from *The Cycle of Spring*

FOCUS

Rabindranath Tagore was a great Indian writer; he won the most coveted literature award in the world—the Nobel Prize. Tagore was a major poet, dramatist, essayist, short story writer, novelist, and philosopher. He was born in Calcutta, India, in 1861, and died in 1941.

Tagore received outstanding reviews of his writing by the English poet, William Butler Yeats, who wrote: "An innocence, a simplicity that one does not find elsewhere in literature . . ." Ezra Pound, American critic and poet, wrote of Tagore, ". . . There is in him the stillness of nature." Gandhi, the great Indian leader, hailed Tagore as "The Great Teacher."

The Cycle of Spring, which appears here, is an unusual play that is somewhat similar in style to the absurd theater made popular by European playwrights, Pirandello, Camus, Genet, and Cocteau. In this brief excerpt, Rabindranath Tagore takes the point of view of the poet, and tries to persuade the King to live his life to the fullest and not to worry about growing old and dying. The poet insists that if we feel we are alive, we shall go on living, because the movement of life is unceasing. Therefore, to go on living, *we must make our life worth this eternity.*

The poet explains to the King:

> *In the play of the seasons, each year,*
> *the mask of the Old Man, Winter, is*
> *pulled off, and the form of Spring is revealed*
> *in all its beauty. Thus we see that*
> *the old is ever new.*

As you read the following excerpt from *The Cycle of Spring,* consider how Tagore's explanation of poetry compares with the work of other poets that appears in this book.

from *The Cycle of Spring*

Poet! . . . Do something. Do anything.
Have you got anything ready to hand? Any play toward?
Any poem? Any masque? Any—

Yes, King, I have got the very thing. But whether it is a drama,
or a poem, or a play, or a masque, I cannot say.

Shall I be able to understand the sense of what you have written?

No, King, what a poet writes is not meant to have any sense.

What then?

To have the tune itself.

What do you mean? Is there no philosophy in it?

No, none at all, thank goodness.

What does it say then?

King, it says "I exist." Don't you know the meaning of the first
cry of the new-born child? The child, when it is born, hears at once
the cries of the earth and water and sky, which surround him,—and
they all cry to him, "We exist," and his tiny little heart responds, and
cries out in its turn, "I exist." My poetry is like the cry of that new-
born child. It is a response to the cry of the Universe.

Is it nothing more than that, Poet?

No, nothing more. There is life in my song, which cries, "In joy
and in sorrow, in work and in rest, in life and in death, in victory
and in defeat, in this world and in the next, all hail to the 'I exist.'"

H.O.T. RESPONSES

1. Poet Archibald MacLeish said, "A poem must not mean, but be." Locate the three sentences uttered by the Poet in *The Cycle of Spring*, that have the exact meaning of MacLeish's line.

2. In your own words, explain the meaning of the Poet's statement:

   My poetry is like the cry of that
   new-born child.

3. The philosopher Descartes once wrote, "I think, therefore I am." Write a contrasting statement from the point of view of the Poet. (Try to write a statement parallel to Descartes'.)

4. Why do you think the Poet in this play is so insistent that there is no philosophy in poetry?

CREATIVE PRODUCT

1. Write a poem that defines your own feelings about poetry.

2. Write a continuation of the dialogue between the Poet and the King with members from your cooperative group. Read the complete play and compare your version to the original.

3. Act out your own version of *The Cycle of Spring*.

4. Create a mask that illustrates *The Cycle of Spring* or the old becoming reborn.

LOTTIE E. PORCH

from *A WomanSong*

FOCUS

Lottie E. Porch is a poet and playwright. She is the author of a novel in progress, *LoriAnn,* which appears in Unit Four.

A WomanSong is Lottie Porch's newest play, from which the following excerpt is taken. Her play explores phases of womanhood and the lives of Mahalia Jackson, Zora Neale Hurston, and Ella Baker.

Her first play, *Rhythms of Life: A Historical Journey,* was performed at the Harlem Abyssinian Church in New York City.

Plays by Lottie Porch that are available to be read or produced include:

The Man was King; If you Hear His Voice; A Child Shall Lead Them; Visions of Malcolm; Benjamin Banneker: The Man Who Put D.C. on the Map; Story Songs, The Tradition of African American Praise Singing.

from *A WomanSong*

Special:	Pastor, the other day we were studying in class about Nat Turner, John Brown, and all the people who helped the slaves be free. But so many of them got killed, and when I asked mama, she said,
Earleatha:	They say the good die young.
Special:	Another time I had a dream about fish. Mama told me,
Earleatha:	They say that means somebody having a baby.
Special:	When I git scared cause it's thundering and lightning outside. Mama say,
Earleatha:	They say God is talking; Somebody made him mad.
Special:	Well, I just wanna know who is "They?" Did God put some real, real, smart people up a hill some-where to sit down and watch us and make these decisions?

© 1996 by The Center for Applied Research in Education

from *A WomanSong*

(cont'd)

Preacher: Now at first,
I didn't know just what to say.
I could have brushed her question aside.
But you know,
I think there's something in that
For all of us to learn.

First of all
Everybody's got a mind. Thoughts.
A gift from God
To use along with their bodies.
And that mind—is a mighty powerful thing!
Got to know how to use it right
Keep it clean, strong,
Moving along.

Now, even the poor souls
That are kinda slow
They got minds too.
But sometimes theirs
Needs a little more prodding.
A little more tenderness,
A little more care.
But that's okay;
They're special
In they own way.

Anyway—like I said,
The mind's a mighty powerful thing.
Cause the thoughts you really believe—
Well, those are the ones that come true.
Take for instance Deacon Stanley.
Doctors told him
He would never walk again
But after that stroke,
Stanley worked on his-self.
And now he's a-walkin,
And he's a-talkin'.
He's on the mend.
All because of
What he believed.

Hattie: Oh, fix it Rev, fix it.

Others: Hallelujah, Amen, (and so on)

from *A WomanSong*
(cont'd)

Preacher: See the problem comes
When half the folks
Don't want to use their brain.
They're content to let
Others speak for them.
And think for them.
Won't go out there
And see for themselves
Feel for themselves, and know.

Man: Well

Preacher: So, the other half gits left
Doin' all that brain work.
And folks believe
Whatever THEY say.
So child, anybody who thinks,
Can be part of THEY.
When you use your mind
All you can
And couple it with muscle 'n faith,
Why it's then
You become a part of THEY,
And you determine what THEY say.
The power you see,
Is yours inside,
To be brave or strong,
To have joy and pride,

Congregation: Oh yes!

Preacher: To make the rules for the world
In which you live,
Giving love, sharing, caring,
Being free to forgive.

THEY is you child.
Honey, THEY is me.
Long as we are being
All God wants us to be.
Long as we are shaping
Our own reality.

from *A WomanSong*
(cont'd)

So you really don't have to worry
About who is THEY.
You ain't even got to worry
About what THEY say.
All you need to do
Is be the best little girl you can.
Mind your parents.
Say your prayers.
And keep on thinking,
And Asking,
And Breathing,
And Growing.
And Bay-bee, pretty soon,
You be THEY."

Special: Reverend, you mean—
If I think real hard,
Search my heart and pray,
Then when I grow up,
I can begin to say
What THEY say?

Preacher: Sho' 'nough, Baby.

Special: Well, I already been thinking.

Earleatha: (aside) Lord, this child!

Special: And it seems to me
God put you here
To help us in all kinda ways
And that's the truth
The way I see it."

Preacher: "Yes, child . . .
I suppose I am here to help
Or at least,
That's what They say."
God Bless you.
Let us pray . . . .

(As the lights dim out we hear, "Sweet Hour of Prayer.")

Preacher: Lord, bless us and keep us. Dismiss us from this
place, but never from thy sight.

307

H.O.T. RESPONSES

1. Have you ever wondered who "they" might be just as Special wondered? Explain your rationale for "they."

2. What do you think of the Preacher's explanation for "they"?

3. Are there other sayings or expressions that people use that need explaining? Can you mention a few? Once you and members of your cooperative group have listed some, explain what you think they mean.

4. Describe the feelings you get from reading this scene. What kind of congregation is this? How does Special respond?

5. How does the Preacher's language create a mood? Describe this mood.

CREATIVE PRODUCT

1. Create a scene from a play that reflects your own religious group.

2. Create a scene in which a teacher and students interact about a problem.

3. Act out *A WomanSong* with your cooperative group.

MOTOKIYO ZEAMI

The Damask Drum

© 1996 by The Center for Applied Research in Education

FOCUS

Motokiyo Zeami lived from 1363 to 1443 and is considered to be the playwright who, with his father Kiyotsugu Kan'Ami, developed Noh drama to its highest form. Zeami wrote over two hundred plays of which one hundred still exist. Zeami was first recognized for his acting talents by the powerful Shogun, a military ruler; he became a member of the court where he received training in poetry, religion, and Noh drama. *Noh* means talented performance, and these dramas are plays that combine prose, poetry, and dance. Zeami and his father turned the Noh drama into a dramatic art form and according to Zeami:

> *The purpose of the art of Noh is to serve as a means to pacify people's hearts and to move the high and the low alike, which brings prosperity to all of us and promotes a long life.*

As you read *The Damask Drum,* see if it performs according to Zeami's explanation of the purpose of the Noh drama.

THE DAMASK DRUM

Characters

A COURTIER   THE PRINCESS   AN OLD GARDENER

COURTIER: I am a courtier at the Palace of Kinomaru in the country of Chikuzen. You must know that in this place there is a famous pond called the Laurel Pond, where the royal ones often take their walks; so it happened that one day the old man who sweeps the garden here caught sight of the Princess. And from that time he has loved her with a love that gives his heart no rest.

Someone told her of this, and she said, "Love's equal realm knows no divisions," and in her pity she said, "By that pond there stands a laurel-tree, and on its branches there hangs a drum. Let him beat the drum, and if the sound is heard in the Palace, he shall see my face again."

I must tell him of this.

Listen, old Gardener! The worshipful lady has heard of your love and sends you this message: "Go and beat the drum that hangs on the tree by the pond, and if the sound is heard in the Palace, you shall see my face again." Go quickly now and beat the drum!

GARDENER: With trembling I receive her words. I will go and beat the drum.

COURTIER: Look, here is the drum she spoke of. Make haste and beat it! [*He leaves the* Gardener *standing by the tree and seats himself at the foot of the "Waki's pillar."*]

GARDENER: They talk of the moon-tree, the laurel that grows in the Garden of the Moon . . . . But for me there is but one true tree, this laurel by the lake. Oh, may the drum that hangs on its branches give forth a mighty note, a music to bind up my bursting heart.

Listen! the evening bell to help me chimes;
But then tolls in
A heavy tale of day linked on to day,

CHORUS [*speaking for the* GARDENER]: And hope stretched out from dusk
  to dusk.
But now, a watchman of the hours, I beat
The longed-for stroke.

GARDENER: I was old, I shunned the daylight,
I was gaunt as an aged crane;
And upon all that misery
Suddenly a sorrow was heaped,

311

The Damask Drum

(cont'd)

The new sorrow of love.
The days had left their marks,
Coming and coming, like waves that beat on a sandy shore . . .

CHORUS: Oh, with a thunder of white waves
The echo of the drum shall roll.

GARDENER: The after-world draws near me,
Yet even now I wake not
From this autumn of love that closes
In sadness the sequence of my years.

CHORUS: And slow as the autumn dew
Tears gather in my eyes, to fall
Scattered like dewdrops from a shaken flower
On my coarse-woven dress.
See here the marks, imprint of tangled love,
That all the world will read.

GARDENER: I said "I will forget,"

CHORUS: And got worse torment so
Than by remembrance. But all in this world
Is as the horse of the aged man of the land of Sai;
And as a white colt flashes
Past a gap in the hedge, even so our days pass.
And though the time be come,
Yet can none know the road that he at last must tread,
Goal of his dewdrop-life.
All this I knew; yet knowing,
Was blind with folly.

GARDENER: "Wake, wake," he cries,—

Chorus: The watchman of the hours,—
"Wake from the sleep of dawn!"
And batters on the drum.
For if its sound be heard, soon shall he see
Her face, the damask of her dress . . .
Aye, damask! He does not know
That on a damask drum he beats,
Beats with all the strength of his hands, his aged hands,
But hears no sound.
"Am I grown deaf?" he cries, and listens, listens:
Rain on the windows, lapping of waves on the pool—
Both these he hears, and silent only
The drum, strange damask drum.
Oh, will it never sound?

© 1996 by The Center for Applied Research in Education

The Damask Drum

(cont'd)

I thought to beat the sorrow from my heart,
Wake music in a damask drum; an echo of love
From the voiceless fabric of pride!

GARDENER: Longed for as the moon that hides
In the obstinate clouds of a rainy night
Is the sound of the watchman's drum,
To roll the darkness from my heart.

CHORUS: I beat the drum. The days pass and the hours.
It was yesterday, and it is to-day.

GARDENER: But she for whom I wait

CHORUS: Comes not even in dream. At dawn and dusk

GARDENER: No drum sounds.

CHORUS: She has not come. Is it not sung that those
Whom love has joined
Not even the God of Thunder can divide?
Of lovers, I alone
Am guideless, comfortless.
Then weary of himself and calling her to witness of his woe,
"Why should I endure," he cried,
"Such life as this?" and in the waters of the pond
He cast himself and died.

[GARDENER *leaves the stage.*]
[*Enter the* PRINCESS.]

COURTIER: I would speak with you madam.

The drum made no sound, and the aged Gardener in despair has flung
himself into the pond by the laurel-tree, and died. The soul of such a
one may cling to you and do you injury. Go out and look upon him.

PRINCESS [*speaking wildly, already possessed by the* Gardener's *angry ghost,
which speaks through her*]: Listen, people, listen!
In the noise of the beating waves
I hear the rolling of a drum.
Oh, joyful sound, oh joyful!
The music of a drum.

COURTIER: Strange, strange!
This lady speaks as one
By phantasy possessed.
What is amiss, what ails her?

The Damask Drum

(cont'd)

PRINCESS: Truly, by phantasy I am possessed.
Can a damask drum give sound?
When I bade him beat what could not ring,
Then tottered first my wits.

COURTIER: She spoke, and on the face of the evening pool
A wave stirred.

PRINCESS: And out of the wave

COURTIER: A voice spoke.

[The voice of the Gardener is heard; as he gradually advances along the hashigakari it is seen that he wears a "demon mask," leans on a staff and carries the "demon mallet" at his girdle.]

GARDENER'S GHOST: I was driftwood in the pool, but the waves of
   bitterness

CHORUS: Have washed me back to the shore.

GHOST: Anger clings to my heart,
Clings even now when neither wrath nor weeping
Are aught but folly.

CHORUS: One thought consumes me,
The anger of lust denied
Covers me like darkness.
I am become a demon dwelling
In the hell of my dark thoughts,
Storm-cloud of my desires.

GHOST: "Though the waters parch in the fields
Though the brooks run dry,
Never shall the place be shown
Of the spring that feeds my heart."
So I had resolved. Oh, why so cruelly
Set they me to win
Voice from a voiceless drum,
Spending my heart in vain?
And I spent my heart on the glimpse of a moon that slipped
Through the boughs of an autumn tree.

CHORUS: This damask drum that hangs on the laurel-tree

GHOST: Will it wound, will it sound?

[He seizes the Princess and drags her towards the drum.]

Try! Strike it!

© 1996 by The Center for Applied Research in Education

The Damask Drum

(cont'd)

CHORUS: "Strike!" he cries;
"The quick beat, the battle-charge!
Loud, loud! Strike, strike," he rails,
And brandishing his demon-stick
Gives her no rest.
"Oh woe!" the lady weeps,
"No sound, no sound. Oh misery!" she wails.
And he, at the mallet stroke, "Repent, repent!"
Such torments in the world of night
Abõrasetsu, chief of demons, wields,
Who on the Wheel of Fire
Sears sinful flesh and shatters bones to dust.
Not less her torture now!
"Oh agony!" she cries, "What have I done,
By what dire seed this harvest sown?"

GHOST: Clear stands the cause before you.

CHORUS: Clear stands the cause before my eyes; I know it now.
By the pool's white waters, upon the laurel's bough
The drum was hung.
He did not know his hour, but struck and struck
Till all the will had ebbed from his heart's core;
Then leapt into the lake and died.
And while his body rocked
Like driftwood on the waves,
His soul, an angry ghost,
Possessed the lady's wits, haunted her heart with woe.
The mallet lashed, as these waves lash the shore,
Lash on the ice of the eastern shore.
The wind passes, the rain falls
On the Red Lotus, the Lesser and the Greater.
The hair stands up on my head.
"The fish that leaps the falls
To a fell snake is turned,"
I have learned to know them;
Such, such are the demons of the World of Night.
"O hateful lady, hateful!" he cried, and sank again
Into the whirlpool of desire.

H.O.T. RESPONSES

In your cooperative group, discuss the following:

1. How must the old gardener make his love known to the Princess?

2. Why does the Princess make such a promise to a commoner like the Gardener?

3. Why does the drum make no sound?

4. Explain the meaning of the line: "From the voiceless fabric of pride!"

5. The ghost of the gardener returns from the pond wearing a demon's mask. Why does he become a demon?

6. What is the function of the Courtier and the Chorus?

7. Notice that the chorus plays an important role in Greek drama, English drama, and Japanese Noh drama. Why do you think the chorus has played such a role in world drama?

8. What is the purpose of this play?

CREATIVE PRODUCT

1. This play has a tragic end. Write a different ending, one that has a more pleasant outcome.

2. Write a poem about *The Damask Drum.*

3. Based upon Zeami's explanation of the Noh drama, create one to be acted out in class. (This can be a collaborative effort.)

4. Create your own Noh masks to wear as you act out your original Noh play.